# Tyndale New Testament Commentaries

## Volume 11

# Philippians

To my students, both past and present

# TYNDALE NEW TESTAMENT COMMENTARIES

## VOLUME 11

SERIES EDITOR: ECKHARD J. SCHNABEL
CONSULTING EDITOR: NICHOLAS PERRIN

---

# PHILIPPIANS

## AN INTRODUCTION AND COMMENTARY

### JEANNINE K. BROWN

Academic
An imprint of InterVarsity Press
Downers Grove, Illinois

Inter-Varsity Press, England
36 Causton Street, London SW1P 4ST, England
Website: www.ivpbooks.com
Email: ivp@ivpbooks.com

InterVarsity Press, USA
P.O. Box 1400, Downers Grove, IL 60515, USA
Website: www.ivpress.com
Email: email@ivpress.com

Inter-Varsity Press, England, publishes Christian books that are true to the Bible and that
communicate the gospel, develop discipleship and strengthen the church for its mission in the world.

IVP originated within the Inter-Varsity Fellowship, now the Universities and Colleges Christian
Fellowship, a student movement connecting Christian Unions in universities and colleges throughout
Great Britain, and a member movement of the International Fellowship of Evangelical Students. That
historic association is maintained, and all senior IVP staff and committee members subscribe to the
UCCF Basis of Faith. Website: www.uccf.org.uk.

InterVarsity Press®, USA, is the book-publishing division of InterVarsity Christian Fellowship/
USA® and a member movement of the International Fellowship of Evangelical Students. Website:
www.intervarsity.org.

Unless otherwise stated, Scripture quotations are from the New International Version.

First published 2022

Set in Garamond 11/13pt
Typeset in Great Britain by Avocet Typeset, Bideford, Devon
Printed and bound in Great Britain by Ashford Colour Press Ltd, Gosport, Hampshire

UK ISBN: 978–1–78974–266–4 (print)
UK ISBN: 978–1–78974–267–1 (digital)

US ISBN: 978–1–5140–0504–0 (print)
US ISBN: 978–1–5140–0505–7 (digital)

**British Library Cataloguing-in-Publication Data**
A catalogue record for this book is available from the British Library.

**Library of Congress Cataloging-in-Publication Data**
A catalog record for this book is available from the Library of Congress.

# CONTENTS

# GENERAL PREFACE

The Tyndale Commentaries have been a flagship series for evangelical readers of the Bible for over sixty years. Both the original New Testament volumes (1956–1974) as well as the new commentaries (1983–2003) rightly established themselves as a point of first reference for those who wanted more than is usually offered in a one-volume Bible commentary, without requiring the technical skills in Greek and in Jewish and Graeco-Roman studies of the more detailed series, with the advantage of being shorter than the volumes of intermediate commentary series. The appearance of new popular commentary series demonstrates that there is a continuing demand for commentaries that appeal to Bible study leaders in churches and at universities. The publisher, editors and authors of the Tyndale Commentaries believe that the series continues to meet an important need in the Christian community, not the least in what we call today the Global South with its immense growth of churches and the corresponding need for a thorough understanding of the Bible by Christian believers.

In the light of new knowledge, new critical questions, new revisions of Bible translations and the need to provide specific guidance on the literary context and the genre of the individual passages as well as on theological emphases, it was time to publish new commentaries in the series. Three authors have revised their commentaries that appeared in the second series. The original aim remains. The new commentaries are neither too short nor unduly long. They are exegetical and thus root the interpretation of the text in its historical context. They do not aim to solve all critical questions, but they are written with an awareness of major scholarly debates which may be treated in the Introduction, in Additional Notes or in the commentary itself. While not specifically homiletic in aim, they want to help readers to understand the passage under consideration in such a way that they begin to see points of relevance and application, even though the commentary does not explicitly offer these. The authors base their exegesis on the Greek text, but they write for readers who do not know Greek; Hebrew and Greek terms that are discussed are transliterated. The English translation used for the first series was the Authorized (King James) Version, the volumes of the second series mostly used the Revised Standard Version; the volumes of the third series use either the New International Version (2011) or the New Revised Standard Version as primary versions, unless otherwise indicated by the author.

An immense debt of gratitude for the first and second series of the Tyndale Commentaries was owed to R. V. G. Tasker and L. Morris, who each wrote four of the commentaries themselves. The recruitment of new authors for the third series proved to be effortless, as colleagues responded enthusiastically to the opportunity to be involved in this project, a testimony to the larger number of New Testament scholars capable and willing to write commentaries, to the wider ethnic identity of contributors, and to the role that the Tyndale Commentaries have played in the church worldwide. It continues to be the hope of all those concerned with this series that God will graciously use the new commentaries to help readers understand as fully and clearly as possible the meaning of the New Testament.

Eckhard J. Schnabel, Series Editor
Nicholas Perrin, Consulting Editor

# AUTHOR'S PREFACE

During my college experience with InterVarsity Christian Fellowship, I was given the Tyndale commentary written by Ralph Martin as I prepared to lead a small-group Bible study on Philippians. This was the very first commentary I owned, and I fell in love with Paul's letter to the Philippians during that year of Bible study. I am grateful for the opportunity in God's providence to write this second edition on Philippians in the Tyndale series.

I want to thank a group of students who read the drafts of the commentary in a course on Philippians in spring 2021. Their joy in studying the text and willingness to engage with my ideas as they were fresh off the page spurred me on and sharpened my work. I am also grateful to my teaching assistants, Jenelle Lemons and Narah Larson, for their careful editing and thoughtful input. My editor, Eckhard Schnabel, provided invaluable feedback; and the team at Inter-Varsity Press was wonderful to work with from beginning to end.

Paul's letter to the Philippians continues to speak to the global church today. It offers guidance to contemporary churches seeking, in their specific cultural and societal contexts, to live out their distinctive identity in the Messiah and to pattern their lives together on the example of Jesus. Additionally, I would suggest that Paul's way of addressing this beloved congregation is a model of Christian leadership for those called to shepherd God's people today. It is with this pastoral vision in mind that I dedicate this book to my students at Bethel Seminary – both past and present. May your relationship with those you lead be the kind that Paul celebrates in this letter: 'my brothers and sisters, you whom I love and long for, my joy and crown, stand firm in the Lord in this way, dear friends!' (Phil. 4:1).

Jeannine Brown

# ABBREVIATIONS

| | |
|---|---|
| AB | Anchor Bible |
| ANTC | Abingdon New Testament Commentaries |
| *BBR* | *Bulletin for Biblical Research* |
| BDAG | *A Greek–English Lexicon of the New Testament and Other Early Christian Literature*, ed. W. Bauer, F. W. Danker, W. F. Arndt and F. W. Gingrich, 3rd edn (Chicago: University of Chicago Press, 2000) |
| BECNT | Baker Exegetical Commentary on the New Testament |
| *BibInt* | *Biblical Interpretation* |
| BNTC | Black's New Testament Commentaries |
| *ChrCent* | *Christian Century* |
| *CTR* | *Criswell Theological Review* |
| *DNTB* | *Dictionary of New Testament Background*, ed. Craig A. Evans and Stanley E. Porter (Downers Grove: InterVarsity Press, 2000) |
| *DPL* | *Dictionary of Paul and His Letters*, 2nd edn (Downers Grove: InterVarsity Press, forthcoming) |
| *EBR* | *Encyclopedia of the Bible and Its Reception*, ed. Hans-Josef Klauck et al. (Berlin: Walter de Gruyter, 2009) |
| *EvQ* | *Evangelical Quarterly* |
| *ExAud* | *Ex Auditu* |
| *Int* | *Interpretation* |

| | |
|---|---|
| *JBL* | *Journal of Biblical Literature* |
| *JETS* | *Journal of the Evangelical Theological Society* |
| *JSNT* | *Journal for the Study of the New Testament* |
| JSNTSup | Journal for the Study of the New Testament Supplement Series |
| *JTS* | *Journal of Theological Studies* |
| L&N | *Greek–English Lexicon of the New Testament: Based on Semantic Domains*, ed. Johannes P. Louw and Eugene A. Nida, 2nd edn (New York: United Bible Societies, 1989) |
| LXX | Septuagint (pre-Christian Greek version of the Old Testament) |
| MM | *The Vocabulary of the Greek Testament Illustrated from the Papyri and Other Non-Literary Sources*, ed. J. H. Moulton and G. Milligan (Grand Rapids: Eerdmans, 1930–82) |
| *NIB* | *The New Interpreter's Bible*, ed. Leander E. Keck, 12 vols. (Nashville: Abingdon, 1994–2004) |
| NICNT | New International Commentary on the New Testament |
| NIGTC | New International Greek Testament Commentary |
| *NovT* | *Novum Testamentum* |
| NovTSup | Supplements to Novum Testamentum |
| SBLGNT | *The Greek New Testament: SBL Edition*, ed. Michael W. Holmes (Atlanta: SBL, 2010) |
| SNTSMS | Society for New Testament Studies Monograph Series |
| SP | Sacra Pagina |
| *TLNT* | *Theological Lexicon of the New Testament*, C. Spicq, tr. and ed. J. D. Ernest (Peabody: Hendrickson, 1994) |
| TNTC | Tyndale New Testament Commentaries |
| *TynBul* | *Tyndale Bulletin* |
| *TZ* | *Theologische Zeitschrift* |
| WBC | Word Biblical Commentary |
| *ZNW* | *Zeitschrift für die neutestamentliche Wissenschaft und die Kunde der älteren Kirche* |

## Bible versions

| | |
|---|---|
| CEB | The Common English Bible. © Copyright 2011 by the Common English Bible. All rights reserved. Used by permission. |
| CJB | Complete Jewish Bible. Copyright © 1998 by David H. Stern. |
| CSB | The Christian Standard Bible. Copyright © 2017 by Holman Bible Publishers. Used by permission. Christian Standard Bible®, and CSB® are federally registered trademarks of Holman Bible Publishers, all rights reserved. |
| ESV | The ESV Bible (The Holy Bible, English Standard Version), copyright © 2001 by Crossway, a publishing ministry of Good News Publishers. Used by permission. All rights reserved. |
| GNT | The Good News Bible, The Bible in Today's English Version. New Testament © 1966, 1971, 1976 by the American Bible Society. |
| GNV | Geneva Bible, 1599 Edition. Published by Tolle Lege Press. GenevaBible.com All rights reserved. |
| ISV | The Holy Bible: International Standard Version®. Copyright © 1996–2007 by The ISV Foundation of Fullerton, California, USA. Used by permission of Davidson Press, LLC. ALL RIGHTS RESERVED INTERNATIONALLY. |
| NASB | The NEW AMERICAN STANDARD BIBLE®, Copyright © 1960, 1962, 1963, 1968, 1971, 1972, 1973, 1975, 1977, 1995 by The Lockman Foundation. Used by permission. |
| NET | The NET Bible, New English Translation, copyright © 1996 by Biblical Studies Press, LLC. NET Bible is a registered trademark. |
| NIV | The Holy Bible, New International Version (Anglicized edition). Copyright © 1979, 1984, 2011 by Biblica. Used by permission of Hodder & |

# SELECT BIBLIOGRAPHY

## Commentaries on Philippians

Bird, Michael and Nijay K. Gupta (2020), *Philippians*, New Cambridge Bible Commentary (Cambridge: Cambridge University Press).

Bockmuehl, Markus (1997), *The Epistle to the Philippians*, BNTC (London: A. & C. Black).

Cohick, Lynn. H. (2013), *Philippians*, Story of God Bible Commentary (Grand Rapids: Zondervan).

Fee, Gordon D. (1995), *Paul's Letter to the Philippians*, NICNT (Grand Rapids: Eerdmans).

Flemming, Dean (2009), *Philippians*, New Beacon Bible Commentary (Kansas City: Beacon Hill).

Fowl, Stephen E. (2005), *Philippians*, Two Horizons New Testament Commentary (Grand Rapids: Eerdmans).

Gupta, Nijay K. (2020), *Reading Philippians: A Theological Introduction*, Cascade Companions (Eugene: Cascade).

Hansen, G. Walter (2009), *The Letter to the Philippians*, Pillar New Testament Commentary (Grand Rapids: Eerdmans).

Hawthorne, Gerald F. (1983), *Philippians*, WBC 43 (Waco: Word).

Hellerman, Joseph H. (2015), *Philippians*, Exegetical Guide to the Greek New Testament (Nashville: B&H Academic).

Holloway, Paul A. (2017), *Philippians*, Hermeneia (Minneapolis: Fortress).

Hooker, Morna (2000), 'Philippians', in *NIB* 11 (Nashville: Abingdon), pp. 467–549.

Hunsinger, George (2020), *Philippians*, Brazos Theological Commentary on the Bible (Grand Rapids: Brazos).

Keown, Mark J. (2017), *Philippians*, Evangelical Exegetical Commentary, 2 vols. (Bellingham: Lexham).

Lightfoot, J. B. (1953), *Saint Paul's Epistle to the Philippians: A Revised Text, with Introduction, Notes, and Dissertations*, repr. (Grand Rapids: Zondervan).

Martin, Ralph P. (1959), *The Epistle of Paul to the Philippians*, TNTC (Grand Rapids: Eerdmans).

Migliore, Daniel L. (2014), *Philippians and Philemon*, Belief: A Theological Commentary on the Bible, 1st edn (Louisville: Westminster John Knox).

Osiek, Carolyn (2000), *Philippians, Philemon*, ANTC (Nashville: Abingdon).

Reumann, John (2008), *Philippians: A New Translation with Introduction and Commentary*, AB (New Haven: Yale University Press).

Silva, Moisés (2005), *Philippians*, BECNT, 2nd edn (Grand Rapids: Baker).

Stubbs, Monya A. (2007), 'Philippians', in Brian K. Blount, Cain Hope Felder, Clarice Jannette Martin and Emerson B. Powery (eds.), *True to Our Native Land: An African American New Testament Commentary* (Minneapolis: Fortress), pp. 363–379.

Tamez, Elsa (2017), 'Philippians', in Elsa Tamez, Cynthia Briggs Kittredge, Claire Miller Colombo and Alicia J. Batten, *Philippians, Colossians, Philemon*, Wisdom Commentary (Collegeville: Liturgical), pp. 1–122.

Thielman, Frank (1995), *Philippians*, NIV Application Commentary (Grand Rapids: Zondervan).

Thurston, B. and J. M. Ryan (2005), *Philippians and Philemon*, SP (Collegeville: Liturgical).

Works, Carla Swafford (2012), 'Philippians', in Carol A. Newsom, Sharon H. Ringe and Jacqueline E. Lapsley (eds.), *Women's Bible Commentary*, 3rd edn (Louisville: Westminster John Knox), pp. 581–584.

## Other commentaries, books, monographs and articles

Achtemeier, Paul J. (1990), '*Omne Verbum Sonat*: The New
Testament and the Oral Environment of Late Western
Antiquity', *JBL* 109, pp. 3–27.

Alexander, Loveday (1989), 'Hellenistic Letter-Forms and the
Structure of Philippians', *JSNT* 37, pp. 87–101.

Barclay, John M. G. (2017), *Paul and the Gift* (Grand Rapids:
Eerdmans).

Barr, James (1961), *The Semantics of Biblical Language* (Oxford:
Oxford University Press).

Bauckham, R. (2008), *Jesus and the God of Israel* (Grand Rapids:
Eerdmans).

Becker, Eve-Marie (2020), *Paul on Humility*, tr. and ed. Wayne
Coppins (Waco: Baylor University Press).

Becknell, Thomas and Mary Ellen Ashcroft (1995), *The Beginning of
Wisdom: Prayers for Growth and Understanding* (Nashville: Moorings).

Bertschmann, Dorothea H. (2018), 'Is There a Kenosis in This
Text? Rereading Philippians 3:2–11 in the Light of the Christ
Hymn', *JBL* 137, pp. 235–254.

Bockmuehl, Markus N. A. (1996), 'A Commentator's Approach to
the "Effective History" of Philippians', *JSNT* 18, pp. 57–88.

Bormann, Lukas (1995), *Philippi: Stadt und Christengemeinde zur Zeit
des Paulus* (Leiden: Brill).

Boyce, James L. 'Rhetoric and the Word of God: Treasure in
Earthen Vessels', in David S. Cunningham (ed.), *To Teach, to
Delight, and to Move: Theological Education in a Post-Christian World*
(Eugene: Cascade, 2004), pp. 201–222.

Brackley, Dean (1988), 'Downward Mobility: Social Implications
of St. Ignatius's Two Standards', *Studies in the Spirituality of the
Jesuits* 20, pp. 1–50.

Brewer, Raymond Rush (1954), 'The Meaning of *Politeuesthe* in
Philippians 1:27', *JBL* 73, pp. 76–83.

Brown, Jeannine K. (2009), 'Apostle, I: New Testament', *EBR* 1,
pp. 471–476.

——— (2017), 'The Love between Paul and the Philippian
Believers', in Paul N. Jackson (ed.), *Devotions on the Greek New
Testament*, vol. 2 (Grand Rapids: Zondervan), pp. 93–95.

———— (2019), 'Reconstructing the Historical Pharisees: Does
  Matthew's Gospel Have Anything to Contribute?', in Darrell
  L. Bock and J. Ed Komoszewski (eds.), *Jesus, Skepticism, and the
  Problem of History: Criteria and Context in the Study of Christian
  Origins* (Grand Rapids: Zondervan), pp. 164–182.
———— (2020), *The Gospels as Stories: A Narrative Approach to Matthew,
  Mark, Luke, and John* (Grand Rapids: Baker Academic).
———— (2021), *Scripture as Communication: Introducing Biblical
  Hermeneutics*, 2nd edn (Grand Rapids: Baker Academic).
———— (forthcoming), 'Letter to the Philippians', *DPL*.
Brown, Jeannine K., Carla M. Dahl and Wyndy Corbin
  Reuschling (2011), *Becoming Whole and Holy: An Integrative
  Conversation about Christian Formation* (Grand Rapids: Brazos).
Brown, Jeannine K. and Nicklas Fox (forthcoming),
  'Hermeneutics/Interpreting Paul', *DPL*.
Brown, Jeannine K. and Kyle Roberts (2018), *Matthew*, Two
  Horizons New Testament Commentary (Grand Rapids:
  Eerdmans).
Brown, Jeannine K. and Steven J. Sandage (2015), 'Relational
  Integration: Relational Integration as Developmental and
  Intercultural 2', *Journal of Psychology & Theology* 43, pp. 179–191.
Brueggemann, Walter (1999), 'The Liturgy of Abundance, the
  Myth of Scarcity', *ChrCent* 116, pp. 342–347.
Capper, B. J. (1993), 'Paul's Dispute with Philippi: Understanding
  Paul's Argument in Phil 1 – 2 from His Thanks in 4:10–20',
  *TZ* 49, pp. 193–214.
Childs, Brevard S. (2008), *The Church's Guide for Reading Paul: The
  Canonical Shaping of the Pauline Corpus* (Grand Rapids:
  Eerdmans).
Croy, N. C. (2003), '"To Die Is Gain" (Philippians 1:19–26): Does
  Paul Contemplate Suicide?', *JBL* 122, pp. 517–531.
Cunningham, David S. (ed.) (2004), *To Teach, to Delight, and to Move:
  Theological Education in a Post-Christian World* (Eugene: Cascade).
Daley, Brian (2006), *Gregory of Nazianzus* (London: Taylor &
  Francis).
deSilva, David (2016), 'Appeals to "Logos", "Pathos", and
  "Ethos" in Galatians 5:1–12: An Investigation of Paul's
  "Inventio"', in Stanley E. Porter (ed.), *Paul and Ancient Rhetoric:*

*Theory and Practice in the Hellenistic Context* (New York: Cambridge University Press), pp. 245–264.

Droge, Arthur J. (1988), '*Mori Lucrum*: Paul and Ancient Theories of Suicide', *NovT* 30, pp. 262–286.

Du Mez, Kristin Kobes (2020), *Jesus and John Wayne: How White Evangelicals Corrupted a Faith and Fractured a Nation* (New York: Liveright/Norton).

Eastman, Susan Grove (2008), 'Imitating Christ Imitating Us: Paul's Educational Project in Philippians', in J. R. Wagner, C. K. Rowe and A. K. Grieb (eds.), *The Word Leaps the Gap: Essays in Scripture and Theology in Honor of Richard B. Hays* (Grand Rapids: Eerdmans), pp. 427–451.

—— (2011), 'Philippians 2:6–11: Incarnation as Mimetic Participation', *Journal for the Study of Paul and His Letters* 1, pp. 1–22.

—— (2017), *Paul and the Person: Reframing Paul's Anthropology* (Grand Rapids: Eerdmans).

Edwards, Dennis R. (2013), 'Good Citizenship: A Study of Philippians 1:27 and Its Implications for Contemporary Urban Ministry', *ExAud* 29, pp. 74–93.

Elliott, J. K. (1993), *The New Testament Apocrypha* (Oxford: Oxford University Press).

Fee, Gordon D. (1989), '*Laos* and Leadership under the New Covenant', *Crux* 25, pp. 3–13.

—— (1998), 'To What End Exegesis? Reflections on Exegesis and Spirituality in Philippians 4:10–20', *BBR* 8, pp. 75–88.

Fellows, Richard G. (2016), 'Name Giving by Paul and the Destinations of Acts', *TynBul* 67, pp. 247–268.

Fellows, Richard G. and Alistair C. Stewart (2018), 'Euodia, Syntyche and the Role of Syzygos: Phil 4:2–3', *ZNW* 109, pp. 222–234.

Fitzgerald, J. (ed.) (1996), *Friendship, Flattery, and Frankness of Speech: Studies on Friendship in the New Testament World*, NovTSup 82 (Leiden: Brill).

Flemming, Dean (2011), 'Exploring a Missional Reading of Scripture: Philippians as a Case Study', *EvQ* 83, pp. 3–18.

Foster, Paul (2009), 'Πίστις Χριστοῦ Terminology in Philippians and Ephesians', in Michael F. Bird and Preston M. Sprinkle (eds.), *The Faith of Jesus Christ: Exegetical, Biblical, and Theological Studies* (Peabody: Hendrickson), pp. 91–109.

Fowl, Stephen E. (1990), *The Story of Christ in the Ethics of Paul*, JSNTSup (Sheffield: JSOT).

—— (2002), 'Know Your Context: Giving and Receiving Money in Philippians', *Int* 56, pp. 45–58.

Fredrickson, David E. (2013), *Eros and the Christ: Longing and Envy in Paul's Christology* (Minneapolis: Augsburg Fortress).

Fredriksen, Paula (2015), 'Why Should a "Law-Free" Mission Mean a "Law-Free" Apostle?', *JBL* 134, pp. 637–650.

Gehring, Roger W. (2004), *House Church and Mission: The Importance of Household Structure in Early Christianity* (Peabody: Hendrickson).

Gorman, Michael J. (2007), '"Although/Because He Was in the Form of God": The Theological Significance of Paul's Master Story (Phil 2:6–11)', *Journal for Theological Interpretation* 1, pp. 147–169.

—— (2013), 'Paul and the Cruciform Way of God in Christ', *Journal of Moral Theology* 2, pp. 64–83.

Green, Joel B. (2007), *1 Peter*, Two Horizons New Testament Commentary (Grand Rapids: Eerdmans).

Gupta, Nijay K. (2020), *Paul and the Language of Faith* (Grand Rapids: Eerdmans).

Heen, Erik M. (2004), 'Phil 2:6–11 and Resistance to Local Timocratic Rule', in Richard A. Horsley (ed.), *Paul and the Roman Imperial Order* (Harrisburg: Trinity Press International), pp. 125–153.

Heilig, Christoph (2014), 'Methodological Considerations for the Search of Counter-Imperial "Echoes" in Pauline Literature', in John Anthony Dunne and Dan Batovici (eds.), *Reactions to Empire: Sacred Texts in Their Socio-Political Contexts* (Tübingen: Mohr Siebeck), pp. 73–92.

Hellerman, Joseph (2009), 'ΜΟΡΦΗ ΘΕΟΥ as Signifier of Social Status in Philippians 2:6', *JETS* 52, pp. 779–797.

Henderson, Timothy (2010), 'Beware of Overlooked Allusions: A New Proposal for Intertextuality in Philippians 3', Paper presented at Annual Meeting of the Upper Midwest Region of the SBL, St. Paul, MN, 10 April 2010.

Holloway, P. A. (2001), *Consolation in Philippians: Philosophical Sources and Rhetorical Strategy*, SNTSMS 112 (New York: Cambridge University Press).

Hooker, Morna D. (1971), 'Interchange in Christ', *JTS* 22, pp. 349–361.

—— (1985), 'Interchange in Christ and Ethics', *JSNT* 8, pp. 3–17.

Hurtado, Larry W. (1998), *One God, One Lord: Early Christian Devotion and Ancient Jewish Monotheism*, 2nd edn (Edinburgh: T&T Clark).

Jeremias, Joachim (1963), 'Zu Phil 2:7: *Heauton Ekenōsen*', *NovT* 6, pp. 182–188.

Johnson, Luke Timothy (2020), *Constructing Paul: The Canonical Paul* (Grand Rapids: Eerdmans).

Kennedy, George A. (1984), *New Testament Interpretation through Rhetorical Criticism* (Chapel Hill: University of North Carolina).

Keener, Craig S. (2020), *Acts*, New Cambridge Bible Commentary (Cambridge: Cambridge University Press).

Klauck, Hans-Josef (2006), *Ancient Letters and the New Testament: A Guide to Context and Exegesis* , tr. and ed. Daniel P. Bailey (Waco: Baylor University Press).

McAuley, D. (2015), *Paul's Covert Use of Scripture: Intertextuality and Rhetorical Situation in Philippians 2:10–16* (Eugene: Pickwick).

McCaulley, Esau (2020), *Reading while Black: African American Biblical Interpretation as an Exercise of Hope* (Downers Grove: InterVarsity Press).

Martin, R. P. (1967), *Carmen Christi* (Cambridge: Cambridge University Press).

Mason, Steve (2000), 'Pharisees', *DNTB*, pp. 782–787.

Morris, Leon (1956), '*Kai Hapax Kai Dis*', *NovT* 1, pp. 205–208.

Nanos, Mark D. (2009), 'Paul's Reversal of Jews Calling Gentiles "Dogs" (Philippians 3:2): 1600 Years of an Ideological Tale Wagging an Exegetical Dog?', *BibInt* 17, pp. 448–482.

Nikki, Nina (2019), *Opponents and Identity in Philippi*, NovTSup (Leiden: Brill).

Nongbri, Brent (2009), 'Two Neglected Textual Variants in
    Philippians 1', *JBL* 128, pp. 803–808.
Novenson, Matthew V. (2005), 'Re-Mapping the Universe: Paul
    and the Emperor in 1 Thessalonians and Philippians', *JSNT*
    27, pp. 301–322.
——— (2012), *Christ among the Messiahs: Christ Language in Paul and
    Messiah Language in Ancient Judaism* (New York: Oxford
    University Press).
Oakes, P. (2001), *Philippians: From People to Letter*, SNTSMS 110
    (Cambridge: Cambridge University Press).
Patterson, Jane Lancaster (2015), *Keeping the Feast: Metaphors of
    Sacrifice in 1 Corinthians and Philippians* (Atlanta: SBL).
Peterlin, Davorin (1995), *Paul's Letter to the Philippians in the Light of
    the Disunity in the Church* (New York: Brill).
Peterman, Gerald W. (1997), *Paul's Gift from Philippi: Conventions of
    Gift-Exchange and Christian Giving* (Cambridge: Cambridge
    University Press).
Peters, Ted (1994), *Sin: Radical Evil in Soul and Society* (Grand
    Rapids: Eerdmans).
Rapske, Brian (1994), *The Book of Acts and Paul in Roman Custody*
    (Grand Rapids: Eerdmans).
Reed, Jeffrey T. (1997), *A Discourse Analysis of Philippians: Method and
    Rhetoric in the Debate over Literary Integrity* (Sheffield: Sheffield
    Academic).
Sandage, Steven J., Mary L. Jensen and Daniel Jass (2008),
    'Relational Spirituality and Transformation: Risking Intimacy
    and Alterity', *Journal of Spiritual Formation & Soul Care* 1,
    pp. 182–206.
Sandage, Steven J., D. Rupert, G. S. Stavros and N. G. Devor
    (2020), *Relational Spirituality in Psychotherapy: Healing Suffering and
    Promoting Growth* (Washington, DC: American Psychological
    Association).
Schnabel, Eckhard J. (2004), *Early Christian Mission: Paul and the
    Early Church* (Downers Grove: InterVarsity Press).
Scott, Ian W. (2009), *Paul's Way of Knowing: Story, Experience, and the
    Spirit* (Grand Rapids: Baker Academic).
Smit, Peter-Ben (2013), *Paradigms of Being in Christ: A Study of the
    Epistle to the Philippians* (London: Bloomsbury T&T Clark).

Smith, Julien C. H. (2020), *Paul and the Good Life: Transformation and Citizenship in the Commonwealth of God* (Waco: Baylor University Press).

Stowers, S. (1991), 'Friends and Enemies in the Politics of Heaven', in J. M. Bassler (ed.), *Pauline Theology*, vol. 1 (Minneapolis: Fortress), pp. 105–121.

Sumney, Jerry L. (2007), 'Paul and Christ-Believing Jews Whom He Opposes', in Matt Jackson-McCabe (ed.), *Jewish Christianity Reconsidered: Rethinking Ancient Groups and Texts* (Minneapolis: Fortress), pp. 57–80.

Thiselton, Anthony C. (2000), *The First Epistle to the Corinthians*, NIGTC (Grand Rapids: Eerdmans).

Wallace, Daniel B. (1996), *Greek Grammar beyond the Basics: An Exegetical Syntax of the New Testament – With Scripture, Subject, and Greek Word Indexes* (Grand Rapids: Zondervan).

Weima, Jeffrey A. D. (2016), *Paul the Ancient Letter Writer: An Introduction to Epistolary Analysis* (Grand Rapids: Baker Academic).

Wenham, Gordon J. (1979), *The Book of Leviticus*, New International Commentary on the Old Testament (Grand Rapids: Eerdmans).

Willis, Wendall Lee (2012), 'The Shaping of Character: Virtue in Philippians 4:8–9', *Restoration Quarterly* 54, pp. 65–76.

—— (2019), 'Paul, the Gift and Philippians', *Horizons in Biblical Theology* 41, pp. 174–190.

Wright, N. T. (1986), '*Harpagmos* and the Meaning of Philippians 2:5–11', *JTS* 37, pp. 321–352.

—— (2013), *Pauline Perspectives: Essays on Paul, 1978–2013* (Minneapolis: Fortress).

—— (2015), 'Joy: Some New Testament Perspectives and Questions', in Miroslav Volf and Justin E. Crisp (eds.), *Joy and Human Flourishing: Essays on Theology, Culture and the Good Life* (Minneapolis: Fortress), pp. 39–62.

—— (2019), *History and Eschatology: Jesus and the Promise of Natural Theology* (Waco: Baylor University Press).

Zoccali, Christopher (2011), '"Rejoice, O Gentiles, with His People": Paul's Intra-Jewish Rhetoric in Philippians 3:1–9', *CTR* 9, pp. 17–31.

—— (2017), *Reading Philippians after Supersessionism: Jews, Gentiles, and Covenant Identity* (Eugene: Cascade).

,

# INTRODUCTION

The letter to the Philippians is Paul's warm and celebratory expression of his affection and concern for his sisters and brothers in Christ in Philippi. The church at Philippi is one that Paul and his fellow itinerant ministers had been instrumental in founding, probably over a decade before he pens this letter to them. In it, he assures these dear friends that his ministry of the gospel and joy in the Lord are unhindered, in spite of being 'in chains' and so far away from them. His deep desire for this congregation is that they live out their unity in Christ with one another by practising the countercultural virtue of humility. As they encounter any suffering for their singular loyalty to Jesus their Messiah and Lord, this unity will cause them to 'stand firm in the Lord' (4:1). Throughout Philippians, Paul holds up a number of exemplars or models for these believers, with Jesus being the model par excellence who renounced his status advantages and humbled himself to show concern for 'the interests of [the] others' (2:4). The letter to the Philippians, though relatively brief, includes a rich tapestry of theological and pastoral motifs that encourage the church at Philippi to embrace knowing Christ more deeply and to adopt his mindset for their communal life together.

## 1. Hermeneutical considerations

Exegetical commentaries do not, as a rule, include any kind of extended discussion of their hermeneutical vantage point.[1] This may simply be due to the expectation that an exegetical commentary will address, as a matter of course, historical enquiry, literary (including linguistic, grammatical, syntactical and discourse) analysis and theological assessment (i.e. the author's distinctive point of view on matters of faith). Yet any savvy reader of the many commentaries on Philippians will soon discover that each commentator exemplifies a particular exegetical and hermeneutical method, with accompanying underlying, though often unstated, assumptions. While there is often much in common on a macro level (e.g. the shared assumption that a certain amount of historical reconstruction is necessary for understanding Philippians), inevitably there are distinctions among the commentaries on a whole range of hermeneutical matters. For example, one can detect how important any particular commentator considers a word's history to be for determining its meaning in Philippians by a quick look at the space allotted to diachronic analysis – that is, a word's development over time.

My goal in this initial section is to make explicit my method for approaching Philippians. Along with my fellow commentators on Philippians, I follow the exegetical practice of a close reading of the text of Philippians, coupled with historical reconstruction of the situations of Paul and the Philippians around the time of the letter's composition. Careful attention to the historical and literary facets of the letter leads to an understanding of Paul's theology in Philippians, which is both pastoral and practical.[2] Paul's theological reflection in Philippians centres on God's work in Christ to bring

---

1. For examples, see Bockmuehl, pp. 42–45; Fowl, pp. 1–8; Tamez, pp. 1–3.
2. Brown and Fox, 'Hermeneutics', forthcoming.

salvation to humanity. His theology issues in exhortations for the community of faith to live out in the present their already granted salvation in the light of their future hope. Given this general sense of how history, literature and theology function together in Philippians, I explore in this section my reflections on the interpretive issues related to the Philippians' situation, Paul's authorship, Paul's language and Paul's theology.

### a. Reading the Philippians' situation

To understand Philippians well, contemporary readers will need to reconstruct something of the situation of the Philippians – their cultural context and their church setting (see 2b). While such historical reconstruction always involves 'approximating' the Philippians' context,[3] historical work is essential for understanding the letter well. Since every reading supplies a context, the question is not whether an interpreter will sketch a backdrop for Philippians, it is whether he or she will do so intentionally with the benefit of solid historical evidence, or instead assume a backdrop apart from careful historical analysis.

An initial question for reconstructing the Philippians' setting involves the specific sources to be used. The letter is, of course, a primary resource, especially for considering the implied audience – the Philippian audience we discern from the contours of the letter itself. Evidence from outside the letter would then support internal evidence in corroboratory fashion. Evidence external to the letter itself could include (1) Paul's other letters, with a recognition of the rhetorical and contingent nature of those writings (e.g. 1 Thess. 2:1–2; 2 Cor. 8:1–5); (2) archaeological and inscriptional evidence from ancient Philippi; (3) evidence from other writers of the time, with the proviso that these authors represent particular points of view. The book of Acts provides a highly relevant example of the last category (given its focus on Paul's ministry) and fits the genre of ancient historiography. Judicious use of Acts 16, the Lukan account of how the church at Philippi began,

---

3. See Bockmuehl, p. 43.

can helpfully corroborate and augment what we hear in the letter to the Philippians.[4]

In the work of historical reconstruction, a balanced approach is important – one that avoids the ends of a spectrum from under-constructing to over-constructing the setting. *Under-constructing* ignores the need for deducing facets of the original setting, often with the assumption that all that is needed is a 'plain reading' of the text. Yet, since every reading necessarily presumes or supplies a setting for that reading, there is no such thing as context-less interpretation. As Bockmuehl aptly observes, 'It is too early to risk forgetting that many of this past century's gravest injustices have been the consequence of callously ahistorical and unhistorical misappropriations of texts for ideological purposes.'[5]

The other side of the spectrum involves a tendency to *over-construct* the historical setting. By this term, I refer to deducing particulars of the original setting from textual details apart from consistent or sustained evidence. For example, to assume that the Philippians have an issue with grumbling because Paul calls them to refrain from grumbling (2:14) probably goes beyond the evidence across the letter, especially in the light of 'grumbling' as a likely echo from the Old Testament testimony of Israel's wilderness journeying, used in Philippians 2:14–16 where a number of such echoes occur (see comment on 2:14).

A challenging area for reconstruction in Philippians is the identity of 'opponents' Paul references quite briefly across the letter (1:28; 3:2; 3:18–19; see 2f). A key question is whether these references point to one, two or three distinct groups influencing the Philippians negatively in some way. Another question is how much these brief and fairly oblique references should be read in the light of Pauline opponents in other letters of his (e.g. Galatians, 1 and 2 Corinthians).

---

4. For a discussion of the genre and usefulness of Acts as history, see Keener, *Acts*, pp. 1–29.

5. Bockmuehl, p. 44. McCaulley offers some examples in *Reading while Black*, pp. 18, 168–169.

## b. Reading Paul aided by the 'implied author'

A crucial interpretive issue of the authorship of Philippians in relation to other Pauline letters is how much, if at all, these other writings should have an impact on our understanding of Philippians. It might seem obvious that it would be advantageous to study Paul's other letters to help understand Paul's language, thinking and theology. Yet the question of Pauline authorship of the thirteen canonical letters ascribed to Paul muddies the waters. Are only the six other 'assured' letters from Paul's pen relevant for assisting in interpretation of Philippians? Or can we draw from Ephesians, Colossians and 2 Thessalonians as well? What about the 'pastorals'? And does it matter whether the interpreter sees Paul's theology as remaining stable over the course of his letters, or whether Paul's theology develops over time (across his letters)?

Given this thorny set of issues, I have found it helpful to draw on the literary concept of the implied author for setting and weighting priorities for studying Philippians (or any other individual letter). This concept identifies a discrete, textually derived portrait of Paul in each of his letters, suggesting that there is value in delineating that persona as a primary task for interpreting the letter at hand.[6] This would set out as a first and primary endeavour sketching the persona of Paul and his message derived from Philippians, with assistance from his other letters (1) to provide important historical information to fill in gaps in Philippians (similar to using Acts 16 to augment historical reconstruction for understanding Philippians); and (2) as a secondary task to understand better Paul's thinking and practice (e.g. from literary and theological angles). The latter task tends to move beyond consideration of Philippians to reflect on either (or both) the 'historical Paul' or the 'canonical Paul'.[7]

---

6. Brown (*Gospels as Stories*, p. 193) defines the implied author as the 'textually derived construct for understanding the author, which is distinct from the empirical (flesh-and-blood) author. The implied author is the writing persona presupposed in the [text] itself.'

7. See Childs' discussion on the relationship between these two in *Reading Paul*, pp. 1–10.

One strategy for focusing on the implied author (the implied Paul) of Philippians involves discerning how the Philippian recipients of the letter may have 'experienced' Paul as they heard the letter read aloud in their gatherings. Bringing their previous relationship to and experience of Paul to that reading, their sense of Paul from the letter would have built upon the Paul they knew. We have no indication that these Philippian believers would have had access to any of Paul's previous letters, so we should be cautious about reading the 'implied author' of other letters into Philippians. It is important to strike a balance between utilizing other letters for historical reconstruction and literary analysis, and steering clear of imposing the characterization of Paul derived from other letters on the implied Paul of Philippians. As Bockmuehl suggests, 'Physical or mental icons of Paul are invariably present whenever anyone reads or hears any of his letters, while at the same time our view of the apostle is distinctively coloured by each document.'[8] The goal is to allow Philippians to lead the way for understanding the Pauline 'icon' that emerges from it.

When the Paul of Philippians is unduly coloured by readings of Paul from his other letters, a skewed portrait can emerge. For example, Romans and Galatians (along with the Corinthian correspondence) have exerted significant influence on Pauline studies and the church's appropriation of Paul. As a result, Paul is sometimes viewed as a polemicist, not afraid to speak bluntly and often lacking in warmth and tact. Some interpreters have tapped into this sort of Pauline portrait for Philippians, reconstructed from the internal evidence of disunity among the Philippians as well as from potential hints of discord between Paul and this church surmised from 2:25–30 and 4:10–20. As Osiek observes (though disavows), 'some commentators [see] conflict everywhere in the letter'.[9] Yet these possible clues about relational problems between Paul and the Philippians pale in comparison with the explicit and sustained evidence of the loyal and warm relationship that pervades the

---

8. Bockmuehl, 'History', p. 65.

9. Osiek, p. 78. Examples of interpreting conflict behind some or much of the letter include Capper, 'Dispute', and Peterlin, *Disunity*.

letter. As I will suggest in this commentary, Paul writes to the Philippians 'in almost wholly commendable terms'.[10]

## c. Reading Paul's language

New Testament studies of the past sixty years has seen a shift in emphasis from attention on individual words to a focus on larger segments and whole discourses. Since the seminal work of James Barr in his *Semantics of Biblical Language* (1961), scholars have come to recognize that meaning does not adhere in individual words but in their contexts, immediate and extended. In this light, the interpretive process very much resembles a hermeneutic circle or spiral, in which the whole (a discourse) informs the parts (individual words) and the parts inform the whole. In this commentary, any focus on particular words and their meanings will be assessed within the wider contexts in which a word occurs.

Increased attention to linguistics informs the way we understand how words work.[11] As we think of individual words, it is important to realize that most words have more than one *sense* or meaning. In Philippians 3:15, Paul refers to believers who are 'mature' or 'perfect' (including himself in this group), using the Greek adjective *teleios*. This word has more than one sense, with 'mature' and 'perfect' expressing two of its possible senses ('initiated' into a religion is another; BDAG, p. 995). Commentators disagree on which sense Paul is using in Philippians, with some who argue for 'perfect' suggesting Paul is being ironic to call out perfectionist tendencies within the Philippian congregation (e.g. NET: 'those of us who are "perfect" . . .').

As we recognize that most words have more than one sense, we should be cautious about asserting that any particular word has a *basic sense*, a meaning that underlies any other senses of the word. Instead, a word might have a primary use in any particular author or corpus (e.g. the Pauline letters). For example, Paul frequently uses the Greek word *sarx* (often translated 'flesh') to denote the realm of human captivity to sin, as contrasted with the realm of the

---

10. Thurston and Ryan, p. 16.
11. For a fuller discussion, see Brown, *Scripture*, pp. 179–186.

Spirit inaugurated in the Messiah (e.g. Rom. 7:5; 8:3–9). Yet Paul can use *sarx* without any negative connotation, as he does in Philippians 1:22 and 24, for his physical 'body'. Neither usage is more *basic*; both are possible senses depending on context.

The fallacy that any particular word has a basic meaning lends itself to the assumption that it is important to identify the 'literal' meaning of a word. Yet if words have multiple senses, not a single basic sense, referring to the 'literal' meaning of a word is confusing at best.[12] Paul calls the Philippian believers *adelphoi* quite a number of times across the letter (e.g. 1:12; 3:1; 4:1, 8). This term refers to siblings, either male siblings ('brothers') or as a generic for siblings of both genders ('brothers and sisters').[13] Context determines which reference is in view; and, given Paul's audience of both female and male believers, he is clearly addressing both when he refers to the Philippians as *adelphoi*. It is inaccurate to claim that 'brothers' is the literal meaning of *adelphoi*. Instead, in any particular context, *adelphoi* can mean 'brothers' (e.g. Matt. 4:18; and singular 'brother' for *adelphos* at Phil. 2:25) or 'siblings' (i.e. 'brothers and sisters').[14]

Additionally, words do not mean the sum total of all their possible senses, a fallacy Barr called 'illegitimate totality transfer'.[15] For example, Paul uses *logizomai* in Philippians 4:8 to call his audience either to 'think about' what is virtuous and excellent or to 'evaluate' what is virtuous and excellent (BDAG, p. 597). While I argue in the

---

12. Sometimes 'literal' is used to refer to a strict or wooden rendering of the Greek intended to visualize Greek word order or phrasing in English. At a few points in the commentary, I use the language 'rendered woodenly' to illuminate Greek grammatical issues.

13. Masculine linguistic gender was used for the generic in Koine Greek to indicate a person, either male or female, or for a group that includes both genders.

14. In fact, we could note that Paul uses this term in Philippians 'non-literally', that is, metaphorically, since he is not claiming that the Philippians are his physical relatives but his spiritual (metaphorical) siblings; i.e. family members with kinship ties.

15. Barr, *Semantics*, pp. 218–222.

commentary for the latter sense, what is least likely is that Paul means to call forth all possible senses of the word in a single occurrence. He means either one sense or the other; not both (authors play on words only sparingly). Another example is the term *apostolos* (Phil. 2:25), which can indicate that Epaphroditus is the Philippians' 'messenger' or their 'apostle', with the latter having a semi-technical sense within New Testament usage. In the context of Philippians 2, it seems fairly clear that 'messenger' (the non-technical sense) is what Paul intends, so we should not read 'apostle' into this occurrence in addition to 'messenger'.

A few linguistic terms regularly used in the commentary are defined here.

- *Cognate*: A word that shares its root with another word; for example, the related noun and verb forms of the same word, such as *chara* ('joy') and *chairō* ('rejoice').
- *Hapax* (shortened from the Greek, *hapax legomenon*): A word that occurs only once in a particular corpus; in this commentary, used of words that occur only once in the New Testament or once in the Pauline letters.
- *Sense*: What is meant or denoted by a word; for example, *kyrios* denotes 'one who is in a position of authority, *lord*, *master*' (BDAG, p. 577).
- *Referent*: What a word points to outside its linguistic (literary) context; for example, in Philippians 2:11, *kyrios* is used specifically to refer to Jesus Christ.

### d. Reading Paul's theology

Some commentary series, like this one, include discrete attention to the task of contextualizing the messages of the biblical text being studied for a contemporary audience (see Theology sections). This is an appropriate task given that Paul is already theologically and Christologically motivated. As Gupta frames it, Paul's

> overarching goal was for his readers/auditors to faithfully, joyfully, and freely embrace the fullness of the gospel . . . [and] those who read Paul's letters from a perspective and purpose of faith are encouraged to read

them *theologically* towards better knowledge of God and deeper
communion with God.[16]

Given the wide variety of ways theology is understood and
accomplished, there is no single, monolithic approach to the
contextualizing task. In this commentary, an important starting
point is the recognition that Paul is writing pastoral or practical
theology to his church audiences. In Philippians, as in Paul's other
letters, we already see Paul 'theologizing', and we see him doing so
in the light of the specific issues and needs of his audience.[17] Given
the inherently theological character of Paul's writings, one way of
addressing theology is to focus on Paul's specific theological reflection in this letter – the theology of Philippians (for examples, see
Theology on 2:5–11 and on 4:2–9).[18] Another way of conceiving the
task is to hear how Paul's thinking in Philippians fits his
theologizing more broadly, across any number of his letters; this is
the task of exploring Pauline theology (e.g. Theology on 1:1–11).
Another approach, one that has gained significant traction in biblical studies in recent decades, is to attend to the history of
interpretation of the text in question.[19] This approach highlights
ways a text has been understood across the church's history.

Finally, an approach used in this commentary at a number of
points involves constructive theological reflection that engages
with the ideas of Philippians from the vantage point of 'contemporary interests, methods, and concerns' and with 'a variety of
voices'.[20] While it is always the case that interpreters bring their
own experiences and perspectives to their engagement with the
biblical text, the approach of constructive theology makes this
vantage point explicit and pursues a conversation with the text with
contemporary interests in mind. For example, in my theological

---

16. Gupta, pp. 9–10.
17. Brown and Fox, 'Hermeneutics', forthcoming.
18. See Bockmuehl's caution about such a narrow endeavour (pp. 41–42).
19. See, for example, Bockmuehl, pp. 43–45; Bockmuehl, 'History'; and
    Silva, pp. 26–34.
20. Brown and Roberts, *Matthew*, p. 381.

reflections on Philippians 2, I engage with the interrelationships of Paul, Timothy, Epaphroditus and the rest of the Philippian believers in conversation with psychological literature on anxiety (see Theology section on 2:19–30). And in the Theology sections on 2:12–18 and 3:1–11, I address how Philippians might be thoughtfully engaged with in relation to Paul's Jewish identity and Israel's continuing place as God's people, in the light of contemporary concerns about anti-Semitism in biblical interpretation (e.g. replacement theologies).

## 2. Historical matters[21]

### a. Author

Paul is the self-declared author of the letter (1:1); and Philippians is one of seven Pauline letters whose authorship is uncontested by contemporary scholarship (along with Romans, 1 and 2 Corinthians, Galatians, 1 Thessalonians and Philemon).[22] While Paul joins his name with Timothy's ('Paul and Timothy . . . to . . .'), implying equal authorial standing, it becomes clear from Paul's first-person address throughout the letter and his references to Timothy in the third person (2:19–23) that Timothy co-sponsors rather than co-writes Philippians. Of all such co-sponsors of Paul's letters, Timothy is mentioned most often (2 Cor. 1:1; Col. 1:1; 1 Thess. 1:1; 2 Thess. 1:1). There is no indication that Paul relies on an amanuensis for this letter, as he does for Romans (Rom. 16:22) and probably does for other letters that offer a concluding line written in his own hand (1 Cor. 16:21; Col. 4:18; 2 Thess. 3:17; cf. Gal. 6:11).

If we draw on the concept of the implied reader (see 1b), the Philippian letter illumines a portrait of its author, Paul, as deeply

---

21. Many of the ideas explored and detailed in parts 2 and 4 of this introduction are based on my work in Brown, 'Philippians' (forthcoming).

22. For a recent proposal that accounts for the significant differences among all thirteen letters by proposing a number of 'Pauline schools' involving relevant co-sponsors and amanuenses that worked with Paul, see Johnson, *Constructing Paul*, pp. 90–92.

invested in and attached to his siblings in Christ who reside in Philippi. His tone across the letter to this church is one of affection (e.g. 1:3–8; 2:12; 4:1) and concern for their well-being (e.g. 2:28; 4:6–7, 17). Paul offers his own assurances that he is faring well and even rejoicing as he considers his own situation, in spite of being in prison (e.g. 1:12; 2:17–18; 4:18). Any harsh language from Paul is reserved for potential threats from the outside to the well-being of these dear believers in Christ (1:28; 3:2, 18–19).

The portrait of Paul offered by Philippians aligns in some fairly obvious but important ways with what we learn about Paul from other parts of the New Testament (Acts and his other letters). First, when writing Philippians Paul is in prison (1:7, 13–14, 17). This is also the case for three other Pauline letters: Philemon, Ephesians and Colossians. Acts attests to Paul routinely being imprisoned for his preaching of the gospel: in Philippi (Acts 16:19–40), in Jerusalem (21:27 – 23:22), in Caesarea (23:23 – 26:32) and in Rome (28:11–31). Paul also attests to frequent imprisonments in 2 Corinthians 11:23 (cf. Rom. 16:7; 2 Tim. 1:8).

Second, the autobiographical character of Philippians 3:5–6 provides information that contributes to a portrait of Paul, with many of the descriptors in 3:5–6 corroborated elsewhere in the New Testament. Paul's identification of himself as from 'the people of Israel' and 'of the tribe of Benjamin' (Phil. 3:5) aligns with his self-identification in Romans: 'I am an Israelite myself, a descendant of Abraham, from the tribe of Benjamin' (Rom. 11:1). Paul identifies himself as a Pharisee (Phil. 3:5), which is attested in Acts 23:6 (cf. 5:34); and he refers to his 'zeal [in] persecuting the church' (Phil. 3:6). Similarly, Paul, as characterized in Acts, claims, 'I was just as zealous for God as any of you are today. I persecuted the followers of this Way to their death, arresting both men and women and throwing them into prison' (Acts 22:3b–4; cf. Gal. 1:13). Paul's other self-descriptions in Philippians 3 – that he is 'a Hebrew of Hebrews' (3:5) and is 'faultless' regarding a Torah-based righteousness (3:6) – are paralleled in Galatians 1:14, where Paul claims to previously have been 'advancing in Judaism beyond many of my own age among my people and . . . extremely zealous for the traditions of my fathers'.

## b. Audience

The make-up and contours of the Philippian church are most often implicit in Paul's letter to them. Sketching their portrait involves taking the clues we find in the letter and filling in some amount of detail from what we know about the city of Philippi and its inhabitants in the first century AD and from what we can glean from Acts 16, which narrates the inception of the Philippian church through the ministry of Paul and his associates.

### i. The city of Philippi

The city of Philippi (originally, Krenides) was so named in the fourth century BC by Philip of Macedon. He subjugated the city shortly after it had been settled by Greeks who had come from the island of Thasos (c.360 BC). In 168 BC, the Romans conquered and claimed Philippi, and established a Roman province (Macedonia) from the city and its surrounding region (see Acts 16:12; Phil. 4:15). Mark Anthony resettled the city as a Roman military colony in 42 BC, and granted land to veterans of the Roman army. About a decade later (31 BC) Octavian (Augustus) granted citizenship and land to army veterans, after his victory over Anthony at Actium.[23] Some of these veterans had been on the losing side, and Octavian's gifting of citizenship and land to them was an attempt to neutralize them as a threat to his continuing rule.[24] The city of Philippi was a desirable location to obtain and control on a number of counts. It was an agricultural centre, surrounded by fertile farmland which produced grain and wine products. It also sat along a major trade route (the Via Egnatia), running from east to west, and the seaport of Neapolis was only 10 miles to the south-west, offering access to the Aegean Sea and so to Asia Minor (modern-day Turkey; see Acts 16:6–12).

The status of Philippi as a Roman colony had a significant impact on the experience of its residents, which by the time of the mid first century AD consisted of a population of roughly 10,000.[25]

---

23. Schnabel, *Mission*, p. 1152.
24. Fee, pp. 25–26.
25. Oakes approximates the town's population from its geographic size and a comparison with the known population of Pompeii (*Philippians*,

As a colony, Philippi 'carried the status of a city on Italian soil'.[26] This title (*ius Italicum*) meant that Roman law was utilized in local civic life; in addition, it sometimes provided exemption from taxation.[27] Although less than half of the city's residents would probably have been Roman citizens, those living in Philippi and its environs would have felt Rome's presence on a regular basis. The minority Roman population of the city and surrounding countryside would have exerted considerable power and influence in the city's local affairs. Additionally, various Roman institutions, such as the forum, would have assisted in reinforcing Roman power. Philippi, as a Roman colony on Greek soil, seems to be fairly distinct, in that Latin, not Greek, was used by the ruling class. This is evident from inscriptional evidence from first-century Philippi (and note Paul's use of the Latinized form of 'Philippians' at 4:15; see comment there). All of this suggests the significant Roman influence in Philippi when Paul writes his letter. As Oakes suggests, in Philippi 'Romans owned almost all the land. Romans had all the political control in the city. Romans largely monopolised wealth and high status.'[28]

The religious landscape in Philippi at this time included traditional Greek and Roman religious cults such as those of Dionysus, Diana, Apollo and Jupiter; Egyptian and Thracian cults; as well as the Roman imperial cult. In fact, it appears from inscriptional evidence that two of Philippi's temples were devoted to the imperial cult during the first century.[29] The focus of the imperial cult was on worship and veneration of some Caesars along with some of their family members. For example, by the time of the writing of

---

(note 25 *cont.*) pp. 44–45). Many people would also have populated the countryside outside the town.

26. Cohick, p. 16.

27. Martin, p. 16.

28. Oakes, *Philippians*, p. 74. By 'Romans', Oakes includes primarily 'grandchildren and great-grandchildren of veterans or peasant colonists', although a small number of Greeks who had been granted Roman citizenship could function within this category (p. 71).

29. Bormann, *Philippi*, p. 41; Heen, 'Phil 2:6–11', pp. 135–136.

Philippians, former emperors Julius Caesar and Augustus, along with Augustus's wife Livia and his grandson Claudius, had been deified after their deaths and were worshipped at the imperial cult.[30] The influence of the imperial cult was felt across the Roman Empire, and it would have been an institution of some consequence in Philippi.[31] Although not an official (legal) requirement, there would have been some amount of social and political pressure to participate in the imperial cult, with this worship practice very likely considered normative.[32]

*ii. The church at Philippi*
The nature of Paul's relationship with the Philippian believers is evident from both the tone and the content of the letter he writes to them. They appear to have a deep connection with one another, unmarred by antagonism and discord (e.g. 1:7–8; 2:17–18; 4:1). The Philippian congregation had partnered with Paul from the very beginning of their existence as a community (1:5; 4:15), and they chose to contribute financially to Paul's ministry a number of times (4:10, 16; cf. 2 Cor. 8:1–5). Acts 16 narrates the establishment of the Philippian church (*c.* AD 50), with Paul, Silas and Timothy arriving in Philippi, where the gospel message both gains traction and also garners opposition (Acts 16:11–40). In the letter, Paul comments obliquely on that early opposition when he refers to the opposition the Philippians currently face for their allegiance to the gospel: 'you are going through the same struggle you saw I had' (1:30).

Beginning with the evidence from Philippians itself, we can see quite a number of points of coherence between the letter and the book of Acts that can inform our understanding of the Philippian church. These include the following:

1   A positive welcome as well as hostile reception of Paul and his message (Phil. 1:28–30; Acts 16:14, 22–24, 30; cf. 1 Thess. 2:2);

---

30. Bormann, *Philippi*, p. 44; Cohick, p. 18.
31. Heen, 'Phil 2:6–11', pp. 135–136.
32. Nikki, *Opponents*, p. 66; see Bormann, *Philippi*, p. 42.

2   The generosity of the new believers towards Paul (Phil.
    4:10–20; Acts 16:15, 34);
3   Paul's imprisonments (Phil. 1:12–13, 30; Acts 16:23–24);[33]
4   An emphasis on Roman sensibilities or features (Phil. 1:13,
    27; 3:20; 4:22; Acts 16:21, 37);
5   The prominence of women in the church – Euodia and
    Syntyche (Phil. 4:2–3) and Lydia and a female slave (Acts
    16:13–15, 16–18, 40), suggesting the presence of female
    leadership within the Philippian house church(es) (see
    comment on 4:2–3).[34]

In addition to these characteristics, the letter (and Acts)
suggests that the Philippian church was primarily Gentile in
make-up.[35] No synagogue building within the city of Philippi
from the first century has been excavated, and Acts does not
explicitly mention a synagogue building (cf. Acts 16:13, 16). It is
likely that a few people (Jewish and God-fearing; cf. Acts 13:26)
met together in Jewish community in spite of having no formal
meeting location within the city. In support of this scenario,
Acts 16 references Paul and his travelling companions attending
on the Sabbath what seems to have been such a gathering at 'the
place of prayer' ([hē] proseuchē; Acts 16:13, 16), a term often used
for Jewish meetings outside Judea.[36] If this was a Jewish
gathering, then Lydia (originally from Asia Minor) was likely a
'God-fearer' attracted to Jewish worship and practices. Evidence
from the names attributed to church members at Philippians 2:25
and 4:2–3 (along with Lydia's name provided in Acts) may
indicate that these were Greek or Roman members of the community, although some Jews did have Greek or Roman names in
addition to their given (Jewish) name. Paul's minimal use of the
Old Testament in the letter may also indicate a primarily non-
Jewish audience.

---

33. Fowl highlights these first three points of connection (p. 13).
34. Thurston and Ryan, pp. 19–21.
35. Hooker, p. 471.
36. Keener, *Acts*, pp. 385–387; Cohick, p. 16.

If we consider the potential size of the church at Philippi, Paul's quite specific greeting to 'the overseers and deacons' which he adds to his general greeting for all believers (1:1) could suggest a fairly substantial group; for example, over fifty people.[37] In the Graeco-Roman world, the interiors of larger homes (with their courtyards providing additional space) could accommodate up to forty to fifty people.[38] This suggests that there may have been more than one house church in the city that made up 'all God's holy people in Christ Jesus at Philippi' (1:1). In the account of the founding of the Philippian church (Acts 16), we hear that Lydia (16:14–15, 40) invites Paul and his companions into her home (with her entire household or *oikos* being baptized). According to Gehring, textual details indicate that Lydia probably owned her own *domus*, a more spacious city house.[39]

Finally, the ethnic and economic make-up of the Philippian house church(es) would have been quite diverse. While it has some-times been assumed that Philippi and so the Philippian church consisted primarily of veterans of the Roman army (see 2b[i]), Oakes's modelling analysis suggests that only about 40% of the residents of Philippi were Roman citizens (which compares with 14% elsewhere in the Roman Empire).[40] As we consider the specific make-up of the Philippian house church(es), Oakes has also proposed that the Philippian church would have been primarily Greek, not Roman, and would have included a broad social spectrum. Oakes's modelling for the demographics of first-century Philippi, and specifically the church there, suggests that only about one-third of the church was likely to have been Roman, with the majority being Greek (and including some non-Greek slaves).[41] He further proposes significant social diversity in the church reflecting

---

37. Oakes (*Philippians*, pp. 61–62) estimates between 50 and 100.
38. Gehring, *House Church*, p. 141.
39. Gehring, *House Church*, pp. 131–132.
40. Oakes, *Philippians*, p. 61; Hellerman, p. 78.
41. Oakes, *Philippians*, pp. 61, 63. Here, Oakes includes under 'Greek' a number of ethnicities whose language was Greek, including Thracian and Macedonian (p. 18).

the social diversity of Philippi, including colonist farmers, slaves, those living in poverty, people involved in service (e.g. trades), and (potentially) a small percentage of elite Romans.[42] Envisioning such diversity in the church clarifies various features of the letter, including its themes of unity and suffering, and the exhortation to press against preoccupation with status.

### c. Provenance

The primary suggestions for the letter's provenance (Paul's location as he writes Philippians) are Rome, Caesarea and Ephesus. Paul makes it clear in the letter that he is in prison as he writes (1:7, 12–14, 17), although the location of his imprisonment is left unspecified. An imprisoned Paul aligns Philippians with Paul's other so-named 'prison epistles': Philemon, Ephesians and Colossians, though none of these provides clear indication of provenance either. Acts narrates the imprisoning of Paul in four locations: Philippi (Acts 16:19–40), Jerusalem (21:27 – 23:22), Caesarea (23:23 – 26:32) and Rome (28:11–31). Paul himself attests to being in prison quite 'frequently' (2 Cor. 11:23), so it is very possible he was imprisoned in more locations than Acts designates.

In Acts, Paul's lengthier imprisonments occur in Caesarea and Rome (usually dated AD 58–60 and AD 60–63, respectively). Both of these have been suggested as the provenance for Paul's prison letters and so for Philippians. Roman provenance has been traditionally assumed, especially given Paul's references to the 'palace guard' (*praetorium*; Phil. 1:13) and to 'Caesar's household' (4:22). Bockmuehl suggests that Paul's rhetorical purpose for highlighting these two Roman institutions is 'precisely that at a time of persecution for both him and the Philippians, the gospel is none the less advancing even into the very centres of Roman power', an argument that has the most weight if Paul were writing from Rome.[43] The primary problem raised for Roman provenance is the extensive distance for travel between Philippi and Rome (*c.*800 miles or 1,300 km) and the number of trips between Paul and the

---

42. Oakes, *Philippians*, p. 61.
43. Bockmuehl, p. 28.

Philippians implied in the letter and especially in 2:25–30 (see below).

Scholars have raised the possibility of Ephesus as a location for Paul's imprisonment while writing Philippians, and this view has gained traction in recent years.[44] An Ephesian provenance would lessen significantly the distance to travel between Paul and Philippi (c.300 miles or 500 km), and those who hold that Paul wrote Philippians from Ephesus note that the term *praetorium* could be used to refer to a provincial governor's headquarters (with its attending guard; cf. Acts 23:35), as well as to the imperial guard itself stationed in Rome. These proponents also indicate that the language of 'Caesar's household' easily refers to the civil servants of the empire (of Caesar) and not only to the immediate family of the emperor. Proponents of Ephesian provenance locate that imprisonment within Paul's general reference to his frequent imprisonments (2 Cor. 11:23; also cf. 1 Cor. 15:32). Against the view that Paul was writing from Ephesus is the lack of evidence of a *praetorium* (a governor's headquarters) in Ephesus and no direct evidence for Pauline imprisonment there.

We can briefly mention Caesarean provenance, which has also been argued, although it has few proponents among contemporary scholars. In favour of this proposal is the presence of a *praetorium* in Caesarea; as Acts 23:35 notes, Paul was kept 'under guard in Herod's palace' (using *praitōrion*).

In this commentary, Roman provenance is assumed. I consider that the arguments for it are stronger than for either Ephesus or Caesarea. And the arguments against it are not as significant as often suggested. Those who argue against Roman provenance raise two main difficulties. One issue involves Paul's future plans, as expressed in Romans 15:23–24. We read there that Paul intends to travel westwards to Spain rather than return eastwards to areas where he had formerly ministered. This plan expressed to the Roman church (c.AD 56–58) appears to contradict his stated intention to return to the Philippian church (Phil. 1:26; 2:24), if Philippians was written from Rome and so after AD 60 (see 2d). An

---

44. A view held by Thielman, Osiek, and Bird and Gupta, among others.

earlier composition date for Philippians (as in the Ephesus scenario) would alleviate this purported problem. Yet there is no need to hold Paul to his intentions expressed in Romans for a westwards mission rather than a return to the east. After writing of this plan and as he sat in prison, Paul could easily have felt a need to return to some of his churches in the east to encourage them (Phil. 1:25–26) before engaging in a mission to Spain.[45] Paul's future plans as expressed in his letters are, after all, human, contingent plans (cf. Rom. 1:9–13; Jas 4:13–17).

The second and more pressing difficulty raised for Roman provenance has to do with the distance between Rome and Philippi, which involved about 800 miles (c.1,300 km) of travel, requiring at least a month. This significant distance raises problems when coupled with the number of trips back and forth between the Philippians and Paul mentioned in the letter itself, often tallied as five or more trips (Phil. 2:25–30; 4:18). A careful reading of 2:25–30, however, suggests fewer trips than often assumed. Philippians 2:25–27 (cf. 4:18) does not require more than four trips between the Philippians and Paul from beginning to end.

After the Philippians heard news of Paul being in prison (trip 1) and sent Epaphroditus to him (4:18; trip 2), and before Paul sent Epaphroditus back to the church (2:25; trip 3), there is only one necessary trip between Paul's location and Philippi. This single trip would have involved someone bringing news of Epaphroditus's illness to the Philippian church (trip 4). No additional dispatch from the Philippians to Paul is required, since Paul does not mention hearing of their response to this news. Instead, he writes of the distress that Epaphroditus feels 'because you heard he was ill' (2:26), a sensibility on the part of Epaphroditus that could be readily assumed if someone had been dispatched to Philippi with this news. Fee raises the additional possibility that Epaphroditus's illness was contracted during his journey to Rome so that the news of it did not require the entire distance to be traversed. If a travelling companion returned to Philippi with the news (a shortened trip 4), Epaphroditus could

---

45. Fee, p. 36.

have pressed on in spite of his illness to reach Paul, potentially accounting for his close brush with death (2:27, 30).[46] We should also note that Paul's imprisonment in Rome was not of short duration; Acts mentions two years and the narrative concludes before Paul is released (Acts 28:30).

If Paul is imprisoned in Rome when he writes to the Philippians, and given his description of his engagement with the *praetorium* or 'palace guard' (Phil. 1:13), he is in military custody (the Roman *custodia militaris*), rather than the more severe *carcer* (e.g. Acts 16:22–24) or lenient *custodia libera*, which was a kind of house arrest under non-military supervision (e.g. a family member).[47] The last-mentioned was reserved for those of elite status. Military custody would involve being chained, usually by the wrist, to one or two soldiers with heavy iron *manacles*,[48] and so Paul's references to being 'in chains' (1:13, 14, 17) are not metaphorical but a physical description of his experience being continually shackled to his guard(s). In this situation, the presence of friends or family would be crucial for physical and mental preservation. Paul's references to the important roles that Epaphroditus and Timothy have played in his welfare (2:19–30) fit within these difficult realities of imperial imprisonment.

### d. Date
The date for the composition of Paul's letter to the Philippians correlates with the location from which he writes. The date ranges for each of the three primary possibilities for Paul's imprisonment are as follows:

Ephesus: Early to mid 50s
Caesarea: 58–60
Rome: Early 60s

---

46. Fee, pp. 277–278.
47. Rapske, *Roman Custody,* pp. 20–35; also Tamez, pp. 12, 17. See Tamez, pp. 11–18, for a detailed discussion of these types of custody and Paul's experiences as a prisoner while writing Philippians.
48. Rapske, *Roman Custody*, p. 31; Tamez, p. 12.

Given the arguments above that the imprisoned Paul writes from Rome (see 2c), a date of AD 60–63 is most likely.

### e. Occasion and purposes

In spite of being a relatively brief letter, the text of Philippians suggests a number of reasons for the letter's composition. A central 'occasion' of the letter (the situation that has initially 'occasioned' it) is the return to Philippi of Epaphroditus, a member of the Philippian congregation. Paul writes, 'I think it is necessary to send back to you Epaphroditus' (2:25). The church had earlier sent Epaphroditus as their 'messenger' to attend to Paul's needs while he was in prison (2:25). He had brought along financial gifts from the church to support Paul (4:18), and he probably was meaning to stay to provide personal presence and encouragement to Paul as a liaison for the Philippians (see comment on 2:25). But Epaphroditus had become gravely ill, whether on his way to Paul or after his arrival (2:26–27; see 2c). Once he had recovered, Paul moved quickly to return him to the Philippian believers so they would not be worried but would experience joy at the restoration and return of their brother in the faith (2:28–29).

Epaphroditus's return to Philippi would have provided the impetus for Paul to write to the church there. In the first-century world, letters were a primary form of communication for people separated by many miles. If someone were setting off on a journey, it would be routine, even expected, for that person to carry a letter or letters from family or friends at the point of departure to those they wanted to communicate with at the point of destination. In this context, travelling became an opportunity for letter exchange.[49] The return of Epaphroditus provided Paul with an opportunity to communicate with his beloved friends at Philippi on any number of other matters that were on his mind and were for their benefit. These include an expression of gratitude for their gift, assurances about Paul's own situation in prison, encouragement towards unity in spite of opposition, and a number of warnings about certain threats to the congregation's growth in faith.

---

49. Klauck, *Letters*, p. 63.

One purpose of the letter is the opportunity it afforded for Paul to acknowledge the gifts the Philippians had sent through Epaphroditus (4:10–20). In line with conventions in the Graeco-Roman world regarding giving and receiving gifts, Paul does not provide an explicit 'thanks'. Instead, he carefully crafts an implicit expression of gratitude (4:10, 14), while providing a Christological (4:13) and theological (4:18–19) framework for understanding the nature of Christian partnership and reciprocity (see comments on 4:10–20). Although coming at the end of the letter, Paul's gratitude for the gift the Philippians had sent through Epaphroditus (4:18) is an important reason for the letter, and his appreciation is already anticipated in his opening thanksgiving (1:3–5, 7).

Another purpose of the letter is to assure the Philippians that they do not need to be concerned about Paul as he sits in prison. He is keen to let his Philippian friends know that, rather than being troubled by his circumstances, he is encouraged by how his imprisonment, somewhat surprisingly, is advancing the gospel about Jesus even further (1:12–18). And he wants to comfort them with this news.[50] He also assures the Philippian believers that he is convinced his forthcoming trial will result in his vindication, not his execution (1:19–26; 2:24), so that Paul will be able to return to Philippi and be with the believers there again (1:25–26).

Another primary purpose of the letter is to encourage the Philippian congregation towards unity, even as they are facing opposition for their allegiance to Christ. The first exhortation of the letter points in this direction, with its dual focus on living with an undivided loyalty to the gospel of Christ and doing so with a unified stance towards outside opposition (1:27–28). The repetition of Paul's admonitions for unity (1:27; 2:2; 4:2), along with a shared mindset based on Christ's mindset (2:2, 5), suggest that the Philippian house church(es) needed, in particular, to hear and actively respond to this call to unity. At 4:2–3, Paul will address a particular issue between two of his co-workers in Philippi, Euodia and Syntyche, who need the reminder to 'be of the same mind in the Lord' (4:2).

---

50. Holloway, *Consolation*, pp. 45–48.

Finally, Paul writes to warn his siblings in Christ about certain threats that could impede their growth in faith and faithfulness. These warnings come in a few, fairly oblique references to what have been called the Philippian 'opponents' ('those who oppose you', 1:28). Given the brevity and rhetorical shaping of these descriptions, much ink has been spilled in an attempt to identify (1) who these opponents are and (2) whether the multiple hints about them (1:28; 3:2; and 3:18–19) point to a single group or to multiple 'opponents'.

### f. The Philippian 'opponents'

Determining the identity and number of the Philippian 'opponents' is complicated by the brevity of Paul's descriptions of them (1:28; 3:2; 3:18–19; cf. 1:15–17), which requires some amount of 'reading between the lines' for any reconstruction of the situation and interpretation of Paul's meaning. It is rather ironic that the dearth of specifics Paul provides about these 'opponents' accounts for the breadth of discussion about them. In spite of the extended scholarly discussion about these opponents, we should keep in mind that the 'threat of opponents is not Paul's primary reason for writing'.[51]

The first mention of any kind of opposition is Paul's reference to believers in his own context who are attempting to rival Paul in their preaching of the gospel (1:15–17). These believers, however, are not in Philippi but are in the vicinity of Paul's imprisonment (probably Rome; see 2c). So this group is not a part of any opposition the Philippian believers are experiencing.[52]

Paul's initial exhortation to the Philippian church includes a brief reference to 'those who oppose you' (1:28). Paul encourages the church to be unified in their complete allegiance to the gospel of Christ (1:27). As they take on this stance, they will have no need to fear these opponents. While the source of the opposition is not mentioned, it seems likely that it comes from unbelievers in

---

51. Flemming, p. 29.

52. Although Nikki (*Opponents*, p. 138) argues they are the same group ('Jewish Christ-believers') referenced in 3:2 and 3:18–21.

Philippi given Paul's reference to their future destruction if they persist (1:28). Given the confluence of motifs in 1:27–28, the Philippian believers are probably experiencing social ostracization arising from their singular allegiance to Jesus, a common situation for the early church (cf. 1 Pet. 3:15–16). Such undivided loyalty would involve a rejection of all other deities, including participation in the imperial cult, eliminating their temple involvement and all the benefits – religious, social and economic – derived from such associations (see comment on 1:28).[53]

At two points in Philippians 3, Paul mentions people whose negative influence poses a threat of some kind to the Philippian church (3:2 and 3:18–19).[54] Some scholars join these two references to the one in 1:28 and consider all three to be describing a single group of opponents.[55] It is more likely, however, that Paul is describing outsiders (unbelievers) in 1:28 and a 'Judaizing' element or influence from within the early church at 3:2. Paul's reproof describing the latter as 'those dogs, those evildoers, those mutilators of the flesh' (3:2) points in this direction. If so, Paul refers to (the views of) some Jewish Christians, whose goal was to persuade Gentile believers to convert to Judaism and so participate fully in the new messianic community. As I will suggest in the commentary, Paul seems to be referring more to the negative influence of 'Judaizing' ideas than to the actual presence or impending arrival of Judaizers in Philippi (see comment on 3:2). Paul is warning his Gentile audience against this potential threat and provides a counter-example in his own focus on boasting in and knowing Christ alone (3:4–11).

Finally, Paul refers to people who are 'enemies of the cross of Christ', whose 'destiny is destruction . . . god is their stomach, and . . . glory is in their shame', with 'their mind . . . set on earthly

---

53. Oakes, *Philippians*, pp. 89–102.

54. For an argument against reading 3:12, 15 as an allusive reference to a perfectionist element within the Philippian church (another set of 'opponents'), see comment on 3:12.

55. Nikki, *Opponents*, pp. 216–218; Silva also considers this a good possibility and identifies the group as Judaizers.

things' (3:18b–19). More than a few scholars identify this group with the one Paul warns against in 3:2.[56] It proves difficult to reconstruct a clear profile of this group due to Paul's intense rhetoric and general descriptors. Yet it does seem that the moniker 'enemies of the cross', along with the description of a mindset focused only on the present, points to believers who have capitulated to external pressure to avoid any suffering or persecution (and so can be called 'enemies of the cross'). If so, Paul may be speaking rather generally about any believers, at Philippi and elsewhere, who are being led in a dangerous direction by their desire to avoid suffering for the cause of Christ (see comments on 3:18–19). The general warning could, then, include any Gentiles in Philippi who might be tempted to become proselytes in Judaism to avoid societal pressures (see comment on 3:2). Whatever their specific identity (or identities), these people are divided in their loyalties and no longer have the eschatological mindset Paul exemplifies and commends (3:7–21).

## 3. Literary matters

### a. Genre

Ancient letters ranged from formal epistles, which virtually functioned as treatises and were intended for a wide audience, to personal letters, often quite brief and covering an array of everyday, often mundane subjects. Philippians fits somewhere in the middle of that spectrum. It has a strongly relational tone and is fairly informal at a number of points (e.g. 1:12–18; 2:19–30), suggesting its personal nature. Additionally, its audience is quite specific – the church community in Philippi. Yet its length is not insubstantial; and it addresses a number of significant theological and ethical themes, carefully woven across the letter. And as we can see from other Pauline letters, he does consider his audience-specific letters appropriate for the edification of other church communities (Col. 4:16).

As an example of a first-century letter, Philippians demonstrates a basic epistolary structure and elements: identification of writer(s)

---

56. E.g. Osiek, pp. 102–103; Smit, *Paradigms*, p. 75.

and recipient (1:1); greeting (1:2); prayer and/or thanksgiving (1:3–11); body (1:12 – 4:20); and personal news, greetings and well-wishes (4:21–23). We can also note some amount of adaptation of these conventional elements in the letter. For example, the prayer/thanksgiving section is quite well developed (a regular Pauline practice) as compared with typical ancient letters (1:3–11). The concluding greetings and well-wishes, on the other hand, are quite brief (4:21–23) in comparison with other Pauline letters. The body of an ancient letter would address whatever topics and concerns the author wanted to communicate to the recipient. In Philippians, Paul addresses a number of discrete topics, but with a sense of thoughtful arrangement (e.g. alternating exhortations with exemplars) and with later parts of the letter recapitulating earlier ideas and themes (e.g. 4:2–20).

In the first-century world, there was quite a variety of types of letters. Determining if Philippians resembles a specific kind of letter has produced no consensus to date. The most common suggestion is that Philippians is a letter of friendship, whose typical features included (1) reference to the 'absence' the two friends or parties were experiencing (see Phil. 1:27; 2:12); (2) expression of affection, even longing (e.g. 1:7–8; 2:26); (3) a focus on unity and reciprocity (e.g. 1:27 – 2:4; 4:2–3, 10–20); and (4) recognition of enmity that provides a backdrop to friendship (e.g. 1:28; 3:2, 18–19).[57] A common difficulty raised for identifying Philippians as a letter of friendship is its lack of any specific language for friendship, such as *philia* ('friendship') or *philos* ('friend').[58]

Alexander has argued that Philippians is a family letter, a type of letter centred on exchanging news between parties and focused on a concern for the welfare of the recipient. Alexander suggests that Paul has 'adapted and expanded' this genre form to bolster the familial connections between himself and the church at Philippi.[59] Another suggestion comes from Holloway, who proposes that Philippians resembles Graeco-Roman 'consolations',

57. Stowers, 'Friends', pp. 109–113. See Fee, pp. 2–14.

58. On the friendship theme in Philippians, see 4c.

59. Alexander, 'Philippians', p. 95.

and specifically the consolatory letter. In this letter type, an author aims to lessen the grief of the recipient and does so through rational argument.[60]

The lack of scholarly consensus regarding whether the internal evidence of Philippians supports its inclusion within any particular epistolary type might suggest that Philippians offers a mixed form or that it simply does not fit cleanly into one of these or other categories. As Klauck concludes, 'among the letter types, none of which is ideally realized in Philippians, one can consider next to the friendly letter also the family letter, and perhaps even the administrative letter'.[61] It is important to note that the various scholars who argue that Philippians is a particular type of ancient letter bring their understanding of that genre to bear interpretively on the letter's structure and substance.[62]

There are at least two embedded genres within the letter that have potential ramifications for interpretation: a virtue list and poetry (for the virtue list of 4:8, see comment there). The most significant hermeneutically is the poetic refrain in Philippians 2:6–11. Some scholars argue that this section, traditionally identified as a Christological hymn, falls short of identification as poetry and is instead an example of elevated prose.[63] While its identification as a pre-existing Christian hymn is unconvincing, a number of its features suggest that at least 2:6–8, if not the entire section, should be identified and interpreted as poetry.[64] First and foremost, the careful balancing of lines is apparent and fits the genre of Jewish poetry. The first line pair is balanced by virtue of its contrasting ideas (i.e. antithetical parallelism):[65]

---

60. Holloway, *Consolation*.

61. Klauck, *Letters*, p. 340.

62. E.g. Fee, p. 3; Holloway, *Consolation*, pp. 161–164.

63. Fee (p. 41) calls it 'exalted – even poetic – *prose*'.

64. Bockmuehl, p. 116; Fowl, *Story*, pp. 16–17; Hansen, p. 122. For the argument against identifying 2:6–11 as a pre-existing hymn, see Fowl, pp. 108–113.

65. This translation of 2:6–8 is my own (see Context for 2:6–8).

6a Who, though being in the form of God,
6b did not consider equality with God as something to be
exploited

Two lines (7c and 8a) are clearly synonymous:

7c Being made in the likeness of human beings
8a and being found in appearance as a human being

And two sets of lines are balanced by the use of a participle (of means) to extend and clarify an initial action of Christ:

7a rather, he emptied himself
7b by taking the form of a slave

and,

8b he humbled himself
8c by becoming obedient to death

Additionally, these two line sets, though not adjacent, share a close structural correspondence to each other: a (past tense) verb + 'himself' + a participle clause.

Another feature of poetry present across 2:6–11 is a decided preference for synonyms to express key ideas rather than a repetition of terms, which might account for the number of unusual (for Paul) terms employed in 2:6–8.[66] For example, to indicate the idea of Christ's 'form' or 'likeness', Paul uses three distinct, though closely related, terms: *morphē* ('nature' or 'form'), *homoiōma* ('likeness') and *schēma* ('appearance'). Given the tendency in poetry towards a use of synonyms, the differences in nuance among these terms should not be unduly pressed. When repetition is used in poetry, however, it often functions as an indicator of structure; for

---

66. Brown, *Scripture*, pp. 145–146. Bockmuehl (p. 119) suggests that the 'several untypical ideas and terms in the passage . . . could well be the result of its poetic style' (cf. 1 Cor. 13).

example, providing clues for delineating stanzas. The twofold use of *morphē* ('nature' or 'form') provides a structural clue for the poem, marking a key contrast: Christ is in the 'form' of God (2:6a) and he takes the 'form' of a slave (2:7b). This repetition marks the first and last lines of what is probably the first stanza (2:6a–7b).[67] The narrative cast to this Christ poem has antecedents in the Old Testament and other Jewish literature (e.g. Pss 77; 105; 106; Wis. 10).

### b. Reading Paul's rhetoric

'Paul's rhetoric' refers to his persuasive design in Philippians or any of his letters. While within the classical tradition rhetoric referred to persuasion developed in speech or oratory, its patterns and practices could also apply to written works.[68] An issue that contemporary Bible readers might raise for understanding the impact of ancient rhetoric on Paul's letters is the tendency in modern discussions to associate 'rhetoric' with deception. When we say someone is being highly 'rhetorical', we usually mean that he or she is emphasizing form over substance, sometimes to the point of being manipulative.[69] Yet the study of rhetoric was the culminating stage of a Graeco-Roman education and, even though there were differing opinions about rhetoric within the philosophical tradition (e.g. some critique of form over substance), it would have been understood more broadly and positively than the term often communicates today.

Much of the focus of rhetorical criticism in New Testament studies has been on structural and stylistic matters, with the suggestion that formal rhetorical practices were used in at least some of Paul's letters. Nevertheless, the application of rhetorical analysis for understanding the structure of Paul's epistles, including Philippians, has yielded little consensus. Most of the letter defies easy classification when using rhetorical categories related to a letter's organization (e.g. *exordium, narratio, confirmatio, peroratio*).

---

67. For other repeated terms that provide structural clues for the Christ poem, see the commentary.
68. Cunningham, *To Teach*, p. 14. See deSilva, 'Appeals', pp. 248–249; and Smit, *Paradigms*, pp. 31–33.
69. Boyce, 'Rhetoric', p. 205.

The use of rhetoric, however, should not be confined to structural and stylistic analysis, what deSilva refers to as a displaced emphasis on 'form over function'.[70] In support of a broader application, we could note that Aristotle's *Rhetoric* addresses formal issues only in his final, shorter book. The first two longer books focus on the creation and development of arguments.[71] It is in this area that rhetorical analysis offers a fruitful companion to exegetical work.

Three primary categories within rhetoric highlight how speakers or writers conceive of and develop their persuasive design: *ethos*, *pathos* and *logos*. Even speakers and hearers who were not formally trained in rhetoric would have understood and drawn upon these basic constructs. In fact, Kennedy suggests that these categories are something of a universal phenomenon.[72] *Ethos* refers to the speaker's character and reputation, while *pathos* involves 'the emotions and tendencies that can be expected of an audience'.[73] *Logos* consists in the internal logic and content of the speech, with this category often being the primary focus of exegetical work in New Testament letters. Nevertheless, by including attention to *ethos* and *pathos* in the textual analysis of a letter, the interpreter can tap into tone as well as semantics – the emotive sense of a text as well its cognitive sense. In his attention to *logos*, *pathos* and *ethos*, deSilva describes the purpose of this kind of analysis as

> identifying and entering into the inner argumentation of the text, discerning varying kinds of appeal that make the text an address to the 'whole person' of the hearer (i.e. to his or her mind, feelings, and connection with the speaker).[74]

In this commentary, I offer a concluding paragraph on 'Paul's rhetorical emphases' under Context for each section of the letter. I

---

70. DeSilva, 'Appeals', p. 245. Also, Boyce, 'Rhetoric', p. 203.
71. Boyce, 'Rhetoric', p. 203.
72. Kennedy, *Rhetorical Criticism*, p. 15.
73. Cunningham, *To Teach*, p. 18.
74. DeSilva, 'Appeals', p. 247.

do so by using the three categories of ethos, pathos and logos (without italics, since these terms have moved from Greek into English use). I do so because I have found it helpful to consider how Paul draws on his own situation and his existing relationship with the Philippian believers to persuade them towards particular dispositions and actions. For instance, he has enough relational capital with the Philippians to ask them expectantly to 'make my joy complete by being like-minded' (2:2). It also proves helpful to consider how Paul might be expressing himself to evoke and/or address the emotions of his audience. Paul's extended discussion of the illness and return of Epaphroditus to Philippi (2:25–30) relies on Paul's assumption that the rest of the Philippian church was concerned for the well-being of this fellow believer (2:26, 28). Paul returns Epaphroditus to Philippi so that the Philippians 'may be glad' (2:28). Holloway goes so far as to suggest that Paul's main objective in the letter was their consolation.[75] Interpretively, insights can be gained from analysing how logos, ethos and pathos work together within Paul's rhetorical design.

### c. Integrity of the letter

The 'integrity' of a letter refers to its unity – its coherence as a single letter written on a single occasion. In the recent history of interpretation, the integrity of Philippians has been an open question. Those who think that the canonical Philippians contains two or more Pauline letters base that conclusion on two textual anomalies: the seemingly abrupt change of tone and direction at 3:1a and 3:1b–2, as well as the unexpected placement of Paul's expression of gratitude for the Philippians' gift at the end of the letter (4:10–20). As a result, some have suggested that 3:2–21 (or up to 4:3) and 4:10–20 are distinct letters, written at different times. Reumann, for example, proposes that Paul wrote a first letter to Philippi, comprising 4:10–20, in the early to mid 50s. A second letter, consisting of much of the canonical Philippians, was written and sent in the mid 50s. Finally, the polemically driven 3:2–21 was written shortly thereafter to address Jewish-Christian missionaries

---

75. Holloway, *Consolation*, p. 55.

pressing for the circumcision (i.e. the conversion) of Gentile Christ-followers.[76]

Yet the textual features that have given rise to theories of multiple letters can be adequately addressed by the oral and aural characteristics of Philippians. Specifically, the letter was intended to be read out to the Philippian church – a routine practice in that context – potentially by its carrier, Epaphroditus, or one of the church's leaders. This aural cast of the letter helps to explain what seems to be an abrupt transition in 3:1, which begins with *to loipon*, often used to indicate 'finally'. Achtemeier has proposed that in the aural reading of Philippians, such a decisive conjunction would helpfully signal a significant change of topic (as occurs in 3:1–21).[77]

Issues of orality could also account for Paul's decision to wait until its conclusion to address the gift he has received from the Philippians. In a context where the letter was read out, Paul's carefully worded thanks would have left a strong impression on the Philippians (intentionally so, it seems), especially coupled with the very brief concluding greetings.[78] Additionally, there are a significant number of literary connections between 1:3–11 and 4:10–20, suggesting that these opening and concluding sections together serve as 'a well-crafted frame', and supporting the letter's unity.[79] All in all, a close reading of the text as it stands (the canonical Philippians), with historical realities in view, supports the letter's integrity.

### d. Structure

Each of Paul's letters has a distinctive structure and pattern of thought. Philippians has a quite personal cast to it, beginning and ending as it does with Paul's reflections on his own situation in prison (1:12–26) and his grateful response to the gift he has received

---

76. Reumann, pp. 16–17.

77. Achtemeier, 'Oral Environment', p. 26. For further discussion of this shift of tone, see comment at 3:1.

78. Fee, p. 17. See Context on 4:10–20.

79. Fowl, p. 192.

from the Philippian congregation (4:10–20).[80] In much of the rest of the body of the letter, Paul follows a flexible pattern of alternating exhortations and exemplars. He begins with a series of exhortations in 1:27 – 2:4, followed by the paradigm of Christ himself – the pinnacle of exemplars (2:5–11). The following sketch visualizes this interchange across the letter (for a full outline, see Analysis):

| | |
|---|---|
| Exhortations | 1:27 – 2:4 |
| Exemplar: Jesus | 2:5–11 |
| Exhortations | 2:12–18 |
| Exemplar: Timothy | 2:19–24 |
| Exemplar: Epaphroditus | 2:25–30 |
| Exemplar: Paul | 3:1 – 4:1 |
| Exhortations (summative) | 4:2–9 |

It should be noted that the exemplar segments typically include some direct exhortation, as in 2:5, 29; 3:2, 16 (cf. 4:1).

Attention to exemplars for the formation of an audience is a common rhetorical strategy in the Graeco-Roman context (expressed by the Latin *exemplum* and the Greek *paradeigma*). According to Smit, Paul uses exemplars not only for moral purposes but for the identity formation of the Philippian congregation. In Philippians, Paul desires 'to steer an entire community in a particular direction' and he does so by means of exemplars.[81]

### e. Use of the Old Testament
There is a fairly modest use of the Old Testament in Paul's letter to the Philippians. This is especially apparent when comparing the significant number of citations and allusions to the Old Testament in Galatians, 1 and 2 Corinthians and Romans. In these letters, Paul regularly draws on the Scriptures, often with his characteristic introductory formula 'it is written' (*gegraptai*; used around thirty

---

80. And framed by the letter's introductory and closing greetings and well-wishes in 1:1–11 and 4:21–23.

81. Smit, *Paradigms*, p. 4.

times in these four letters). Although there are no such explicit citations in Philippians, Paul does allude to a number of Old Testament texts or images, and he does so by using the Septuagint (the Greek Old Testament, also referred to as the 'LXX'). He has multiple purposes for drawing on the Scriptures, including to inform his Christology and to shape the Philippians to live more fully their identity as the people of God.

One of the clearest allusions, and one that contributes significantly to Christology, comes from Isaiah 45:23 ('every knee should bow . . . and every tongue acknowledge') at the conclusion of the 'Christ poem' (Phil. 2:6–11, specifically 2:10–11). Paul draws on this Isaianic text – with a clear contextual message in Isaiah 45 that Israel's God is the only true God – to affirm the exaltation of Jesus the Messiah and his inclusion in the divine identity and sovereignty and so the appropriateness of ascribing worship to him.[82] This allusion provides an example of a Christological use of the Old Testament (for another example, see Gen. 1:26 in Phil. 2:7).

A number of allusions occur in Philippians 2:12–18, with Paul drawing on this cluster of Old Testament texts and images to shape the Philippians' communal identity. In this section focused on exhortation, Paul brings together more than one allusion or echo from texts focused on Israel's time in the wilderness. He alludes to Deuteronomy 32:5 to shape the identity of the Philippians to live blamelessly as 'children of God . . . in a warped and crooked generation' (Phil. 2:15). They are to contrast with that particular generation of Israel described as 'blemished' (Deut. 32:5, LXX) by being 'unblemished' or 'without fault' (Phil. 2:15). They are also to avoid 'grumbling' (Phil. 2:14), a characteristic of the wilderness generation (e.g. Deut. 1:27). And Paul may draw as well on Deuteronomy 32:47 in his reference to the Philippians holding firmly to 'the word of life'. Paul also seems to be echoing Daniel 12:3 ('shine . . . like stars', Phil. 2:15); and Isaiah 65:23 ('not . . . labour in vain', Phil. 2:16); and he uses temple imagery of a 'drink offering' and 'sacrifice and service' drawn from the Old Testament. This web of allusions and echoes illustrates the storied nature of much of Paul's

---

82. Bauckham, *Jesus*, p. 38.

use of the Old Testament. Paul can certainly cite or allude to particular scriptural texts, yet even as he does so he could be hearing these in their wider storied setting. And at some points, he is tapping into a part of Israel's story to shape his audience, as he does in Philippians 2:14–16.[83]

Other recognizable Old Testament allusions or echoes in Philippians include (1) Job 13:16 at Philippians 1:19; (2) possibly Psalm 22:16 at Philippians 3:2; (3) Psalm 69:28 or Daniel 12:1 at Philippians 4:3; and (4) Psalm 145:18 at Philippians 4:5. Fee points to an interesting gap in Old Testament usage in Philippians 3. Specifically, he notes that there is a decided lack of Old Testament argumentation in this 'polemic' chapter that begins by addressing the issue of 'Judaizing', where we might most expect Paul to marshal it (cf. Galatians and Romans in this regard). Instead, Paul 'offers himself as an example of one who [held a Judaizing perspective] but had given it all up for Christ', suggesting that Philippians 3:2–11 should be read less polemically than has been done.[84]

Whether or not Paul expects his primarily Gentile recipients to recognize each of these, often brief, allusions or echoes remains a debated question among New Testament scholars. I suggest that the Philippians who had come to trust in Jesus the Messiah had taken on Scripture (the Old Testament) – its stories and texts – as their own, which were probably communicated primarily aurally through the teaching of Paul and others. And Paul's preaching would have included in some way the larger story of those Scriptures. So it would not be far-fetched to imagine that the Philippians could have recognized some of Paul's allusions, as they would have fitted well with Paul's ways of teaching when he had been with them (see comment on 2:14).[85] What we can affirm in any case is that Paul's communicative intentions can regularly be more clearly discerned if we pay attention to the ways he uses and adapts scriptural texts, stories and images.

---

83. See Brown, *Gospels as Stories*, pp. 112–116.

84. Fee, p. 17.

85. See Brown, *Gospels as Stories*, p. 110.

### f. The Greek text and its translation

Although this commentary is not aimed at a scholarly audience, it is necessary to give some attention to textual criticism – that is, making determinations about the original text of Philippians. The earliest extant copy of Philippians comes from around AD 200 (p[46]). This papyrus manuscript is an important textual witness for Philippians, along with early majuscules (e.g. ℵ, A, B, D) and quite a number of minuscules. All extant Greek manuscripts witnessing to Philippians include the Pauline letters as an entire group, that is, a corpus (not just Philippians), with the corpus having been brought together sometime during the late first or early second century AD.[86] Bockmuehl notes that the Greek text of Philippians is 'free from major text-critical uncertainties', making the work of textual criticism less difficult than in some other parts of the New Testament.[87]

In this commentary, I address eleven text-critical issues in Philippians, with my goal being to focus on any discrepancies among the manuscripts that have particular literary or theological import-ance (e.g. 1:11; 3:12). I was also aware of the need to explain any major divergences among English translations that arise from textual questions (4:13). For the eleven instances of text-critical dis-cussion in the commentary, see comments (in some cases footnotes) on 1:11, 14; 2:4, 9, 30; 3:3, 12, 16; 4:3, 13, 23.

The translation used in this commentary is the New Inter-national Version (NIV), 2011.[88] Where I consider likely a different reading from the NIV, I note this in the commentary and also explain the rationale for the NIV's rendering. A few particular translation issues warrant some initial comment here and provide examples of the kinds of issues that arise in translating the Greek of the New Testament.

The NIV and almost all other English versions translate *Christos* as 'Christ' in Philippians and through the New Testament epistles. While I understand the rationale and have no particular issue with

---

86. See Fee, p. 23.

87. Bockmuehl, p. 40.

88. Translations of the Septuagint are my own.

this choice, I do find it helpful at points in the commentary to highlight that *Christos* is itself a translation of the Hebrew title for the anticipated Jewish 'Messiah'. I follow Novenson in his demonstration that *Christos* sits somewhere between a title and a name; it is an 'honorific' which retains at least some of its associations as a title.[89] Also, given a tendency in popular parlance to hear Christ as nothing more than Jesus' (last) name, I have found it helpful to remind myself and my audience of the title, Messiah, and its function as a corporate reality within Pauline theology (see comment on 1:5).

Another translation issue that has been a matter of some debate is how to render the Greek word *doulos*. In the commentary, I suggest 'slave' as a helpful rendering of *doulos* in 1:1 (NIV's 'servant'). While 'servant' is possible, I am swayed by Paul's use of *doulos* in 2:7 for Christ, who took 'the very nature of a' slave. Deeply resonant for Paul and his audience would have been the status connotations of this language. Christ in his exalted status ('in very nature God', 2:6) descends to the status of a slave, especially seen in his death on a cross – the form of execution for slaves. Given this status connotation at 2:7, I believe Paul follows in Christ's footsteps by calling himself and Timothy 'slaves of Christ Jesus' (1:1).

A term that provides something of a challenge to render in English is *kauchēma* and its verbal cognate, *kauchaomai* ('boast' and 'to boast'). Given that the English word 'boast' (traditional rendering) routinely carries a connotation of *excessive* pride, it can be helpful to use a different English term to render the Greek terms. I have suggested the idea of celebration in the commentary at a few points (see 1:26; 2:16; 3:3; cf. Bockmuehl's 'jubilation').[90] For other notable translational issues, see comments on 1:27a (*politeuomai*) and 2:25 (*leitourgos* and *leitourgia*).

## 4. Theological messages and themes

The letter to the Philippians has a rich tapestry of theological messages and themes, some fairly distinctive within the Pauline

---

89. Novenson, *Christ*. See comment on 1:1.
90. Bockmuehl, p. 95.

corpus (e.g. joy) and others that correspond to significant themes of his other letters (e.g. the centrality of the gospel and the significance of imitation). There are layers of themes even within a single topic or area, such as Christology or eschatology. For this reason, I delineate six core thematic, theological emphases that serve as constellations or clusters for numerous other motifs, with all of these interwoven across the discourse of Philippians. The six emphases are Christology, eschatology, friendship, communal discernment, unity and resilience in response to suffering, and Christian imitation.

### a. Christology

In Philippians, as in Paul's other letters, Christology is central. Even when Paul is focusing on what we might identify as pragmatic issues (e.g. his imprisonment, details about the dispatch of Timothy and Epaphroditus, his gratitude for their gifts), his central preoccupation with Jesus the Messiah shines through. The arrival of Jesus, Israel's Messiah, has changed everything. Unsurprisingly then, Paul routinely refers to *Christos* (the Greek translation of the Hebrew for 'Messiah') across Philippians (thirty-seven times), either on its own or with 'Jesus' ('Christ Jesus' or 'Jesus Christ'). While it has been argued that *Christos* functions more as name than title in Paul, Novenson is persuasive in his argument that the term functions as an 'honorific' and so can retain its messianic connotations (see comment at 1:1). If it were simply a (double) name, it would have a set order. Yet in Paul's other letters, as in Philippians, Paul freely interchanges *Iēsous* ('Jesus') and *Christos*.[91] In Philippians, Paul prefers the order *Christos Iēsous* (thirteen times), yet still uses *Iēsous Christos* often enough (eight times). So we should take seriously Paul's thoroughgoing use of *Christos* to signal 'the Messiah'. Paul's Christology centres on the arrival of the promised Messiah, sent by Israel's God, who has inaugurated Israel's long-awaited redemption and the restoration of all humanity and all creation. And we can hear overtones of Jesus' messianic role in many of the references to

---

91. Novenson, *Christ*, pp. 91–92, 99–101.

*Christos* across Philippians. For example, to 'preach Christ' (1:15–17) is to proclaim this messianic story.

An important way Paul uses *Christos* in Philippians is to reflect the communal reality that those who believe in and follow Jesus the Messiah have been incorporated into his life, death and resurrection. They participate 'in the Messiah'. Paul signals this spiritual reality with the language *en Christō* ('in the Messiah'). For example, in his opening and closing greetings, he addresses 'God's [holy] people in Christ Jesus' (1:1; 4:21). He identifies their standing as a community 'in the Messiah', whose life is enfolded into the life of Messiah Jesus. As such, all the Messiah's benefits belong to them as well (e.g. 3:14; 4:7; see comments on 1:5; 2:1). This communal reality joins together God's people in unity, just as they enjoy relational union with the Messiah.

Paul also uses *kyrios* or 'Lord' across the letter to refer to Jesus and to indicate his present exalted status. Paul tells the story of the exaltation to Lordship of Jesus the Messiah in the 'Christ poem' of 2:6–11 (on its genre, see 3a). This text is the Christological centrepiece in Philippians. Whether Paul borrows and adapts an early Christian hymn or these stanzas are his own construction (see Context on 2:5–11), this passage provides a distinctive offering for Pauline Christology, especially as it highlights the pre-existence of the Messiah.

The first movement of the poem traces Christ surrendering the advantage of 'equality with God' to embrace the identity and condition of humanity (2:6–8). Although some scholars have read 2:6 as describing Christ's Adamic (human) identity before the fall and dispute that the hymn refers to Christ's pre-existence, the only allusion to Genesis 1:26 comes in the poem's second stanza addressing Christ's incarnation (2:7c/8a).[92] The first lines of the poem establish Christ in the 'nature' or 'form' of God, and at this early point there is little to connect to Adam (though some see an oblique reference in 2:6b). The first stanza (2:6a–7b) suggests a descent in status (an 'emptying', 2:7a) of the greatest magnitude – from 'the form of God' to 'the form of a slave' – the very lowest status.[93]

---

92. Fee, p. 209.
93. My translations (see NIV footnotes).

The poem's second stanza (2:7c–8d) expresses the particulars of the incarnation. It is at this point we hear an allusion to Genesis, with Christ 'being made in human likeness' (*homoiōmati anthrōpōn*, 2:7; cf. LXX Gen. 1:26). In the incarnation, Christ 'humbled himself', embracing his divinely appointed mission even to the point of death (2:8). 'Christ was obedient to God in his service to humanity.'[94] The last line of the second stanza confirms the slavery metaphor of 2:7 by indicating the kind of death of the Messiah: 'even death on a cross'. Crucifixion was quintessentially the form of execution intended for slaves in the Roman-occupied world.

The second half of the Christ hymn (2:9–11) portrays the exaltation and Lordship of Christ. God's exaltation of Messiah Jesus after his self-humbling puts him in the 'highest place', as God grants him 'the name that is above every name' (2:9). That phrase alludes to the divine name (Yahweh) used across Isaiah 45:18–24 and heard in language borrowed from Isaiah 45:23, where it is affirmed that, *before Yahweh*, 'every knee will bow . . . every tongue will acknowledge God' (LXX). Now, in Philippians 2:10–11, it is *before Jesus* that 'every knee should bow . . . and every tongue acknowledge' him. Jesus is exalted to the place of universal authority and so is worthy of worship, alongside Israel's God (see comment on 1:1). This is the import of the pronouncement 'Jesus Christ is Lord' (*kyrios*, 2:11). Lordship, through this Isaiah allusion, speaks to Christ's participation in 'the divine sovereignty'.[95] The Messiah, who began in the place of 'equality with God', became a human being (Jesus of Nazareth). His fully faithful life and death resulted in God's exaltation of Messiah Jesus to the highest place: to the place of Lordship over all things.

The surprising conclusion to the Christ poem is not the return of Christ to the place of divine authority – a place the poem has affirmed as Christ's starting point (2:6); it is that a human being (Jesus of Nazareth) is exalted to the place of divine authority and receives the name 'Lord'. The exaltation of Jesus Christ to universal Lordship is an affirmation of his divine–human identity.

---

94. Stubbs, p. 371.
95. Bauckham, *Jesus*, p. 200.

Christ's exaltation to universal Lordship also presses against false claims of lordship that would have been pervasive in Philippi, in its Roman-saturated culture. If Jesus is *the* exalted Lord, then Caesar cannot be lord in spite of his claims to lordship (see comment on 2:10–11). Paul's consistent use of *kyrios* to describe Messiah Jesus affirms this truth (e.g. 1:2; 2:11, 19; 3:8, 20; 4:23). Another implicit critique of the power of Caesar may be implied in Paul's use of 'Saviour' for Jesus (*sōtēr*, 3:20), especially since this term does not occur much elsewhere in the Pauline epistles and given Roman claims that the emperor was the people's saviour (see comment on 3:20).[96]

While Paul employs the 'Christ poem' within the flow of Philippians 2 to inform key values, such as humility, to be embraced by the Christian community (2:5; cf. 2:1–4), we should not lose sight of its importance for Pauline Christology. Christ, though fully God, embraced becoming human – a meteoric descent of status, even to the point of the most shameful kind of death. As Paul affirms elsewhere in the letter, Christ's death and resurrection paves the way for the present salvation and future resurrection of believers. It is the exalted and ruling Christ who 'will transform our lowly bodies so that they will be like his glorious body' (3:21). His exaltation in resurrection makes possible their own future resurrection (3:10–11).

A final point about Paul's Christology in Philippians is its profound relationality, an insight drawn from Paul's auto-biographical descriptions in 3:7–11. There, Paul expresses that 'knowing Christ' (3:8) is his greatest desire and focus. This participation in the entire scope of Christ's story – his suffering as well as his resurrection and exaltation – echoes that story as rehearsed in the Christ poem (2:6–11). For Paul, knowing Christ, a reality he can also describe as 'gain[ing] Christ' and being 'found in him' (3:8–9), is the greatest of all experiences. Paul also writes of Christ's affection or compassion that propels his own affections (1:8), Christ's love that provides the greatest comfort (2:1), Christ's nearness to believers (4:5), and the grace that Christ gives (4:23; cf.

---

96. See examples in Oakes, *Philippians*, pp. 138–140.

1:2). This reality of relationship with Christ causes Paul to celebrate ('boast in') Christ, together with his Philippian sisters and brothers (1:26; 3:3). Relationship with Christ brings Paul ultimate joy.

### b. Eschatology

By placing the arrival and work of Christ at centre for understanding theological history, Paul's eschatology in Philippians fits closely with the eschatology offered in his other letters. For Paul, the arrival of Jesus, Israel's Messiah, is the fulcrum of salvation history. This is at the heart of Paul's eschatology – the assumption that in Jesus the last days have begun. What came before, Paul can express in terms of the evil age or the time of 'the flesh', the age when sin wielded inordinate power over humanity. Yet Christ's death has rescued believers 'from the present evil age' (Gal. 1:4). His death and resurrection have inaugurated the 'age to come' (cf. Eph. 1:21), so that Paul can refer to Christians as those 'on whom the culmination of the ages has come' (1 Cor. 10:11).

In Philippians, Paul refers very little to the age of the 'flesh' that is passing away. Only at 3:3–6 does Paul refer to the *sarx* or 'flesh' to indicate his past confidence in his ethnic and religious heritage, a confidence that is no longer appropriate in the light of the arrival of the Messiah.

Paul focuses his eschatology in Philippians on the present time of the Messiah, which has been transformed through Jesus' death, resurrection and exaltation to Lordship (2:6–11; see 4a). Paul and the Philippian believers are living in the *already–not yet* of God's kingdom. Their shared life in the Messiah maps on to the eschatological terrain of *already*, as they participate in the current blessings of the time of the Messiah. And they await what is still *not yet* – their own resurrection and the completion of God's work in them at the 'day of Christ Jesus' (1:6).

Paul's recurring language of the 'day of Christ Jesus' (1:6; cf. 1:10; 2:16) fits with Paul's similar and flexible language across his letters to indicate the still-future arrival of complete salvation for believers (e.g. 1 Cor. 1:8; 5:5; 1 Thess. 5:2; cf. Rom. 2:5, 16). This language resonates conceptually with the 'day of the Lord' motif that emerges in Jewish prophetic literature and signals a future day when Israel's God will bring restoration and judgment (e.g.

Joel 2:31; 3:14; Zech. 13:1; 14:1). Paul focuses the prophetic language of the 'day of the Lord' Christologically to reflect his conviction that the restoration begun in Jesus will be completed on that final day – the day of the Messiah. In the light of that certain future reality, believers can look ahead to their salvation (1:28) without fearing death (1:21–23).

Paul especially focuses attention on the eschatology of 'already but not yet' in Philippians 3:2–21, a section of the letter that illuminates how relationship with Christ changes everything. Paul compares what he had previously found valuable in his heritage and religious commitments (3:4–6) with his present experience of knowing Christ and participating in Christ's sufferings as well as in his resurrection (3:7–10). In reality, there is no comparison; for Paul, all else is worthless when compared with 'the surpassing worth of knowing Christ Jesus my Lord' (3:8). This present reality of knowing Christ also leads to the future possibility of 'attaining to the resurrection from the dead' (3:11). Paul views all else as inconsequential when compared with his goals of knowing Christ and reaching the day of resurrection.

In Philippians 3:12–14, Paul exemplifies a finely tuned balance of living in the time between the already and the not yet. He concedes more than once that he has not yet arrived at the goal of resurrection and exaltation, which still lies in the future (cf. 3:20–21). Yet this only seems to invigorate Paul's eagerness to reach his goal; he earnestly presses on 'to take hold of that for which Christ Jesus took hold of me' (3:12). And he calls the Philippians to do the same – to live in a way consistent with what they 'have already attained' (3:16). For Paul, this eschatological mindset is a key sign of Christian maturity (3:15).

Towards the end of Philippians 3, Paul provides a warning about some believers (or former believers) who are now living as 'enemies of the cross' (3:18). Paul goes on to describe this group as those who have abandoned the eschatological mindset he has been characterizing. In contrast to a true eschatological mindset, the mindset of these 'enemies of the cross' (i.e. antagonistic to suffering) is focused on 'earthly things' (3:19). To combat any similar capitulation on their part, Paul exhorts the Philippians to embrace their true eschatological identity: 'our citizenship is in heaven'

(3:20). He points them to the still future arrival of Jesus their Saviour and their own final-day resurrection (3:21). Paul will, in chapter 4, encourage them that 'the Lord is near' (4:5), likely signalling both the nearness of the day of the Lord Jesus and his closeness to believers in the present.

Paul's eschatologically focused mindset provides the capacity to reframe life in the present, even and especially the suffering that Paul and the Philippians are experiencing (1:28–30). First, suffering fits within Paul's eschatological framework as a sign of the present experience of the *not yet*. This means that suffering has a time stamp on it. When 'the day of Christ' arrives, all suffering will be past tense. From the vantage point of that final day, 'our present sufferings are not worth comparing with the glory' that awaits (Rom. 8:18). Paul can even refer to suffering as 'light and momentary troubles' (2 Cor. 4:17) from that future perspective. Suffering is not a virtue or a 'good' to be carried into the eschaton. It is a remnant of the present evil age that is already passing away in Christ.

Second, Paul considers any suffering that comes from remaining loyal to Christ and his gospel (1:27–28) as integral to participating in Christ's sufferings (3:10). Participation in the Messiah involves sharing in his entire story – suffering and resurrection, death and life (2:6–11; 3:10–11). There is no embracing a theology of glory without joining in a theology of the cross (Rom. 8:17; 2 Cor. 1:5). As Christ's identification with humanity involved sacrifice for the sake of mission as well as service to others (2:7–8), so also believers' identification with Christ involves these same dispositions and realities. 'The thought of a spiritual union with Christ in His death and resurrection . . . is at the very heart of Paul's experience and teaching.'[97] In this light, Paul can even refer to the Philippians' suffering because of their allegiance to Christ as something that has been 'granted' to these believers (1:29). To be joined in union with Christ to this extent – to suffering for and with him – can be understood as a gift.

Finally, Paul considers ministry, what he calls 'the work of the Messiah' (2:30, my translation), worth any suffering it entails. If, in

---

97. Martin, p. 50.

the final day, the Philippians have lived out their identity as God's children and have been a missional light in their own setting (2:15–16), Paul will consider it a joy to have experienced any suffering necessary in his ministry among them: 'even if I am being poured out like a drink offering on the sacrifice and service coming from your faith, I am glad' (2:17). Paul reflects here the integral connection between opposition or suffering and the work of the gospel. As Stubbs suggests, Paul 'does not sacralize suffering. Instead, he collapses the distinction between conviction and action.'[98] If Paul and the Philippians put into action their allegiance to Jesus, they will in all likelihood experience suffering for that conviction.

### c. Friendship

In considering the particular kind of letter that Philippians is, some have identified it as a letter of friendship (see 3a). Whether or not there is adequate evidence for this specific categorization, Paul's use of friendship motifs, corresponding to the Graeco-Roman topic of friendship, is unmistakable. The fabric of friendship in the letter is most evident in the frequent use of the language of *koinōnia* ('participation'; 1:5; 2:1; 3:10) and its cognates *synkoinōnos* (1:7), *synkoinōneō* (4:14) and *koinōneō* (4:15). Paul uses this constellation of terms to highlight the benevolent and reciprocal relationship he shares with his brothers and sisters in Philippi (1:5, 7; 4:14, 15). It is a relationship grounded in the participation and union they all have experienced in Christ (2:1; 3:10) and through the Holy Spirit (2:1). As Fowl expresses it, 'We are called into friendship with each other because of our common friendship in Christ.'[99] Friendship with fellow believers is built on believers' friendship with God received in the representative work and example of Messiah Jesus (2:5–11). Paul highlights union with Christ in Philippians by using the language of being 'in Christ' (*en Christō*; e.g. 1:1; 4:21; see 4a) and in expressions of his own deep desire to 'know Christ – yes, to know the power of his resurrection and participation in his sufferings' (3:10).

---

98. Stubbs, p. 370.
99. Fowl, p. 216.

Paul's letter to the Philippians strikes a tone of friendship, with language of affection and longing permeating the letter (1:7–8; 2:26; 4:1). Paul's consistent expressions of joy contribute to this warm, relational tone, as he rejoices at the thought of his 'dear friends' in Philippi (1:4; 2:17; 4:1, 10) and frequently prompts them to rejoice from their side of the friendship (2:18, 29; 3:1; 4:4). For Paul, 'the proper working of Christian friendship' produces joy.[100] Yet it is not only Paul's joy that fits well the theme of friendship. His own 'relational anxiety' points to his deep friendship with the Philippians, and with Timothy and Epaphroditus (see Theology on 2:19–30). This anxiety arises from the concern for a friend's well-being, including that person's emotional and spiritual welfare (e.g. 2:20, 26, 27–28). The depth of the relationship shared by Paul, Timothy, Epaphroditus and the Philippians brings with it concern for the circumstances and well-being of the other.

The friendship between Paul and the Philippians centres around the gospel of Christ, a reality made especially clear at the conclusion of the letter (4:10–20). There, Paul (implicitly) conveys his gratitude to the Philippian congregation for the gift they had sent to him through Epaphroditus. For Paul, this tangible support for him while in prison is an important expression of their common life together – their 'partnership in the gospel' (1:5). So while Paul uses what we might call more transactional language of finance in 4:14–18, it is nested within a theological framework that places God in Christ at the centre of Christian relationship (4:18–20). Christians are joined in profound friendship anchored in the gospel and in their friendship with God.

### d. Communal discernment

Paul guides the Philippians towards a disposition of communal discernment as they reorient their perspective through the lens of the gospel. This is the shared mindset Paul refers to across the letter – a mindset that involves attitudes and emotions, dispositions and thinking.[101] Early on, Paul has offered a prayer for the

---

100. Fowl, p. 209.
101. Fee, pp. 89–90.

Philippian community to 'discern what is best' (1:10). This focus on discernment reappears in the exhortation towards a shared mindset that is oriented around Christ's own mindset (*phroneō*, 2:5). The Philippian believers are called to consider together how to live with one another (*phroneō*, 2:2; 4:2) and in their particular cultural location (4:8) in a way that coheres with the story of Christ – with the gospel. Fowl suggests the language of 'practical reasoning' for *phroneō* and describes it as a 'pattern of practical reasoning involv[ing] a common perspective on their situation and how it fits into the divine economy and the practical implications of that perspective'.[102]

In addition to *phroneō*, Paul uses two other words in Philippians that contribute to this constellation of terms around the concept of discernment: *hēgeomai* ('consider', 2:3, 6, 25; 3:7–8) and *logizomai* ('consider', 3:13; cf. 4:8). Each term is used to promote a reorientation from prior dispositions, actions and ways of thinking towards a Christ-focused perspective. Paul provides his own example of a changed point of view, as he narrates past ways of understanding his privileges and accomplishments (3:4–6) and compares them with his present preoccupation with knowing and gaining Christ and arriving at the day of resurrection (3:7–11). He 'considers' (*hēgeomai*, used three times in 3:7–8) his life and goals quite differently from his current vantage point of being 'in the Messiah' ('in him', 3:9). Paul's temporal location in the time after the Messiah's arrival but before the final consummation means he discerns or carefully 'considers' (*logizomai*, 3:13) that location in the way he lives. For Paul, Christ Jesus provides the supreme example of a mindset of discernment, as Christ considered (*hēgeomai*) taking on human likeness more important than capitalizing on the advantages of his divine prerogatives and status (2:6).

Towards the end of the letter, Paul calls the Philippians to a posture of discernment related to their cultural context. They are to weigh 'the good' on offer in that context (4:8), and they are to do so in the light of the gospel (4:9).[103] Paul again uses the verb *logizomai*

---

102. Fowl, p. 90 (in reference to Phil. 2:2, 5).
103. Fee, p. 416.

for the activity of considering or weighing what is 'excellent or praiseworthy' (4:8; see comment there). This is a communal task, with the Philippian congregation discerning together God's wisdom and direction for them. And they are to seek discernment from a posture of unity, from a shared mindset. Again, it is the gospel – the story of Jesus – that grounds this common mindset. Paul entrusts this communal discernment to God, who will bring wisdom and clarity to the community as its members grow in maturity (3:15).

### e. Unity and resilience in suffering

As is already evident from the discussion of communal discernment (4d), a prominent theme in Philippians is communal unity. This central theme is integrally connected to Paul's initial exhortation of the letter to live out singular loyalty to the gospel (1:27). By doing so, the Philippian believers will be able to 'stand firm in the one Spirit, striving together as one for the faith of the gospel' (1:27). Only a profound unity of focus and direction can result in the entire church working together as if they were one person. In a series of exhortations, Paul demonstrates how such singular unity is possible: through a shared mindset and affection informed by the virtue of humility that highly values others and looks out for their interests (2:2–4). This 'shared mindset' (*to auto phronēte*, 2:2; see 4d) is based on imitation of Christ, whose mindset was infused with humility and was worked out in other-focused giving and action (2:5–8). Paul draws on the same language (*to auto phronēte*) later in the letter, to implore two co-workers, Euodia and Syntyche, towards a shared mindset 'in the Lord' (4:2). Paul also warns about practices that disrupt unity and so should be avoided, such as 'grumbling', 'arguing' (2:14), and placing confidence in anything other than Christ himself (3:3, 7–8). Dispositions that contribute to unity include an eschatologically oriented mindset (3:12–21) and joy (2:18; 4:4).

Paul grounds his exhortations to unity in the unity believers already share 'from being united with Christ' (translating *en Christō*, 2:1). This phrase, *en Christō*, points to the present reality of the believer's union with Christ, which forms the basis for the Christian's unity with all other believers. All who trust the Messiah are together

'in the Messiah' (*en Christō*). And all who trust in the Messiah share
in the 'one Spirit', who makes possible Christian oneness (1:27; 2:1).

From the outset, the theme of Christian unity is connected to
resilience in suffering. By 'striving together as one for the faith of
the gospel', the Philippian congregation will have the capacity to
address any fear or anxiety that arises from opposition (1:27–28).
Remaining loyal to Christ and the gospel in first-century Roman
Philippi was no easy task. Within a polytheistic landscape such as
Philippi, people would divide their allegiances among any number
of gods, including giving attention to the demands of the imperial
cult. In such a setting, civic and religious expectations promoted
loyalty to and worship of multiple deities, even if someone might
maintain a preference for or special connection to one particular
god. What was little understood or accepted was allegiance to only
one god (and that one not recognized as part of the Greek or
Roman pantheon), as promoted by those who worshipped Messiah
Jesus exclusively. When Christians proclaimed Christ and Christ
alone as Lord, they were rejecting a primary religious and civic
duty. So it would be unsurprising that opposition and even persecution could follow, some of which may very well have been
economic in form.[104] As Cohick suggests, 'Confessing Christ was
one way [for service providers and shopkeepers] to scare away
patrons and often resulted in the believer leaving the pagan trade
guild or being ostracized from others doing similar work.'[105]

Although Paul explicitly mentions the Philippians' suffering due
to such opposition only once in the letter (1:28), the motif of suffering emerges elsewhere. First, Paul identifies with their suffering,
suggesting that their struggle is similar to his own (1:30). Second,
Paul portrays a counter-example at 3:18–19 to the singular allegiance he calls the Philippians to embrace. There, he references
'enemies of the cross' – an image that seems to point to some who
have compromised their loyalty to Christ so as to avoid opposition
and suffering. With their 'mind . . . set on earthly things' (3:19), they

---

104. Oakes, *Philippians*, p. 99. See comment on 1:28.
105. Cohick, p. 19. She notes the tendency of privileged readers to
    'spiritualize the suffering motif' of the New Testament.

have lost sight of the supreme value of Christ and his gospel (3:8), which would help them not only to endure suffering but to see it as a kind of gift (1:29) of deeper identification with Christ (3:10).

Resilience in suffering, then, comes from the community having a right mindset about what is supremely valuable – 'knowing Christ' (3:8) and identifying with him in all ways, including participating in his sufferings (3:10). Resilience in suffering also comes from putting suffering in perspective. While it may be a present reality for many or most of the Philippian believers, it is not their final state. By having an eschatological mindset, they can see ahead to their transformation, resurrection and exaltation (3:11, 20–21; see a fuller discussion of suffering at 4b). Finally, and to return to the theme of unity, the burden of suffering is lightened with the help and solidarity of a united community (1:27–30). Paul paints a vivid picture of such unity of purpose, even if attended by opposition and suffering, when he writes, 'even if I am being poured out like a drink offering on the sacrifice and service coming from your faith, I am glad and rejoice with all of you' (2:17).

What emerges in Philippians is a portrait of a church being encouraged to endure suffering, when it is necessary for remaining true to the gospel and to Christ, who himself provides an example of missional suffering that the Philippians are to be ready to emulate (2:8). With a shared mindset grounded in Christ's own mindset, the Philippian believers will be able to 'stand firm in the Lord' (4:1).

### f. Christian imitation

Imitation was an important pedagogical and discipleship practice in the first-century world. And it fitted equally well within both Graeco-Roman and Jewish contexts. As Keown notes, in the ancient world, 'before the printing press and electronic media, life was taught more by way of models than simply instruction'.[106] Paul emphasizes imitation both implicitly and explicitly in Philippians. Implicitly, he provides a number of exemplars who model a way of life for the congregation. His commendation of Timothy provides

---

106. Keown II, p. 241; see comment at 3:17.

a path to follow, especially Timothy's pattern of looking out for the interests of others, which, Paul claims, corresponds to looking out for the interests of Christ himself (2:20–21; cf. 2:4). Timothy also models serving in the work of the gospel (2:22). Epaphroditus is characterized similarly (2:25–30) and so offers another example for the Philippians to follow. Additionally, the Philippians are to emulate Paul's mindset, especially as he models the reorientation of his entire existence towards the ultimate value of knowing Christ and being found in Christ (3:4–14).

When Paul calls the Philippian church to follow Christ as exemplar his message becomes more explicit: 'In your relationships with one another, have the same mindset as Christ Jesus' (2:5). This community of believers, residents of a Roman colony, are to embrace the countercultural disposition of humility (2:3–4), and they are to do so precisely because their exalted Messiah and Lord set the pattern of humility and renunciation of status on behalf of humanity (2:6–11). Jesus is the role model par excellence; only as other believers imitate him are they worthy of emulation (cf. 3:10–11 with 2:6–11).

Paul also expressly exhorts the Philippian believers to follow his lead (3:17a); he is not shy about calling for imitation of his own example. While this might sound arrogant to modern sensibilities, it would have had no such negative connotation for Paul and his audience. Not only does Paul regularly call his churches to imitate himself (1 Cor. 4:16; 11:1; 2 Thess. 3:7–9; cf. 1 Thess. 1:6), he makes it clear that he does so only as he himself is imitating Christ (1 Cor. 11:1; Phil. 3:10). And, as he emphasizes towards the end of Philippians, believers are to follow him in the ways of the gospel (what they have 'learned or received or heard from me, or seen in me', 4:9). The Philippian believers are to imitate Paul, as well as all others who live out the gospel and its values (3:17b; cf. 2:29).

As the foundation for imitation of Christ and of Christian exemplars in Philippians, Christ himself makes the move to imitate humanity by taking upon himself the human condition (2:7–8). In the Christ poem, Paul portrays Christ as 'shar[ing] fully in the desperate contingency, suffering, and death of Adam's heirs'.[107]

---

107. Eastman, 'Imitating Christ', p. 445.

Because of Christ's identification with humanity, believers are brought into Christ's own story of humility and exaltation, suffering and resurrection. Because of Christ's imitation of humanity, humanity is empowered to imitate Christ.

# ANALYSIS

## 1. OPENING: GREETING, THANKSGIVING AND PRAYER (1:1–11)

A. Paul's greeting to the Philippian believers and leaders (1:1–2)

B. Paul's gratitude to God for the Philippians (1:3–6)

C. Paul's deep affection for the Philippians (1:7–8)

D. Paul's prayer for their growth in love towards wisdom and righteousness (1:9–11)

## 2. PAUL'S SITUATION AND PERSPECTIVE CONCERNING THE GOSPEL (1:12–26)

A. Assurance of the gospel's progress in spite of imprisonment (1:12–14)

B. Joy in the gospel being preached, whatever the motive (1:15–18a)

C. Expectation of release from prison and continuing ministry (1:18b–26)

## 3. EXHORTATIONS: TO SINGULAR LOYALTY AND STEADFAST UNITY IN SUFFERING (1:27 – 2:4)
A. Singular loyalty to Christ and the gospel (1:27a)
B. Unified stance towards opposition (1:27b–30)
C. Mindset of unity and humility towards one another (2:1–4)

## 4. JESUS AS EXEMPLAR: THE ULTIMATE SERVANT (2:5–11)
A. Jesus as model for believers' mindset (2:5)
B. Jesus' descent in humility (2:6–8)
C. Jesus' glorification to Lordship (2:9–11)

## 5. EXHORTATIONS: TO OBEDIENCE, UNITY, MISSION AND JOY (2:12–18)
A. The work of salvation (2:12–13)
B. God's holy children on mission (2:14–16)
C. Joy over commingled service (2:17–18)

## 6. TIMOTHY AND EPAPHRODITUS AS EXEMPLARS: SERVICE TO OTHERS (2:19–30)
A. The model provided by Timothy (2:19–24)
B. The model provided by Epaphroditus (2:25–30)

## 7. PAUL AS EXEMPLAR: A CONTRAST TO OPPONENTS OF THE GOSPEL AND THE CROSS (3:1 – 4:1)
A. Paul's experience of prioritizing Christ (3:1–11)
   i. Warning against confidence 'in the flesh' (3:1–3)
   ii. Paul's former confidence in his Jewish identity (3:4–6)
   iii. Paul's Christ identity and identification (3:7–11)
B. Paul's exhortation to an eschatological mindset (3:12 – 4:1)
   i. Living with the final day and end goal in view (3:12–16)
   ii. Positive and negative examples of living eschatologically (3:17 – 4:1)

## 8. SUMMATIVE EXHORTATIONS: TO UNITY, JOY, PEACE, WISDOM AND IMITATION (4:2–9)

A. Shared mindset for two co-workers (4:2–3)
B. Joy and peace in the Lord (4:4–7)
C. Wise evaluation of virtues, imitation of behaviour (4:8–9)

## 9. PAUL'S SITUATION AND PERSPECTIVE CONCERNING THE PHILIPPIANS' GIFT (4:10–20)

A. Joy in their gift and contentment in all circumstances (4:10–13)
B. The Philippians' participation with Paul and God's abundance (4:14–20)

## 10. CONCLUDING GREETINGS (4:21–23)

# COMMENTARY

## 1. OPENING: GREETING, THANKSGIVING AND PRAYER (1:1–11)

*Context*

In this opening, Paul greets the audience of his letter, naming Timothy as its co-sponsor, and indicates the Philippian church, along with its leadership, as its recipients. Paul thanks God for them and for their partnership in the good news about Jesus, expressing his deep affection for them and his confidence in God's work among them. He prays for their love to grow and lead to discernment in the present and holiness and righteousness when God's full restoration arrives.

The opening to the letter follows expected epistolary conventions, with a greeting leading into a thanksgiving and prayer. In ancient letters, this part of the letter (its proem) might consist of such elements as a 'prayer-wish', 'thanksgiving', 'remembrance' and/or an 'expression of joy'.[1] We can see these elements in

---

1. Klauck, *Letters*, p. 42.

Philippians 1:3–11, though quite extended from what might be expected in typical letters.

Although Paul is following – as well as adapting – epistolary conventions in his greeting and thanksgiving, his shaping of these expressions is by no means merely routine. Rather, a number of ideas that will be thematic in the body of the letter are thoughtfully introduced in the opening.

- The self-description of Paul and Timothy as 'servants' or 'slaves' (*douloi*, 1:1) anticipates Paul's reference to Christ's descent to the lowest human status, that of a 'slave' (*doulos*) in 2:7.
- The reference to 'overseers and deacons' (1:1) may foreshadow Paul's attention to the church's leadership in 4:2–3, where Paul addresses Euodia, Syntyche, Clement 'and the rest of my co-workers' (cf. 2:25 where Epaphroditus is identified as a co-worker).
- Paul indicates he prays 'with joy' (*chara*, 1:4), introducing a pervasive theme in the letter of rejoicing (*chara/chairō*, 1:18, 25; 2:2, 17, 18, 28, 29; 3:1; 4:1, 4, 10).
- Paul affirms the 'partnership' (*koinōnia*, 1:5) he has with the Philippians, introducing another key motif (from the noun and its cognates): 1:7 ('share'); 2:1; 3:10; 4:14, 15 (see comment on 1:5).
- The partnership in view is their shared commitment to the 'gospel' – the good news about Jesus – a term that is pervasive in the early parts of Philippians (1:5, 7, 12, 16, 27; see also 2:22; 4:3, 15).
- Paul also expresses his confidence in God's work evident in and among the Philippian believers: the 'good work' begun by God in them will be brought to completion at the final day (1:6). Paul refers to the efficacious work of God (or of Christ) at other key points in the letter (2:13, 30; 3:21).
- Twice in his prayer, Paul points his audience ahead to 'the day of Christ' (1:6, 10; cf. 2:16). This eschatological vision of the final restoration ahead is consistently on Paul's horizon in Philippians (1:28; 2:16; 3:10–11, 12–16, 20–21; 4:5).

- Paul first draws on the language of *phroneō* in the letter opening ('feel' at 1:7), a verb he will use ten times in the letter to express the development of a 'mindset' that is appropriate to the Christian life (e.g. 2:2, 5; 3:15, 19; 4:2, 10).[2]

*Paul's rhetorical emphases in Philippians 1:1–11:* Paul's rhetoric (see Introduction 3b) in the letter's opening, not unexpectedly, lands on ethos and pathos. Paul establishes his ethos by fostering his connection with the Philippian believers, first by emphasizing his (low) status as 'servant' (or 'slave'; 1:1) and then by assuring them of his deep gratitude and affection for them (1:3–8). These assurances bridge into pathos – the stirring of the audience's emotions, as they would quite probably feel a reciprocity towards Paul in his expressions of friendship. Pathos is extended through Paul's positive affirmations about the Philippian church and his expressed desire for their well-being. He affirms their status as 'God's holy people' (1:1), as well as their 'partnership in the gospel' with Paul (1:5). His prayer sets forth his desire for their present and eternal well-being, with its final note of praise to God, inspiring his readers towards love and praise. It is also in the prayer of 1:9–11 that logos most clearly emerges, with an implicit reasoning that the Philippian community needs to continue to grow from love into discernment and into holiness.

## Comment
## A. Paul's greeting to the Philippian believers and leaders (1:1–2)

**1.** Paul begins by identifying himself and Timothy as the co-sponsors of the letter. While naming both himself and Timothy in the opening could signal their status as co-writers, it becomes clear from the body of the letter with third-person references to Timothy (2:19–24) that Paul is the sole author of Philippians (see Introduction 2a). Timothy's role, illuminated in 2:19–24, involved serving alongside Paul 'in the work of the gospel' (2:22) and for the

---

2. Fee, pp. 89–90.

'welfare' of the Philippians and the 'interests . . . of Jesus Christ' (2:20–21). Timothy would also fulfil the role of surrogate for Paul, travelling to Philippi to see how the church was doing and to minister to and with them, if Paul were not (yet) to be released from prison (2:19, 23–24).

It is significant that Paul chooses the language of *servants of Christ Jesus* (or 'slaves') to describe Timothy and himself. Although referring to himself as a 'slave' is not unique to this letter's opening (see also Rom. 1:1; Titus 1:1), it is not Paul's practice to do so routinely. More commonly he uses the appellation 'apostle' (*apostolos*) in his greetings (1 and 2 Cor.; Gal.; Eph.; Col.; 1 and 2 Tim.). But Paul may feel no need to accent his apostolic authority in his communication with the Philippian church, given their mutually supportive and unstrained relationship (see Introduction 2b). The term *doulos* (and the concept of a slave) will be important within Paul's discourse about Jesus, who will be described as taking on the form of a slave (2:7), so Paul probably introduces it here intentionally. Stubbs defines the metaphor of *doulos* in Paul's use as 'someone who acts in the name of [his or her] master for the sake of the household and someone totally defined by [his or her] mission in the name of the master. The focus is thus on Christ's mission'.[3]

Paul refers to the recipients of the letter as *God's holy people in Christ Jesus at Philippi*, with *God's holy people* (*hagioi*) traditionally rendered as 'saints'. This description highlights the sanctifying work of God in creating a distinctive people and borrows from Israel's identity as a people set apart for God (Exod. 19:4–6; Deut. 7:6; Ps. 135:3–4). The believers in the Philippian church, though primarily Gentile, take on the cast of the people of God in the Hebrew Scriptures as they trust in and are faithful to Jesus, the Jewish Messiah (*Christos*). Although the Greek term *Christos* is typically rendered 'Christ' in the epistles under the assumption that it has become more name than title, it should not be forgotten that it is a title in Jewish use (and so often rendered 'Messiah' in the Gospels). It is likely that Paul retains its messianic

3. Stubbs, p. 367.

connotations, as Novenson has argued in his identification of *Christos* as an 'honorific'. An 'honorific' is not a birth name but is assigned or taken on later, yet it can substitute for the person's name. It is 'a word that can function as a stand-in for a personal name but part of whose function is to retain its associations' beyond the name.[4]

The church *at Philippi* would have met in homes, in one or more households among its members (cf. Acts 16:14–15, 40; see Introduction 2b[ii]). In addition to the Philippian church, Paul singles out *the overseers and deacons* among the letter's audience for special mention, a feature absent from his other letters. Although some have argued that this might signal an element of contention between Paul and these leaders, it is more likely that Paul desires to call the entire Philippian church, with a special emphasis on its leaders, to the unity and common mission that will be thematic across the letter. The inclusion of *overseers and deacons* would fit well the status-consciousness of Philippi (see Introduction 2b[i]).[5] If Paul intends to address preoccupations with status, it may be that Paul's description of himself and Timothy as Christ's 'slaves' (NIV: *servants*) is meant subtly to reshape the identities of these leaders as well. The reference to these two specific groups within the leadership could also signal a later date for the letter in comparison with Paul's other letters (see Introduction 2d). Fee argues that these two groups are the primary, though fluid categories of emerging church leadership in the latter part of the first century (cf. 1 Tim. 3:1–13).[6]

**2.** Paul employs his standard greeting for the Philippian believers: *grace and peace* (e.g. Rom. 1:7; 1 Cor. 1:3; 2 Cor. 1:2; Gal. 1:3; 1 Thess. 1:1). He draws from the common Greek greeting (*chairein*; see Acts 15:23), adapted to *charis*; and he combines it with the Jewish notion of peace (Heb.: *šālôm*; Gk: *eirēnē*). Although this pairing is Paul's standard epistolary greeting, it should not be passed over as perfunctory. The combination for Paul signals the epitome of

---

4. Novenson, *Christ*, pp. 91–92.

5. Hellerman, 'Social Status', p. 783.

6. Fee, 'Leadership', p. 10.

God's action towards humanity (*grace*) and its result of holistic, communal salvation (*peace*).

This extraordinary benevolence comes from *God our Father and the Lord Jesus Christ*. This formulaic phrase is commonplace in Paul's letter openings (Rom. 1:7; 1 Cor. 1:3; 2 Cor. 1:2; Gal. 1:3; Eph. 1:2; 2 Thess. 1:2; Phlm. 3) and speaks of the filial relationship between Jesus and God. Paul often uses this kind of 'binitarian' formula to express his theology (less often a trinitarian formula; e.g. 2 Cor. 13:14).[7] The emphasis in such binitarian expressions is upon the relationship of the God of Israel to Messiah Jesus, who is uniquely God's Son (though believers share in this sonship, as indicated by *our* here; see Rom. 8:14–17) and has been granted rule or Lordship over all creation (Phil. 2:10–11; see 1 Cor. 8:5–6; 15:24–28). As Hurtado has noted, Pauline binitarian greetings 'are commonly thought to represent Paul's use of early Christian liturgical formulas in epistles that were intended to be read out as part of the liturgical gathering of the groups to which they were sent'.[8]

## B. Paul's gratitude to God for the Philippians (1:3–6)

**3–4.** Paul communicates to the Philippians his gratitude to God for them: *I thank my God every time I remember you* (1:3). This indirect address to God (with the recipients directly addressed) fits Paul's epistolary pattern and custom (e.g. Rom. 1:8; 1 Cor. 1:4; 1 Thess. 1:2). His depiction of his prayers for them is effusive, peppered with sweeping language (*every time ... in all my prayers ... I always pray*, 1:3–4) and exuberance (*I ... pray with joy*, 1:4). Paul expresses the mode of his prayers: he prays with joy and with confidence. His joy stems from the Philippians and their 'partnership in the gospel' with him from the time of the inception of their faith to the present (1:5).

---

7. Hurtado (*One God,* p. 135) suggests an early '"binitarian pattern" of devotion and worship, in which Christ is treated as recipient of devotion with God and in ways that can be likened only to worship of a deity' (p. 139).

8. Hurtado, *One God*, p. 139.

**5.** The *partnership* (*koinōnia*) Paul experiences with other believers is a significant Christological theme across his letters, especially as it is grounded in the *partnership* all believers experience 'in Christ' (*en Christō*; i.e. in the Messiah). Thiselton describes this reality, signalled by the term *koinōnia*, as being *shareholders* in Christ,[9] a relational union in which believers share in Christ's benefits (and sufferings; see 3:10) as they dwell in Christ. Paul signals this theme of union with Christ both with the term (*syn*)*koinōnia* (and its cognates; see Context) and with the shorthand 'in Christ' (as in, e.g., 1:1; 3:14; 4:7, 19; also 'in the Lord'; e.g. 1:14, 2:19, 24). The phrase *en Christō* is 'a concept of corporate status which provides the ground for Christian life and destiny'.[10] It is this union with Christ that makes possible the partnership among believers as they share the same unity with one another that they share with Christ. In this context, Paul highlights that the Philippians have shared with him in *the gospel* (*euangelion*), the term used in the New Testament to identify the good news of God's restoration of humanity (Jew and Gentile) enacted in Messiah Jesus, through his life, death and resurrection. Partnership in the gospel includes the joint ministry of Paul and the Philippians in proclaiming and embodying the gospel, and, more specifically, refers to the Philippians' financial support for Paul's ministry (2:25; 4:1–10). It also points to their mutual life together as immersed in and benefiting from Christ's story that is the lifeblood of the gospel. The consistency of their mutual partnership is reassuring to Paul (*from the first day until now*).

**6.** Paul also prays with confidence – a confidence arising from God's initiating and persistent work among this group of believers (cf. 2:12–13). It is Paul's confidence in this divine commitment to believers that assures them they will remain in faith *until the day of Christ Jesus*. Across the letter, Paul will focus on eschatology; he is especially keen to point the Philippians to the final day of resurrection and salvation that awaits them (e.g. 1:10–11, 28; 2:16; 3:10–14, 20–21).

---

9. Thiselton, *Corinthians*, p. 104.

10. Thiselton, *Corinthians*, p. 76.

## C. Paul's deep affection for the Philippians (1:7–8)

**7.** Paul confirms his joy and confidence in the Philippian believers by describing his mutual and warm relationship with them. Having just conveyed God's constancy towards these believers (1:6), Paul justifies (*it is right*) his own devoted stance towards them.[11] His affection – *to feel this way* – renders the Greek phrase *touto phronein*, with *phroneō* being thematic in the letter (see Context). Though its translation is less than straightforward (one English term does not adequately cover all contexts), Fee's suggestion of 'mindset' provides helpful guidance.[12] The scope of Paul's use of *phroneō* is not limited to a person's thinking, just as a mindset involves attitudes, dispositions and emotions. A mindset is a frame of reference, a lens for seeing the world and assessing it. The believer's mindset is to be shaped by the gospel and by Christ's own 'mindset' (2:5). The NIV translates *phroneō* here as *feel this way*, since the term includes Paul's attitude and feelings towards the Philippians that arise from his Christologically focused mindset and the immediate context highlights Paul's affection for these believers arising from his right perspective about them (1:7–8).

The reasons Paul gives for his (appropriate) feelings for the Philippians focus on their reciprocal, abiding relationship and their partnership in the gospel. The first reason (*since*) involves the deep affection between Paul and the Philippians, with the image of 'having someone in one's heart' suggesting relational attachment. The language communicates either Paul's affection for them or their affection for him. The phrase *I have you in my heart* (NIV) could be rendered 'you have me in your heart' (cf. NRSV), since both pronouns surrounding 'have' (a Greek infinitive, which takes its subject and object in the accusative) are in the accusative case. It is the Greek word order that suggests but does not necessitate the NIV's translation ('I/me ... you'). In context, both readings

---

11. Phil. 1:7 begins with a comparative adverb (*kathōs*), which seems to connect God's eschatological commitment to the Philippians to Paul's own devotion or loyalty to them.

12. Fee, pp. 89–90.

commend themselves. Paul will accent his own deep affection for
the Philippian believers in 1:8; and the commitment of the Philippians to Paul is the subject of the rest of 1:7. It is intriguing to
ponder whether Paul might have intended this ambiguity to
highlight their 'warm, reciprocal relationship'. It may be that, 'after
penning this line and rereading the prayer, Paul perceived the
ambiguity and, rather than somehow "fixing" it, decided that it was
the perfect expression of their relationship so valued by both
sides'.[13]

Tied closely to their relationship is Paul's description of the Philippians as those who *share in God's grace with me*. This is the same
participation Paul has already described in 1:5 as 'your partnership
in the gospel', with a cognate of *koinōnia* ('partnership') used here:
*synkoinōnos* – a person who shares or participates with someone else.
The connection between these phrases in 1:5 and 1:7 (with the
repetition of *gospel* in 1:7) implies that Paul understands *grace* to be
comparable to the gospel. In this sense, grace is a shorthand for
what God has accomplished in Christ Jesus to bring about the
restoration of humanity, with emphasis on the effects of that restoration on those who are 'in Christ'.[14] The mutual participation of
believers in the gospel – in God's gracious redemption – is something that runs deep for Paul. It is a cord of connection that cannot
be severed by misfortune or suffering; it weathers any situation. So
Paul speaks of their continuing participation with him – in his state
of imprisonment (*in chains*) and in his commitment in any situation
to *defending and confirming the gospel*. While Paul may be alluding to his
approaching trial and his need to defend himself there, he is
probably using these terms broadly to refer to all the ways the Philippians have partnered with Paul in his ministry, including their
material support (4:18).[15] Across their shared history, this church
has participated with Paul in *God's grace*. By highlighting his defence

---

13. Brown, 'Love', p. 94.

14. Barclay uses 'gift' language to refer to Paul's understanding of *charis*
    and expresses its focal point as the 'life, death, and resurrection of
    Jesus', so that Christ himself is *'the Gift'* (*Gift*, p. 56).

15. Thielman, p. 40.

and confirmation of the gospel, Paul makes it clear that the notion of sharing in the gospel includes not only receiving the benefits of Christ and his community but also joining in 'the work of the gospel' (cf. 2:22) – its advancement (1:12) and proclamation (1:14).

**8.** Paul concludes the thanksgiving section by re-emphasizing his affection for the Philippian church, this time using oath language to express his utter sincerity: *God can testify* (or 'God is my witness'; cf. Rom. 1:9; 2 Cor. 1:23; 1 Thess. 2:5, 10). With these words, Paul communicates his longing for the Philippian church, from whom he is separated by a great distance and by his chains (1:7). He will later refer to a similar longing that Epaphroditus feels for his fellow believers in Philippi (2:26). Once again, Paul connects his own relationship and concern for this group of believers to their shared experience in Christ: *how I long for all of you with the affection of Christ Jesus.* This is Paul's only explicit affirmation in Philippians of Christ's love or affection (*splangchna*) for believers, although it seems quite clear that the love referenced in 2:1 is Christ's love for believers (the pronoun is absent from the Greek),[16] with 'tenderness' (*splangchna*; 2:1) also very probably descriptive of Christ. Also relevant is the Christ hymn or poem of 2:5–11, which Paul will use as an exemplar to highlight the model mindset for believers. The story of Jesus embedded in that poem highlights his self-humbling and sacrifice for humanity's sake. This story of Jesus is, in essence, a story of affection and love in action.

## D. Paul's prayer for their growth in love towards wisdom and righteousness (1:9–11)

**9.** Paul adds intercession to his thanksgiving for the partnership of the Philippians. Given that key ideas from this prayer become prominent themes in the letter, it seems likely that Paul is implicitly identifying areas of needed growth for this community he holds dear. To begin with, the prayer for love addresses the need for the Philippian believers to press towards unity in love and into the

---

16. This is fairly common in Greek, with a prior noun usually assumed as the referent of the implied pronoun.

practice of humility (2:1–4). Paul's prayer for their progress in discernment also fits the pervasive theme of the need to develop a Christlike mindset (e.g. 2:5). The structure of the prayer indicates that their growth in love is the seed that will blossom into wisdom, which will culminate in a mature holiness and righteousness at the final day. In this way, Paul's prayer for (his goals for) the Philippians moves from love to discerning wisdom to the ultimate goal of righteousness.

In line with Paul's affirmation of love rooted in Christ's affection (1:8), Paul begins by praying that their love would *abound more and more*. Though it is common to interpret Paul's prayer for the Philippians' ever-increasing love as focused on or even limited to fellow believers, it is more likely that Paul's expansive language here signals a growth in love to be expressed broadly. It is true that Paul emphasizes across the letter the need for unselfish love to increase towards others within the believing community (e.g. 1:27; 2:1–4, 14; 4:2–3). Yet Paul also casts a wider vision for their abounding love in 4:5, where he desires that their gentleness 'be evident to all' (cf. 1 Thess. 3:12). And undoubtedly Paul would commend a growing love for God in Christ, which though not explicit in the letter, is at least hinted at across the letter (1:29; 2:1, 21; 3:12). So Paul probably has a wide application in mind for their growth in love.

Paul signals the integral connection between loving and knowing in his petition that their *love may abound . . . in knowledge and depth of insight*. In other letters, Paul highlights a potential tension between human knowledge (*gnōsis*) and love (*agapē*), especially when knowledge is wielded apart from love (1 Cor. 8:1–3). Here, however, Paul sees knowledge (*epignōsis*), a term that he usually uses to signal experiential or relational knowledge, contributing to growth in love.[17] Paul uses the term *aisthēsis* (*depth of insight*) only here in his letters. Fowl notes that its use in the Septuagint (in Proverbs especially) is often paralleled with practical wisdom and suggests the term connotes 'moral understanding'.[18] So the use of these two terms, *knowledge* and *depth of insight*, signals that Paul is

---

17. Hellerman, p. 32.
18. Fowl, p. 32 n. 28.

addressing the practice of discernment rather than a kind of professed knowledge that goes no further than the intellect ('head knowledge'). Love and discernment are to function in tandem in the Philippians' relationships with others, with love being the primary marker (see Theology).

**10–11.** The ever-expanding love of the Philippian congregation, when spurred on and informed by practical wisdom, will result in the capacity *to discern what is best*. The verb, *dokimazō*, means to evaluate or discern something, in this case that which is superior (*the best*). The context suggests a moral cast to what is best – those values and virtues that will lead to blamelessness in the final day. This is confirmed by Paul's parallel exhortation near the conclusion of the letter. In 4:8, Paul will call the Philippians to evaluate and reflect upon ('think about') the highest ideals (e.g. 'whatever is pure, whatever is lovely'). The list he provides there corresponds to recognized virtues from Graeco-Roman moral discourse, and the Philippians are exhorted to consider (*logizomai*) such virtues in the light of the truth and testimony they have received from Paul in the gospel (4:9). In 1:9–10, this kind of moral discernment comes as the result of a maturing love and insight. The goal of discernment in Paul's prayer coheres well with the development of a Christlike mindset (see *phroneō* for the call to a shared mindset, 2:2, 5), which, as we have seen, includes dispositions and actions as well as thinking.[19]

The ultimate goal from Paul's perspective is that the Philippians would arrive at *the day of Christ*, having become *pure and blameless . . . filled with the fruit of righteousness*. This final purpose clause highlights the status of the Philippians at the return of Christ (3:20). As the Philippians discern and live out what is best (i.e. values consistent with the gospel), Paul trusts that, when the final day arrives, they will *be pure and blameless*, language that implies a state unmarred by sin. This is not, however, a state grounded in what the Philippians

---

19. To fill out the idea of discerning and pursuing a right mindset (*phroneō*), Paul will draw on the (related) verbs *hēgeomai* ('consider', e.g. Phil 3:7–8) and *logizomai* ('consider', 3:13) across the letter to address this idea of practical reflection on the gospel.

could accomplish on their own. Paul's eschatological vision for 'the day of Christ Jesus' has already surfaced at 1:6, where he confidently anticipates the completion of *God's* saving work among the Philippian believers. The same emphasis on what God has and will achieve for redeemed humanity is signalled in 1:11, where Paul affirms that the Philippians will arrive at a final state of blameless-ness by being *filled with the fruit of righteousness that comes through Jesus Christ*. The Greek participle for *filled* reads best as a participle of means, indicating how they become *blameless*. And the passive verb, *filled*, implies that God is the one doing the filling. Paul prays for the Philippians – for their love in knowledge moving to discernment resulting, finally, in their holiness and righteousness. All of their progress is superintended by God and made possible *through Jesus Christ*, that is, through his representative death on their behalf (2:7–8). Later in the letter, Paul will contrast his own right-eousness with the righteousness whose source is God (3:9), a contrast that clarifies 1:11. All along the Philippians' trajectory of growth for which Paul prays, God is deeply and consistently involved (1:6; 2:12–13), which is the very point of Paul entrusting this process to God in prayer (1:9–11).

Yet Paul does not conclude his prayer with a vision of the Philip-pians in a final state of righteousness, as glorious as that vision might be. As their pathway from love to discernment to righteous-ness has come about through God's initiative, so *the glory and praise* for all of it belongs to God. Paul will continue to reiterate that what God has done in Christ is glorious – it illuminates God's glory (2:11; 4:19). And he will conclude the body of the letter by ascribing glory to God (4:20).[20]

---

20. A significant set of textual variants occurs at 1:11. Although the variant which has God as the recipient of glory and praise seems the most plausible, especially given its early and widespread support, the variant *moi* ('me') in place of *theou* ('God') is difficult to explain as arising in the scribal tradition. Silva suggests the singular reading of p[46] ('to God's glory and my praise') best accounts for the other readings (p. 58). See Nongbri's support for the variant which attributes both glory and praise to Paul ('Variants', p. 808).

*Theology*

Already in the opening to the letter, Paul is theologizing: exploring theology as it emerges from practical and pastoral concerns and questions. As he adapts the typical epistolary greeting, he deepens it to include a Jewish affirmation of communal *šālôm*: 'Grace and peace to you' (1:2). In Jesus the Messiah, God has acted definitively to bring grace and *šālôm* to humanity. Paul also includes Jesus in the greeting with his characteristically binitarian phrasing. The reference to 'God our Father and the Lord Jesus Christ' intimates Paul's fuller engagement ahead with the issue of Christ's relationship with Israel's God in 2:6–11 (see Theology on 2:5–11). We can also observe Paul drawing on Christology as the foundation for his shared experience and partnership with the Philippians. Using language drawn from the Graeco-Roman topics of friendship, patronage and commerce (from the [*syn*]*koinon-* stem), Paul infuses it with theological overtones (see comment on 1:5) to communicate the depth of his relationship with the Philippian church, grounded in their shared experience 'in the Messiah' ('in Christ', 1:1).

Paul's prayer for the Philippians emphasizes the priority of love in the Christian life. This priority of love is evident in his letters in the gratitude Paul expresses for his churches (e.g. Eph. 1:15–16; Col. 1:4; 1 Thess. 1:3; 2 Thess. 1:3; Phlm. 5), as well as in his exhortations (e.g. Rom. 12:9–10; 13:8–10), and is especially evident in his praise of love (1 Cor. 13:1–13). While it may be that Paul prays for love as a priority for the Philippians because as a community they need to hear the call to turn from selfish ambition to prioritize the other (2:2–4), we should not lose sight of the link he forges between their love and their communal discernment and holiness. Love provides the proper disposition for discerning and then living out 'what is best', especially when guided by relational knowledge (1:9–10).

The direction in Paul's prayer (love to discernment to holiness) contravenes possible and sometimes common misconceptions about the Christian life. First, it avoids dichotomizing holiness and love. Holiness, narrowly conceived, has sometimes been understood as avoidance behaviour – a listing of what Christians are prohibited from doing. If love is foundational to holiness, we will need to expand our understanding of biblical holiness. Moving from 'behavioural abstinence' to love as the basis for Christian identity may be challenging, but it is a crucial reorientation, and one that Paul, it seems, would affirm. As Dahl suggests, 'Perhaps one reason "behavioral abstinence" is such a tenacious worldview is that being known for what we don't do is easier in some ways than being known for our love.'[21]

Second, Paul joins love and knowledge closely together (1:9), a connection that is all the more intriguing given the sometimes ambiguous relationship between the two across the Pauline corpus. At times, Paul can emphasize the tension between knowledge and love, as he does in 1 Corinthians 8:1–3, when commenting on the Corinthians' use of knowledge (*gnōsis*) in ways that harm a weaker brother or sister: 'knowledge puffs up while love builds up' (8:2). In his ode to love in that same letter, Paul stresses that knowledge without love is worthless (1 Cor. 13:2). Even when he is not expressly critiquing a certain kind of (or a certain way of pursuing) knowledge, Paul routinely prioritizes love over knowledge (1 Cor. 8:3; see NIV footnote). Christ's love 'surpasses knowledge' (*gnōsis*; Eph. 3:19); and love is the culminating virtue (2 Cor. 8:7–8). The argument of Colossians 2:2 runs in similar fashion to Philippians 1:9: love leads to understanding and knowledge. As Scott comments on Colossians 2:2–3, 'Love is thus the key to achieving right understanding – not just moral understanding, but understanding of Christ.'[22] In Philippians 1:9, love, accompanied by knowledge and insight, is the springboard to discerning what is best.

It is instructive in this regard to ponder again the direction of Paul's prayer for the Philippians: love leads to discernment. As Osiek notes, 'We would expect knowledge to lead to love, but Paul puts it the other way around.'[23] Love is not something to be added to a list of Christian virtues; it is the starting point from which all good things – the best things, as Paul suggests – grow. Love, joined by knowledge (1:9), leads to discerning what is best (1:10), which leads to blamelessness and righteousness (doing and being what is best, 1:11). Discernment and holiness are not possible without love.

21. Brown, Dahl and Corbin Reuschling, *Whole and Holy*, p. 100.

22. Scott, *Knowing*, p. 65 n. 68.

23. Osiek, p. 37.

Ranking *love under knowledge* is an easy path to follow, especially in circles that prioritize right doctrine (orthodoxy). In such contexts, it can be tempting to think that imparting knowledge (about the Bible, about the faith) will necessarily produce Christian discipleship and right ways of living (orthopraxy). Yet prioritizing knowledge over love can lead to what Paul warns so vigorously against in 1 Corinthians: a puffing-up kind of knowledge that lacks a building-up kind of love. Prioritizing knowledge over love can also lead to warped views of both, as when knowledge is viewed as a means of tempering the (too) wide embrace of love by pursuing a more 'discriminating love'. What Paul seems to offer in his vision for the Philippians is an inclusive and ever-growing love that leads to discernment (a 'discerning love'). Discerning love, I would suggest, seeks to discern how to love well rather than how far it should extend (and where it should stop). Discerning love is thoughtful, but it is not stingy.

At its core, Christian love is based on the one who has loved us first (1 John 4:19), as Paul intimates at Philippians 2:1, 5–8. Søren Kierkegaard expresses God's initiating work with this indelible portrait:

> When we awake in the morning and turn our thoughts to you – you are the first, you have loved us first. Even if I arise at daybreak and instantly turn my thoughts to you in prayer, you are too quick for me; you have loved me first.[24]

This Christ-infused vision aligns with the ultimate conclusion of Paul's prayer (1:11). God's work among the Philippian believers is based on the work of Christ (it 'comes through Jesus Christ') and will, in that final day especially, bring glory and praise to God.

---

24. In Becknell and Ashcroft, *Wisdom*, p. 141.

## 2. PAUL'S SITUATION AND PERSPECTIVE CONCERNING THE GOSPEL (1:12–26)

*Context*

Paul turns from thanks and prayer for the Philippians to the body of the letter. He finds it important to begin with an extended set of assurances that his present situation in prison is not something that his Philippian friends should be concerned about (1:12–26). This section, focused on Paul's situation and perspective about his imprisonment, parallels the conclusion to the body of the letter (4:10–20), which addresses Paul's situation and perspective related to the Philippians' gift.

Paul's choice to begin with this autobiographical reassurance confirms the warm and personal relationship that Paul shares with these fellow believers (cf. 1:7–8) and indicates that he is aware they would be concerned about his current situation of imprisonment. Paul focuses a gospel-oriented lens on his circumstances and comforts his audience that, from this perspective, all is well (1:12–18a). He also anticipates a release from prison and explores this possibility in the light of how it would benefit the Philippian church (1:18b–26). The 'gospel' has a place of prominence in this passage

(1:12, 14, 16), along with its proclamation (to 'preach Christ', 1:15, 17, 18), continuing the emphasis on the gospel already begun in the letter's opening (1:5, 7).

Paul's threefold reference to his 'chains' in this passage (1:13, 14, 17; also 1:7) indicates he is in prison as he writes the letter to the Philippians. The reference to chains is very probably a physical description rather than simply metaphorical, indicating that Paul is in military custody, chained between two guards (on types of Roman prison, see Introduction 2c). A question that occupies scholars is where Paul is imprisoned as he writes the letter (for other prison epistles, cf. Phlm. 1; also Eph. 3:1; Col. 4:18). Traditionally, Paul has been understood to be imprisoned in Rome, in line with the narrated events of Acts 28:16–31. Evidence internal to Philippians for a Roman imprisonment includes Paul's reference to the Roman *praitōrion* (1:13), and his expression of greetings from 'those who belong to Caesar's household' (4:22). In this commentary, Roman provenance is assumed. For the possibilities of Caesarea or Ephesus, the two other primary suggestions for the location of Paul's imprisonment as he writes to the Philippians, see Introduction 2c.

*Paul's rhetorical emphases in Philippians 1:12–26:* Paul continues to draw on ethos and pathos as he begins the body of his letter. His repeated emphasis in this passage on his unwavering commitment to the progress and preaching of the gospel further establishes his ethos with his audience, who have been affirmed as equally committed to the gospel (1:5, 7). Paul's ethos could be undermined by the shame of his imprisonment; yet he makes it clear that he is 'in chains for Christ' (1:13), a situation that would elevate his standing in the Philippians' estimation. As Paul speaks of rejoicing in the gospel's progress, pathos is evoked, especially as he anticipates returning to Philippi for their 'progress and joy' and their 'boasting'. As he considers the possible outcomes of his imprisonment, he moves to logos to deliberate between life and death and to affirm that either scenario would bring a beneficial outcome (1:21–24).

## Comment

## A. Assurance of the gospel's progress in spite of imprisonment (1:12–14)

**12.** Paul reassures the Philippians (*I want you to know*) that his current circumstance of being imprisoned ('in chains', 1:7, 13) has worked for and not against the gospel. Paul acknowledges the assumption that his imprisonment could easily be considered in wholly negative terms with his use of *mallon* ('rather'), captured by *actually*. Viewed from the right perspective, however, what has happened to Paul has served a greater purpose – *to advance the gospel*. Paul uses a particular grammatical pattern – *ta kat' eme: what has happened to me* – that will recur across Philippians 1 – 2 to refer to his circumstances or to the Philippians' situation (*ta peri hymōn*, 'the matters concerning you', 1:27; 2:19, 20; cf. 2:23).[1] Paul refers to the Philippians as *brothers and sisters* (*adelphoi*), a familial term referring to siblings and his preferred language for fellow believers who now share a deeply affectionate connection (e.g. 3:1, 13, 17; 4:1, 8).[2]

The gospel's advancement or progress (*prokopē*) is of paramount importance to Paul, a commitment the Philippians share, according to Paul's earlier references (1:5, 7). This section of the letter is saturated with gospel language and references. Paul will closely align the preaching of the *gospel* (*euangelion*, indicated by *logos* in 1:14) with the preaching of Christ (1:15, 17, 18). This alignment indicates that, for Paul, Christ and his story (his life, death, resurrection) is

---

1. The construction consists of a plural article (*ta*: 'the things') + preposition (*kata* or *peri*: 'about') + pronoun (*eme* or *hymōn*: 'me' or 'you'). Fee considers this to be a significant structural and semantic marker in the letter (pp. 3, 38, 54–55).

2. Although *adelphoi* is linguistically a masculine noun, it is functioning here as a generic (as the masculine linguistic gender did in ancient Greek) to refer to a group of siblings that included women and men (BDAG, p. 18; see NIV footnote on 1:12). Translation choices such as 'beloved' (NRSV) and 'friends' (GNT) are not inaccurate, but they do lose something of the familial metaphor of Paul's language.

at the centre of the gospel. Paul will also repeat an earlier reference to his imprisonment 'for the defence of the gospel' (1:16; cf. 1:7). For Paul, the vitality of the gospel is a central lens for assessing life's circumstances.

**13–14.** Paul narrates two results of his imprisonment and, more specifically, two demonstrations of the gospel's progress because of it. The first result of Paul's imprisonment has a direct impact on those outside the faith: *the whole palace guard and . . . everyone else* have become aware that Paul is in prison for his commitment and loyalty to Christ. Paul here seems to refer to the word-of-mouth impact of his imprisonment among the guards and even further afield, rather than extensive opportunity for direct proclamation. Paul provides the reason for his imprisonment by including the phrase *en Christō* ('in Christ' or *for Christ*) – a phrase which emphasizes his identity as belonging to Christ and Christ's people (see comment at 1:5). Fowl suggests that 'in Christ' is highly allusive language that can evoke any number of associations. It is 'a sort of verbal shorthand for the body of believers who are "in Christ" and the manner of life appropriate to that body (2:1). It would have been Paul's membership in this body which landed him in jail'.[3] The association of Paul *in chains* and Paul 'in Christ' highlights Paul's participation in all Christ has accomplished, including his sufferings (3:10).[4]

Paul speaks of his imprisonment using the language of *chains* (1:7, 13, 14, 17) and here mentions the *praitōrion*, a Greek transliteration of the Latin *praetorium*, which can refer either to a governor's official residence in an imperial province (e.g. Herod's residence in Caesarea, Acts 23:35) or to the soldiers of the Praetorian Guard in Rome (numbering around 9,000).[5] The latter is more probable here – that is, *the whole palace guard* – given the likelihood that Paul writes from Rome (see Introduction 2c). Providing further evidence, Paul adds *and to everyone else* and so places emphasis on people over a building. The NIV footnote, 'the whole palace', signals the alternative possibility.

---

3. Fowl, p. 39.
4. Fee, p. 113.
5. Bockmuehl, pp. 28, 75.

The second result of Paul's imprisonment involves an increased confidence among believers to make the gospel known. Paul refers to *the brothers and sisters* who are in his vicinity, so in Rome if that is his location,[6] most of whom have gained increased confidence *because of my chains*. The exact connection between Paul's imprisonment and this increased confidence to proclaim the gospel is not made explicit. It may be that these believers have taken on the task of proclaiming the gospel now that the scope of Paul's direct influence has been narrowed (1:15–17). It may also be the case that they have greater boldness based on Paul's boldness that had landed him in prison – his *chains* have inspired them. Adding to their motivation from his circumstances, Paul mentions their increased confidence *in the Lord* (cf. 2:24). Whether they are taking up where Paul has left off or deriving inspiration from him, the Lord is 'the ultimate basis of their confidence'.[7]

The outcome, based on their confidence in the Lord, is that these believers now *dare all the more to proclaim the gospel without fear*. To *dare* (*tolmaō*) indicates boldness or a resolute stance in the face of opposition (BDAG, p. 1010). Paul conveys the heightened courage that has taken hold of these believers by using two adverbs: *perissoterōs* (*all the more*) and *aphobōs* (*without fear*). The proclamation of the gospel continues unabated in spite of Paul's imprisonment; in fact, it is happening more than if Paul were free and unhindered. Paul uses *logos* as a synonym for *euangelion* at the end of 1:14 (*the gospel*), as he does elsewhere (e.g. 2:16; 1 Thess. 1:5–6).[8] In 1:15–17, he will refer to Christ being preached as another such equivalent or shorthand.

---

6. And so would have been the recipients of his letter to the Roman churches (*c.* AD 56–58).

7. Flemming, p. 67.

8. It seems that scribes felt it important to clarify whose *logos* is in view (since the Greek word can mean 'word' or 'message' as well as 'the gospel'), by adding *tou theou* ('of God') in some cases and *kyriou* ('of the Lord') in others.

## B. Joy in the gospel being preached, whatever the motive (1:15–18a)

**15.** In 1:14, Paul has given only a positive portrayal of fellow believers in Rome and their increased confidence to proclaim the gospel. In 1:15–18, we hear a more mixed characterization, with two groups described based on quite different motives: *some preach Christ out of envy and rivalry, but others out of goodwill*. The two negative descriptors, translated *envy* and *rivalry*, are both found in vice lists in the Pauline writings (e.g. Rom. 1:29; cf. 1 Tim. 6:4). Their use here sets up a group of terms Paul employs in the letter as a foil to Christlike behaviour (see discussion at 1:16–17). For example, he will exhort the Philippians to avoid 'selfish ambition' and 'vain conceit' (2:3; cf. 1:17), and he will press against the idea of looking out for only one's own interests (2:4, 21). In 1:15–18, the believers who are preaching Christ with wrong motives are not harming Paul (1:18) but they do provide a striking contrast for the ethical instructions to come.

**16.** Having referenced Roman believers who are preaching Christ 'out of goodwill' (1:15), Paul further clarifies their motive as goodwill directed towards Paul himself: they are motivated by love (*agapē*). Paul has prayed for the Philippians that their love would increase and lead to deeper discernment of what is best. The Roman believers who act out of love towards Paul exhibit such discernment; Paul references their knowledge of his role and theirs in the progress of the gospel. They know that Paul has been consigned to prison *for the defence of the gospel*, so they boldly step up to 'proclaim the gospel' (1:14) on his behalf, out of love for Paul and for Christ. This is the second time Paul has mentioned his role in defending the gospel (as in 1:7). In addition to being a reason for his imprisonment (defending the gospel in his ministry; cf. Acts 21 – 28), *the defence of the gospel* could be an oblique reference to his forthcoming trial (1:19–20).[9] The verb Paul uses, *keimai* (*put*), when followed by *eis* (*for*), can denote being appointed for a task/ destiny (BDAG, p. 537). Paul then would be implying that God had

---

9. Fee writes of 'the (apparent) tribunal referred to in vv. 19–20' (p. 120).

appointed him for the defence of the gospel at his forthcoming trial, further heightening the sense that his imprisonment is not an accidental, inopportune circumstance, but rather a divinely orchestrated opportunity for the gospel to move forwards.

**17.** Paul returns to describing the believers in his own context who *preach Christ out of selfish ambition* (*eritheia*), a way of living for self-interest and self-promotion that may have been an issue in the Philippian community given Paul's admonition against it in 2:3. These believers are insincere in their preaching, since they seem to be preaching the gospel not for Christ's sake but to *stir up trouble* for the imprisoned Paul. Why and how might they do this? Do they mean to demoralize Paul by rivalling his success at preaching the gospel with their own ambition to surpass him?[10] Or do they think that their unhindered preaching of the gospel would offend Paul, who was now not able to move about preaching freely? Whatever the specific ways they might think to cause Paul trouble or anguish, he makes it clear that their ploy has no such effect on him.

**18a.** Paul sets up his sanguine response to these self-perceived rivals with a question: *what does it matter?* He begins an answer by affirming what is most important (*plēn*, 'only', emphasizing the most important thing): that, no matter what, *Christ is preached*. Paul accents once more the two motives for preaching that he has been addressing: *whether from false motives or true*. The situation Paul describes is not one of preaching 'a different gospel' (2 Cor. 11:4; Gal. 1:6) but of disparate motives while preaching the true gospel. For Paul, this is no matter for concern, because the gospel is the heart of the matter. His single-minded focus on its preaching and progress is evident in his seeming indifference to how it moves ahead, whether by his imprisonment or by the false or true motives of others. Fowl helpfully points out in relation to Philippians 4:11 that Paul 'has learned to narrate [his circumstances] as part of the story of God's economy of salvation'.[11] The same disposition seems evident here. In God's story, the good news of the life, death,

---

10. Bockmuehl suggests that 'theirs is a petty, territorial vision; their aim is naked self-advancement' (p. 80).

11. Fowl, p. 195.

resurrection and exaltation of Jesus has changed everything and getting the word out about Jesus the Messiah is more important than whether petty rivalries exist among some of those who are spreading this good news.

Rather than responding with concern, Paul responds with rejoicing. The improbable juxtaposition of prison and rejoicing is compelling, and joy will be an extraordinary and pervasive theme across the letter (*chara or chairō* in 1:4, 18, 25; 2:2, 17–18, 28–29; 3:1; 4:1, 4, 10). Once more, the lens of the gospel shifts Paul's mindset to such an extent that his circumstances are not the final arbiter of his disposition and emotions.

In 1:14–18, Paul has referenced a distinct group that is acting apart from the ideas and examples Paul is commending to the Philippians. Interpreters of the letter routinely explore the identities of all such 'opponents' Paul references in the letter, namely, at 1:15–17; 1:28; 3:2; and 3:18–19. Some see enough continuity among these references to suggest there is a single group of opponents in view. Most, however, identify and reconstruct two or more opposing groups (see Introduction 2f). It is important to note that, in 1:14–18, Paul's self-perceived rivals are active in Paul's location, not in or near Philippi. This distinguishes this group from those mentioned in 1:28 and chapter 3 and may help to explain why Paul responds without distress to his own 'opponents'. Paul's rhetoric about the people he describes in 3:2, 18–19 indicates that he is concerned that some believers in Philippi might succumb to their influence. In 1:14–18, he has no such anxiety; he knows that those preaching out of rivalry are not harming him or their common work for the gospel.

## C. Expectation of release from prison and continuing ministry (1:18b–26)

**18b.** Paul presses further into the theme of rejoicing by affirming his intention to continue rejoicing (using the future tense of the same verb). This reaffirmation begins with a conjunction (*alla*), often used as a strong adversative ('but'). In this case, however, it seems to function as a change of direction in Paul's discourse (BDAG, p. 45), as he moves to deliberate on his possible release from prison. So the translational *Yes* (NIV) captures this shift, especially when followed by the reason for Paul's continuing practice of rejoicing (1:19).

**19.** The reason Paul gives for his continuing experience of joy is his confidence (*I know*) that he will soon be released from prison, which he refers to as his *deliverance* (*sōtēria*). Paul often uses this word to denote ultimate rescue or 'salvation', as he does to signal the present outworking of the Philippians' salvation from God (1:28 and 2:12). Reading *sōtēria* in this sense is possible, as the NIV footnote suggests ('salvation').[12] A more likely interpretation in context, however, understands the rescue in view to be Paul's physical release from prison. This is supported by 1:25–26, where Paul anticipates being present with the Philippians again to encourage them in their faith. These verses (1:19 and 1:25–26) form a frame around this passage and highlight Paul's confidence in his forthcoming release (see comment at 1:25).

Paul draws a phrase from Job 13:16 to express this outcome: 'this will turn out for my deliverance', with 'this' referring to Paul's current circumstances. The text of Philippians shares five Greek words with the Septuagint (*touto moi apobēsetai eis sōtērian*), making it fairly certain that Paul is intentionally alluding to Job 13. In Job 13, Job replies to his 'friends' who have been assuming his guilt, and speaks of his expectation that he will be vindicated or shown to be in the right when he brings his case before God (Job 13:15). 'And this for me will result in vindication' (13:16, LXX). Job then speaks of his judgment (his verdict) being close at hand (13:18). Paul seems to draw on Job's situation, analogous to his own, to point ahead to his own deliverance from his circumstances (in his case, release from prison), and possibly to signal his coming trial and expected vindication. Job and Paul also experience the effects of 'friends' who are actually working in some way against them (Phil. 1:15, 17).[13]

---

12. The other possible reading, 'vindication' (see NIV footnote), fits well with the allusion to Job in this verse and may refer more specifically to a positive outcome for his trial (and so would have a similar sense to *deliverance*).

13. Fee, p. 131 n. 21.

Paul expresses the basis for his anticipated deliverance as *your prayers and God's provision of the Spirit of Jesus Christ*. As Paul has already actively demonstrated (1:3–11), dependence on God is the centrepiece of his theology and praxis. Here, Paul expresses reliance on the Philippians in their prayers to God for his release from prison, while also emphasizing that God is the one who will provide.[14] Paul uses a unique phrase (for him) to communicate the content of God's provision, namely, *the Spirit of Jesus Christ*, though elsewhere he refers to the 'Spirit of Christ' (Rom. 8:9) and the 'Spirit of [God's] Son' (Gal. 4:6). Luke also closely connects the Spirit with Jesus in Acts 16:7 (see also 2:32–33), as he refers to Paul and his team being guided by the 'Spirit of Jesus' (parallel with 'the Holy Spirit' in 16:6) away from Asia Minor and eventually in the direction of Macedonia (16:9–10) and Philippi (16:11–12).

**20–21.** Although Paul anticipates his release, he moves into a deliberative mode at 1:20 to consider two distinct possible outcomes of his imprisonment. It seems that he is ruminating on the outcome of his future trial, with vindication, release and life as one possibility, and conviction and subsequent execution as the other. While Paul has expressed confidence ('I know') about his release or 'deliverance' (1:19), as he moves to contemplate the dual possibilities of either death or release he uses language of expectation and hope to express a desire to be courageous in facing death, if that would prove to be the outcome. The goal of this courageous stance is not indifference to the situations of life – a perspective commended in Stoic philosophy. Instead, Paul's focus is Christ's exaltation in Paul's *body, whether by life or by death* (1:20). For Paul, Christ himself is the lens for assessing what is valuable and of ultimate worth. If Paul were to be convicted at his Roman trial, that would not in itself be reason to *be ashamed* (contra cultural messages of shame at such an outcome). What is important to Paul is that the person of Christ would be exalted – shown to be of ultimate value – whatever the outcome.

---

14. The two nouns (rendered *prayers* and *provision*) share a single article and are governed by a single preposition in the Greek, indicating the integral connection between them.

Paul initially sums up his deliberation in 1:21. In this well-known verse, he anticipates a win–win situation: *to live is Christ and to die is gain*. Paul uses two Greek infinitives, with the first in the present tense and so with the connotation of continuing existence: 'living is Christ' (NET). As Paul will make clear in 3:7–11, his life between the present and the resurrection is infused with meaning because of his relationship with Christ. Knowing the living Messiah and participating in the life of the Messiah means that Jesus is the core, the essence, of Paul's daily experience. Yet as good as present Christ-centred living is, Paul's perspective is that death is actually better for him (*for . . . me*; repeated to emphasize his point of view in 1:22). Paul's later references to final resurrection (3:11, 21) make it clear that he does not view death as an end. Instead, death will lead to bodily life that is restored and transformed (3:21; 1 Cor. 15:20–28). As Paul endures imprisonment, anticipating the possibility of release or execution, he assures the Philippians that either potential outcome will work to his benefit. So they do not need to be troubled about his fate. They can rest assured that their dear brother Paul will be in good hands either way.

**22.** Paul continues his deliberation around his own impending trial and its outcome, moving to explore the benefits for the Philippians if he were to be released (i.e. *go on living in the body*). He anticipates more opportunity for *fruitful labour (karpos ergou)*,[15] which probably refers to his ministry broadly and not just with the Philippian believers. Paul turns again to deliberation – giving a sense of his internal dialogue – and rhetorically raises the question of whether he will choose life or death. Although there is not an explicit question in the Greek clause (rendered woodenly, 'what I should choose I do not know'), the NIV nicely captures the rhetorical moment by framing it as a question: *Yet what shall I choose? I do not know!* Some read in this language of choice that Paul must have had the agency to enact both outcomes. For example, Droge

---

15. Here, *ergou* ('labour', 'work') is probably either a genitive of source ('fruit coming from my work') or an attributed genitive ('fruitful work'; see Wallace, *Greek*, pp. 89–90), with a similar meaning in either case. Paul anticipates continuing ministry and the fruit it will provide.

suggests that Paul is contemplating suicide in these verses.[16] Keown proposes that it is possible that Paul intends to escape and make his way back to Philippi.[17] More likely, Paul uses this language more for rhetorical effect than for precision, as he invites his audience into his deliberation of outcomes to encourage them about his situation and to affirm his confidence that he will see them again. Croy suggests that, in this rhetorical move, Paul draws on the commonplace trope of 'feigned complexity' (*diaporēsis*) to deliberate on a purported question (*what shall I choose?*) to dramatize his line of thought.[18] In the end, Paul leaves his destiny in God's capable hands and expresses his expectation of deliverance given what he understands to be a continued need for his ministry among the believers at Philippi (1:24–26).

**23–24.** As Paul continues his rhetorical deliberation (*I am torn between the two*), he again weighs the relative benefits of two potential outcomes: *to depart and be with Christ* (1:23) or to *remain in the body* (1:24). For the latter phrase, Paul uses the language of *sarx* ('body' or 'flesh'; also at 1:22) as a synonym for *sōma*, which is rendered 'body' in 1:20. In these two occurrences, he does not use *sarx* negatively as he will at 3:3–4. Elsewhere, Paul can use *sarx* as a near technical term to refer to the realm of the human captivity to sin (e.g. Rom. 8:3–13).[19] Paul again affirms the superiority of being *with Christ* after death (see 1:21). From Paul's vantage point, it is *better by far*. Yet the needs of the Philippians press Paul towards the option of release and a return to them: *it is more necessary*. Later, in 2:25, Paul will again speak of what is necessary for the Philippians' well-being (there, he thinks it necessary to return Epaphroditus to the Philippians to alleviate their anxieties). In

---

16. Droge, 'Suicide', pp. 262–286. Croy argues against this view in 'Suicide', pp. 517–531.

17. Keown I, pp. 253–254; also pp. 11–14.

18. Croy, 'Suicide', p. 525.

19. The NIV footnote at Rom. 8:3 defines this technical use of *sarx*: 'In contexts like this, the Greek word for *flesh* (*sarx*) refers to the sinful state of human beings, often presented as a power in opposition to the Spirit.'

both cases, the needs of the Philippians guide Paul's rumination about his own situation.

**25.** As Paul concludes his rhetorical deliberations, he confirms the necessity of his presence and ministry with the Philippians as decisive (*I know that I will remain*). Although some argue that Paul's language here indicates certainty,[20] it is more natural to read *peithō* and *oida* (*convinced, know*) as culminating Paul's introspective dialogue on life and death, which he frames as choices between two options. And he concludes where he began – with the confidence that God will work in his situation for his release (with *oida, I know*, repeated at 1:19, 25). At 2:24, Paul will assure the Philippians that he is confident (*peithō*) that he will be released and so be able to return to them to strengthen their faith. Paul speaks here of his presence with them again as benefiting their *progress and joy in the faith*. The genitive *pisteōs* (*faith* or 'faithfulness') is probably used to modify both nouns (*progress* and *joy*), especially as these nouns are tied together by a single article. Paul hopes to encourage the Philippians to grow in their faith/fulness and to see them rejoicing in it (cf. 2:18; 4:4).[21] At 1:12, Paul has expressed his deep commitment to the progress or advancement (*prokopē*) of the gospel. Now Paul demonstrates his commitment to and care for the progress (*prokopē*) of the Philippians' continuing trust in and commitment to Christ. Paul seems to use *pistis* (*faith*) in Philippians (1:25, 27; 2:17; 3:9) for the believer's response to the gospel, broadly conceived. It involves assent and trust as well as a continuing commitment to Jesus as Lord (i.e. allegiance to Jesus). Gupta affirms this 'large-as-life interpretation of [*pistis* that] goes beyond creed or conceptualization and includes will and action'.[22]

**26.** Paul concludes this section of his letter by articulating the result (*so that*) of his contribution to their spiritual growth and joy. The result is that their boasting or celebration in Christ Jesus will

---

20. Keown I, p. 263; cf. p. 134.

21. The genitive appears to function either as an objective genitive – the progress and joy they have in their faith – or a genitive of source – the progress and joy that come from their faith in Christ.

22. Gupta, *Faith*, p. 88.

only grow when they are reunited with Paul (*through my being with you again*). The language of *kauchēma* and its cognates (e.g. the verb *kauchaomai*) is used often and positively in Paul (over fifty times) to signal boasting in Christ (e.g. Phil. 3:3) or in believers based on Christ's work in them (cf. 2:16). Given the fairly narrow semantic range and often negative associations of the English word 'boast/ ing', it is helpful to hear the possible connotations of exaltation and celebration in the Greek *kauchēma* (see comment on 2:16).[23]

The short phrase *en emoi* has produced long discussions. It is ambiguous, indicating most likely either that Paul will join in their boasting (NRSV) or that they will boast because of Paul (NIV: *on account of me*). Paul is using here two adjacent prepositional phrases both introduced with the preposition *en*: *en Christō Iēsou* (Christ Jesus) and *en emoi* (*me*). Paul's regular use of *en Christō* to signal believers' participation in the life of the Messiah (see comment at 1:5) suggests that he is using the two instances of *en* in different ways. Paul might be indicating that they will revel in Christ Jesus because of Paul (causal, as NIV). Yet this reading seems less likely given that Paul already includes in this verse the idea of his return to the Philippians (*my being with you again*). This would render the *en emoi* redundant.[24] Alternatively, Paul might be including himself with the Philippians as those doing the boasting (an accompanying sense), which the NRSV renders 'that I may share abundantly in your boasting in Christ Jesus'. Whichever reading is intended, it is clear that Paul portrays their future reunion, which he is confident will take place, as a time of ever-expanding joy and celebration centred on Christ Jesus who is the object of their boasting (also 3:3; cf. 2:16 and see comment there).

---

23. Bockmuehl uses 'jubilation' as one translation equivalent and indicates that *kauchēma* here 'means to regard as a source of strength and encouragement' (p. 95).

24. This is not a definitive argument, since Paul repeatedly mentions or implies the benefit they will experience from his release (1:19, 22, 24, 25, 26); i.e. he has already been redundant on this point for emphasis.

## Theology

The gospel is the theological centrepiece of this part of Philippians. Paul refers to the gospel's advancement, defence and preaching (using *euangelion* and *logos*) in 1:12, 14, 16. Additionally, for Paul, preaching the gospel and preaching Christ are one and the same (see 1:15, 17, 18). This begs the question of Paul's precise understanding of the gospel or good news. Given the interchangeability of 'gospel' and 'Christ', we might briefly define the gospel as the good news about Christ. And while Paul often focuses on Christ's death, resurrection and exaltation as the heart of that good news (e.g. Phil. 2:9–11; cf. 1 Cor. 15:3–4), he can expand that vision for particular purposes to be more inclusive of the life and teachings of Jesus (e.g. Phil. 2:6–8; cf. Rom. 1:3; 1 Cor. 7:10). Paul also emphasizes the Holy Spirit as a sign of the arrival of God's restoration (Phil. 2:1; cf. 2 Cor. 5:5). Bringing these strands together, we might define the gospel according to Paul as 'the story of God's promised redemptive work now enacted in the Messiah through the presence and agency of the Holy Spirit'.[25] Paul, in his focus on the gospel at any particular juncture, can highlight relevant parts of that story – its grounding in Old Testament promises, Jesus' life, his death, his resurrection, his current reign, or the Spirit's presence with believers.

Paul's perspective on the circumstances and fluctuations of life is profoundly shaped by the gospel. In Philippians 1:12–18a, Paul focuses on how present imprisonment has propelled the gospel forwards, both by his own witness while in chains as well as by increased attention to preaching the gospel by believers in the vicinity of his imprisonment. While he could view this situation through the lens of his own suffering in prison or the antagonism he is facing from some of these fellow believers, Paul chooses to don the lens of the gospel. By doing so, the crucial question for him is how the gospel is faring. And he believes the Philippians will take comfort from hearing this gospel-shaped perspective on his circumstances.

Paul continues to reflect theologically on his own situation and impending future in his deliberations on the possible outcomes of

---

25. Brown and Fox, 'Hermeneutics', forthcoming.

his trial – if he is freed to continue in ministry or if he is executed
(1:18b–26). He brings a gospel lens to this assessment as well, particularly drawing on the way his situation places Christ further in
the spotlight. Paul's use of the phrase 'to/for me' (*emoi* and *moi* in
1:21, 22, respectively) accents his own gospel-infused point of view
on life and death. From the perspective of the gospel – the good
news of redemption in Christ – neither death nor present existence
encapsulates ultimate reality. God's redemption of Paul has ensured
that death will not be the end; instead, death will gain for Paul the
full presence of Christ (1:23). Although Paul most often refers to
the final state of believers with his frequent references to bodily
resurrection, he does on a few occasions refer to what theologians
call the intermediate state (the experience of a believer after death
but before resurrection; see 2 Cor. 5:1–8). Paul's words here in Philippians are less specific than in 2 Corinthians. He expresses what
he expects will be his experience after death, either immediately
after death in conscious experience of God's presence or when the
final-day resurrection occurs. God's redemption of Paul has also
ensured that the rest of his life will be spent in continuing gospel
ministry – the opportunity to proclaim the good news of redemption through Christ to more people and the chance to see the
Philippians again for their continued progress and joy (1:25).

This last sentiment shows that Paul's commitment to the gospel
is an abiding commitment to the people God has entrusted to him.
The framing of this passage with the language of *prokopē* ('advance',
'progress') highlights Paul's commitment to the development of
both the gospel and the Philippian believers (1:12, 25). For all Paul's
emphasis on the gospel, it must be remembered that the gospel is
a story of our relational God enacting salvation for people through
Christ, the representative human one. Paul's gospel focus is not
devotion to an abstract principle or truth; it is inherently people-
focused, because the gospel is the story of humanity's redemption.
Paul devotes himself to people and to Christ, whose work has made
all the difference. It is not surprising then that this very personal
section of the letter spotlights Paul's deep desire to see Christ
celebrated. He desires that he will possess the courage in whatever
circumstance to exalt Christ (1:20); and he looks forward to a time
when his fellow believers in Philippi will join him in an even

greater celebration of Christ Jesus (when their 'boasting in Christ Jesus will abound', 1:26). Within the New Testament, the language of boasting is particularly Pauline, with a helpful explanation of this notion in relation to Christ provided in 1 Corinthians 1:26–31. For Paul, boasting in human wisdom and status is illegitimate (1 Cor. 1:26–28) and is contrary to the proper focus for boasting, which is 'Christ Jesus, who has become for us' all things: 'wisdom ... righteousness, holiness and redemption' (1:30). Boasting in Christ 'is the paradigmatic activity of the believer'.[26]

---

26. Fowl, p. 54.

## 3. EXHORTATIONS: TO SINGULAR LOYALTY AND STEADFAST UNITY IN SUFFERING (1:27 – 2:4)

*Context*

Paul turns to exhort the Philippian church at 1:27. He has begun the body of the letter by assuring his siblings in the faith that his situation in prison is not a cause for alarm. He himself is encouraged by how his imprisonment has advanced the gospel, and he comforts these friends with his confidence that he will be able to return to them soon to assist in their own progress in Christ (1:12–26). Now he calls them as a believing community to live for the gospel in their own particular situation of experiencing opposition. Paul considers their situations comparable ('the same struggle', 1:30) – his situation in prison and dealing with detractors (1:15–18) and their experience of opposition (1:28). As such, he draws their attention to their unifying reality of suffering on Christ's behalf (1:29). And as Paul moves to exhorting the Philippians to a mindset committed to the good of the other (2:3–4), he has already demonstrated this same disposition in his deep commitment to their 'progress and joy in the faith' (1:24–25).

Paul's refrain continues to be the progress of the gospel (1:7, 12, 18) and the progress of the Philippians' communal faith and life (1:9–11, 25). It is no surprise then that his first exhortation presses for an alignment with the gospel in their communal and unified life together (1:27). As Paul introduces the situation of opposition on the Philippians' side of the equation (1:28), he foreshadows similar references to negative influences that he will warn the Philippians about in chapter 3 (3:2, 18–19), as well as the privilege of suffering on Christ's behalf (1:29; 3:10). His call to unity for the whole church (1:27; 2:2) prepares for his specific advice to Euodia and Syntyche (4:2–3) to have the same Christ-directed 'mindset' (*phroneō*; 2:2; 4:2). He may, in fact, expect his audience already to identify the issue between these two 'co-workers' (4:3) as an implicit backdrop to his initial call to a unified and other-oriented mindset. At 4:1, Paul will also repeat his exhortation for the Philippians to 'stand firm' (*stēkō*, 1:27), further connecting this initial section of exhortation with specific encouragements provided near the conclusion of the letter.

*Paul's rhetorical emphases in Philippians 1:27 – 2:4:* In this passage, Paul begins to engage consistently in logos – his argumentation. His exhortations and accompanying rationales are woven into the letter throughout the next full chapter as he alternates between exhortations and exemplars. In 1:27 – 2:4, Paul introduces central admonitions for the Philippian church, which can be summed up as singular loyalty and a steadfast, other-focused unity in the face of the opposition and even suffering they are facing. Paul draws on the realities they have experienced – salvation from God (1:28), encouragement in Christ and participation in the Spirit (2:1) – to ground his exhortations to them. As he does so, he employs pathos by evoking these experiences (and, presumably, the accompanying emotions of well-being and relationship with the triune God) to motivate their behaviour. He touches on ethos in his identification with them in suffering (1:30) and his assumption that they will want to contribute to his joy (2:2).

*Comment*
## A. Singular loyalty to Christ and the gospel (1:27a)

**27A.** The adverb *monon* ('only') at the beginning of 1:27 makes the transition from Paul's confident anticipation of a reunion with the Philippian believers to their present situation of living out their faith without Paul present with them (1:27b). The translation of *monon* as *whatever happens* nicely signals that whether or not Paul is released and able to travel to Philippi, the church should be living in line with what he has taught them and how he would guide them if he were present.

Paul's first exhortation in the letter holds primacy of place in his appeals to the Philippian congregation. It is no accident, then, that it speaks to Paul's central commitment to the gospel and to the Philippians' particular need to consider their allegiances in the light of the gospel. The verb Paul chooses for this first exhortation – *politeuomai* – occurs only here in the Pauline corpus (cf. Acts 23:1, 'to fulfil one's duty'). It often has the connotation of living loyally as a citizen (BDAG, p. 846).[1] While most English translations render the verb in line with the NIV (*conduct yourselves*; i.e. without referring to citizenship), a few bring in this connotation (e.g. CSB, NLT, TNIV). Two issues are at play, one semantic and one practical. First, and most importantly, does Paul use this word specifically to highlight a connotation of citizenship? Second, given the adverbial phrase *in a manner worthy of the gospel of Christ*, it can be cumbersome to capture in translation the additional connotation (e.g. 'live as a citizen'), since English has no verb corresponding to the noun 'citizen'.

On the substantive issue, it seems likely that Paul chose this word carefully for its connotation of citizen-appropriate conduct. First, this is Paul's first exhortation in the letter and it would be

---

1. Brewer reviews usage from the Maccabean writings (e.g. 2 Macc. 6:1; 11:25; 3 Macc. 3:4; 4 Macc. 2:8; 4:23; 5:16) and from Philo (*On the Confusion of Tongues* 17) to support his view that Paul uses the term with this connotation ('Philippians 1:27', pp. 76–83).

odd if such a specific choice had no significance.[2] Second, Paul
will use the cognate noun in 3:20 (*politeuma*) to remind his
audience that their 'citizenship is in heaven'. This too is a *hapax*
in Paul, occurring only in Philippians and only at 3:20. The two
occurrences, coupled with Philippi's status as a Roman colony
(whether or not the church itself has a large contingent of Roman
citizens), suggest that Paul means to convey something about
living out citizenship.

If this connotation is relevant to Paul's use of *politeuomai*, then
we can move to the question of how to translate the whole
clause. Not having a verb that can signal a way of living as a
citizen produces a fairly wordy rendering; for example, 'Whatever
happens, as citizens of heaven live in a manner worthy of the
gospel of Christ' (TNIV). Problematic in this translation is the use
of 'of heaven' (from 3:20). It would be better to follow Paul's
logic and place the citizenship focus on the gospel itself rather
than importing language from 3:20 into this earlier context. To
do so, it is valuable to notice that the adverb *axiōs* (*worthy*) directly
modifies *politeuomai*. As Smit notes, a person in the ancient world
could be described as 'worthy of a city'.[3] One way of capturing
this connection in English is to use loyalty terminology: 'live in
singular loyalty to the gospel of Christ'.[4] This rendering makes
it quite clear that Paul speaks of living *in a manner worthy of the
gospel* as a guiding (civic) norm. 'Taking the gospel as the measure
for worthy citizenship is striking, given that it is an inner-
Christian criterion that was otherwise acknowledged by no one,
and could be controversial politically.'[5] As cities expected their
citizens to live in undivided loyalty to their laws, norms and
ideals, Paul expects believers in Jesus to live in undivided loyalty

---

2. Brewer provides lexical evidence that Paul does not use this specific
   verb as a synonym for his more usual terms for living as a Christian
   ('Philippians 1:27', p. 77). See also Edwards, 'Citizenship', pp. 76–77.

3. Smit, *Paradigms*, p. 81.

4. Brown, 'Philippians', forthcoming. The notion of living 'worthily' is
   expressed in my translation in the idea of loyalty.

5. Smit, *Paradigms*, p. 81.

to the norms and values implicit in the gospel and to Jesus as Lord.[6]

This exhortation to singular allegiance headlines the major part of the letter that weaves together exhortations and examples (1:27 – 4:9), and informs an understanding of the rest of 1:27–30, which forms a single sentence in the Greek. As such, it signals that citizenship forms the 'central notion of the passage'.[7]

## B. Unified stance towards opposition (1:27b–30)

**27b.** Paul moves on to specify what ensues from alignment of allegiance to the gospel (using a *hina* result clause: *Then*). The outcome will be the Philippians' communal resilience: they will be able to *stand firm . . . striving together as one*. Paul employs language often used in athletic competition: *synathleō*, indicating 'to strive together' (also 4:3), and *agōn* (1:30) for 'struggle' or 'contest' (cf. 1 Cor. 9:24–27).[8] Paul refers to the goal of their unified resolve as *the faith of the gospel*. As at 1:25 (see comment there), Paul seems to be using *pistis* broadly to refer to the Christian's response to God's work in the gospel. As such, gospel 'faith/fulness' can signal acknowledgment of and trust in Christ's work (itself expressed in the gospel) and the Philippians' faithfulness and commitment to the gospel.[9]

In Greek, the two verbs in 1:27b, translated as *stand firm* and *striving together*, bracket two phrases: *in the one Spirit* (*en heni pneumati*) and *as one* (*mia psychē*), with both focused on the unity Paul commends for the Philippian believers. The latter refers to *how* the

---

6. I disagree with those who see in the use of the word itself a call to be 'a good citizen of an earthly state' (e.g. Rome), with the reference to 'the gospel of Christ' providing an additional and parallel requirement to live as citizens of 'the Christian commonwealth' (Hawthorne, p. 69; also Brewer, 'Philippians 1:27').

7. Keown I, p. 279.

8. Hellerman, pp. 79–80. Others hear *synathleō* and *stēkō* (*stand firm*) as military terms.

9. Smith suggests the reading 'striving . . . because of allegiance to the gospel' (*Good Life*, p. 49).

Philippians are called to strive together: working together as a single person (*psychē*) to reach their goal. The first expression, with its reference to *pneuma*, *Spirit* (or 'spirit'), seems to be addressing the spiritual reality of their unity through their sharing of the (one) Holy Spirit (see 2:1; cf. 1 Cor. 12:13), although the NIV footnote provides a viable alternative, 'in one spirit' (cf. 4:23). If the latter rendering is right, Paul is laying emphasis on the importance of their unity by repeating the sentiment using differing expressions.[10]

Paul indicates that, if the Philippians live out their loyalty to the gospel with a unified stance, it will be of no consequence whether he is with them in person or remains apart (*whether I come and see you or only hear about you in my absence*). This motif of Paul's possible return is thematic in the letter (1:26, 27; 2:12, 24). He has just expressed his confidence that he will be restored to them (1:26), yet now he affirms that they can live out their gospel allegiance by relying on one another, even if he is unable to return to strengthen them in person.

**28.** Paul explicitly refers to opponents in the Philippians' setting for the first time. Later, he will highlight antagonists or counter-examples (in 3:2 and 3:18–19), whose specific identities are debated. In 1:27–30, the opponents are quite clearly some people in Philippi outside the church, as Paul refers to contrasting futures: salvation for the Philippian believers and destruction for these particular opponents. Paul encourages the Philippians that they do not need to be *frightened in any way*, and uses unusual and strong language (*ptyromai*): there is no cause for being 'intimidated' (L&N, p. 317) or 'terrified' (BDAG, p. 895). Paul's logic suggests that a unified stance by the church in relation to these opponents will alleviate the deep fears that would naturally arise from such opposition. Paul reassures them that God is on their side and will save them, vindicating their trust in Christ and their commitment to the gospel.

Other than that these opponents are not believers in Christ, their particular identity and activity are left unspecified. Certainly, Paul's Philippian audience would have had no need for him to fill

---

10.  As argued by Silva, p. 89.

in details as they would have been keenly aware of the opposition
they were experiencing for their loyalty to Jesus as Lord. A likely
scenario is that these opponents are residents of Philippi
(neighbours, patrons and even family members) who are responding
negatively to Christian behaviour that would have been at odds
with certain Roman civic and religious values, with these routinely
being intermingled. First, participation in the imperial cult would
have been expected, if not required, of Philippi's residents
(including non-citizens). Additionally, participation in religious
practices and festivities at pagan temples would have been similarly
expected as part of living as faithful members of the *polis*.

Yet these expected activities would have compromised allegiance to the gospel, since their confession was 'Jesus is Lord', an
honour not to be given to Caesar or any other gods (cf. 1 Pet. 3:15).
This singular allegiance (which Paul affirms at 1:27) would
potentially mean the straining or even severing of important relationships with non-believers, including economic, civic and family
relations.[11] The church in Philippi would have been considered odd
at best or, at worst, unfaithful to their civic duties by withdrawing
from such central practices as worship of the gods and engagement
with the imperial cult. Tapping into the close identification of the
early church with its Jewish roots, Oakes suggests that Christians
in Philippi would have been understood to be 'members of a
strange, subversive, Jewish organization'.[12]

The resulting experiences for these believers might include
financial hardship, 'shunning, public embarrassment, non-
recognition of personal honor and status, [and] discrimination in
the patronage system because of their beliefs'.[13] It is also possible
that some amount of official pressure or persecution was part of

---

11. See Oakes (*Philippians*, pp. 89–102) for a detailed description of
    potential scenarios for the various social strata represented in the
    Philippian church. He proposes that economic factors would have
    been the most problematic given Paul's linking of suffering and unity
    in 1:27–30 (p. 99).
12. Oakes, *Philippians*, p. 90.
13. Osiek, p. 50.

the mix for transgressions against the *polis* (cf. Paul's experience narrated in Acts 16:16–24). As Oakes sketches out with clarity, any particular member of the Philippian church may have experienced some of these and not others.[14] In the face of such diffuse opposition, unity among the Philippian believers would not necessarily be easy to attain. Joining together in a united stance, however, would provide the support – tangible and intangible – that any particular individual or family group would need to face pressure or persecution for their faithfulness to Christ.[15]

**29.** Paul not only calls for a unity among the Philippians that can withstand opposition, he also reframes their suffering Christologically – from the perspective of Christ's own suffering. This verse probably connects most directly to the admonition against 'being frightened' by opposition (1:28a), given that 1:28b ('This is a sign . . .') is a parenthetical relative clause. The Philippians need not capitulate to fear, since their experience of opposition and of suffering is not accidental or incidental. They have been *granted* (*charizomai*, referring to a gracious gifting; cf. Rom. 8:32; Phil. 2:9) the opportunity to suffer (*paschō*) for Christ. Paul, in an autobiographical moment (3:10), will share his longing to know Christ, which involves participating in Christ's sufferings (*pathēmata*; cognate noun). Paul intentionally frames identification with Christ's suffering as a gift rather than a calamity, since it presses believers into deeper participation with the Messiah. Paul balances this divine gifting to suffer with the gift of faith in Christ (*to believe in him*), though his primary focus is the role of suffering for the Christian (the two Greek *to hyper* phrases – 'for' or 'on behalf of' – indicate this emphasis).

**30.** Paul concludes this extended thought (the sentence begun in 1:27) by joining his own *struggle* with the suffering of the Philippians

---

14. Oakes, *Philippians*, pp. 89–96.

15. The indefinite relative pronoun *hētis* (*This is a sign*) refers back either to the whole of what is to be the Philippians' united stance, not in fear but in faithfulness to the gospel (i.e. 1:27–28a), or to their *pistis* (*faith* or 'faithfulness'). For the details related to how the gender of the pronoun affects interpretation, see Hawthorne, pp. 72–74.

for their allegiance to the gospel. Their suffering 'for Christ' connects them to Paul, since they are experiencing *the same struggle* Paul has experienced both past and present. The mention of his past struggles (*you saw I had*) probably refers to mistreatment Paul experienced in Philippi when he founded the church there (e.g. as narrated in Acts 16). They have also heard of his present experience in prison (*you . . . now hear that I still have*; cf. 2:25) and have just heard his positive, theological framing of that experience in 1:12–26. As Fowl suggests, the connection fostered in 1:30 indicates that Paul 'wants them to "read" their situation as he "reads" his own'.[16] The suffering they are currently experiencing is not an unfortunate accident. It fits coherently, if somewhat mysteriously (since suffering itself is not a 'good'), within their God-given salvation and their very real identification with Christ as well as with Paul (see Introduction 4b).

## C. Mindset of unity and humility towards one another (2:1–4)

**1.** While 1:27–30 focuses primarily on the Philippians' stance towards outside pressures, 2:1–4 addresses internal relationships: the posture of these believers towards one another. Thematic is the call to unity (anticipated in 1:27b), based on what the Philippians share through Christ, which is where Paul begins (2:1). He frames four parallel conditional clauses to invite his audience into his line of reasoning, which moves naturally from the benefits of their salvation to the need for unity (2:2). Each clause begins with *ei tis* or *ei ti* ('if there is any') followed by a divinely provided benefit.[17]

The first benefit is the *encouragement* tied to being *en Christō* ('in the Messiah'), the Pauline phrase that connotes the relational union between Christ and believers, as well as among believers (see 1:5). The NIV captures this sense with the phrase *being united with Christ*.

---

16. Fowl, p. 70.

17. Because these clauses are quite compressed, divine action is only implied in the second and fourth clauses. See Hawthorne for the range of possible meanings for each clause (pp. 82–85).

Paul begins the fourfold inventory with its Christological centrepiece and continues by highlighting Christ's love as integral to participation in him (*if any comfort from his love*).[18] Paul continues emphasizing the theme of relational participation by identifying their *koinōnia* or *sharing in the Spirit* (cf. 1:27; see comment on 1:5). The final clause mentions more generally the Philippians' experience of *tenderness and compassion*. As Silva notes, 'The clauses are deliberately compressed and vague, since the appeal is primarily emotional ... an impassioned pleading.'[19] While Paul refers to facets of their faith that are current realities, he frames them as conditional (*if*) to lead his audience actively to affirm the truth of these realities and so feel the weight of responding to his exhortations that follow.

**2.** Based on the reality of the graces they share in Christ and through the Holy Spirit, Paul calls the Philippians to unity – a key aspect of the participation they already enjoy and expressed by *en Christō* and *koinōnia*. As Paul often does, he enjoins a disposition that is already a reality for his audience because of their identity in Christ (e.g. Rom. 6:2, 11; Gal. 5:24−25). The language Paul uses in his exhortation highlights the key motif of joy in Philippians: *make my joy complete by being* united (also at 1:4, 25; 2:29; 4:1). His call to unity draws on language already used in the letter, some of it thematic. The fourfold description of unity, in fact, is framed by the term *phroneō*, referring to a mindset that includes dispositions and attitudes as well as a right way of thinking (see comment on 1:7):[20]

> *then make my joy complete by being like-minded* [*to auto phronēte*],
> *having the same love,*
> *being one in spirit*
> *and of one mind* [*to hen phronountes*].

---

18. Although there is no pronoun modifying 'love', it probably follows from the reference to Christ in the previous clause. For the view that Paul refers here to God's love (e.g. Rom. 5:5), and so has a trinitarian emphasis in this verse, see Fee, pp. 180−181.

19. Silva, pp. 87−88.

20. Fee, pp. 89−90.

Using *phroneō* here and across the letter, Paul calls the Philippians to a common mindset: a shared way of looking at and living in the world, through the lens of the gospel (2:5; 3:15; 4:2; cf. 3:19). The other two constructions – *having the same love, being one in spirit* – affirm the importance of working towards this shared stance and common frame of reference. Paul has already prayed that their love would increase (1:9). Now he calls them to unity via a shared love (2:2) grounded in their common experience of Christ's love (2:1). What authentic love will look like in community is fleshed out in 2:3–4. Paul's exhortation to unity *in spirit* (*sympsychoi*) recalls the language of 1:27, where he enjoins them to strive together 'as one' (*mia psychē*). They are to live and act as if they were a single person (*psychē*), integrated and unified in their purpose and direction.

**3–4.** Paul moves from a broad vision of unity for the Philippian church (2:1–2) to specific ways of enacting that vision (2:3–4). He first provides a crucial contrast to building unity by referring to dispositions that foster disunity: *selfish ambition* and *vain conceit*. Paul begins the Greek sentence with the negation *mēden* (*nothing*), to emphasize that these two attributes should in no way describe the Philippian believers. Given that there is no expressed verb in the first clause, the reader can best discern what verbal idea is implied by looking to the context. The related verbs in context have to do with attitudes: *phroneō* ('having a mindset', 2:2); *hēgeomai* (value, 2:3) and *skopeō* ('paying attention to' or *looking to*, 2:4). This suggests that we hear a similar kind of verb implied in 2:3a, such as, 'Consider nothing from (the lens of) selfish ambition or vain conceit.'

The first attitude to avoid, *eritheia* (*selfish ambition*), is one that Paul has already used to describe fellow believers in his own setting (probably Rome) who are competing with Paul in the preaching of the gospel now that he is in prison (1:17). Paul's issue with these self-understood 'competitors' is not their act of preaching, which he celebrates, but their ambition to promote themselves as they do so. Paul refers to *eritheia* elsewhere in vice lists delineating communal behaviours that are antithetical to belonging to Christ (2 Cor. 12:20; Gal. 5:20). Paul's use of *vain conceit* (*kenodoxia*) signals an exaggerated sense of self or excessive ambition (BDAG, p. 538; cf. Gal. 5:26), which plays into the status-conscious Roman environment in

Philippi. Such an attitude of one-upmanship would directly inhibit the unity and communal mindset Paul is commending.

Instead of being shaped by self-promotion and conceit, the Philippians are to foster the opposite disposition. Humility, instead of arrogance, should shape their entire outlook – both thought and action. Paul uses (or may even coin) the term *tapeinophrosynē* to indicate renunciation of status and of self-promotion in pursuit of the good of the community, a stance that would not have been viewed favourably within Graeco-Roman society. Humility was decidedly not a virtue in this milieu.[21] In the rest of 2:3–4, Paul fleshes out his understanding of humility, which involves a preferential valuing of and concerted focus on others.[22] Such humility is deeply communal. As Becker notes, *tapeinophrosynē* 'makes it possible to place the fellowship that follows from the mutual high estimation of the community members over the interests of the individual'.[23]

To value or consider (*hēgeomai*) is language Paul uses, much like *phroneō*, to signal a frame of reference informed by the gospel and focused on care for the other and, certainly in this context, for the needs of the whole community. Paul will affirm that Christ displayed such an other-focused perspective (2:6), and Paul himself will 'consider everything' through a gospel lens at 3:7–8 (cf. *hēgeomai*, 'think', at 2:25). Paul concludes his exhortations by calling the Philippians to be attentive *to the interests of the others (ta heterōn)* and not (only) to their own interests (*ta heatōn*; 2:4).[24] Paul highlights the interests of the self in relation to the whole community by using the singular *each* (*hekastos*) followed by its plural form to emphasize *the others* who are to take precedence over the individual interests of 'each one'.

A relevant text-critical question is the potential inclusion of *kai* ('also') in the final clause of 2:4. The argument for its originality

---

21. Becker, *Humility*, p. 148.
22. Bockmuehl, p. 110.
23. Becker, *Humility*, p. 53.
24. Each phrase begins with a neuter, plural article (*ta*), which indicates the 'things' or 'matters' in view, and so here the *interests* or 'concerns' of the audience.

has strong manuscript support,[25] while its transcriptional evidence is mixed. The *kai* might have been a scribal addition intended to soften the strongly worded either/or of 2:4: 'not looking [only] to your own interests, but also to others' interests'. More likely, given ascetic tendencies in the second- to third-century church, *kai* was omitted (and in alignment with the Pauline sentiment at 1 Cor. 10:24). If this is correct, then Paul expressly allows for attentiveness to one's own matters or interests, but with the clear sense that the needs of others – of the community – are to be prioritized.[26]

To conclude commentary on this passage, we can consider if Paul's heavy paraenetic emphasis on unity in 1:27 – 2:4 reflects a problem of present disunity in the Philippian church. Given his later exhortations to Euodia and Syntyche (4:2–3) towards a similar shared gospel-oriented mindset (*to auto phronēte*; as at 2:2), it is very likely that this disagreement is in view, if not others as well. But Paul, rather than shining a spotlight on any particular instance of disunity, begins with a general and far-reaching call to unity – for the community to live as a single person, with a shared mindset and spirit. Only after he has provided this clarion call to unity, along with a portrait gallery of exemplars for his audience (2:5–11, 19–30), does he move to address more pointedly an exhortation to a unified mindset for his dear fellow workers.

This conclusion about the situation of the Philippian church is based on a number of textual indicators: the specific address of disunity at 4:2–3; the prominence of the call to unity in the letter (1:27b); its repetition and expansion (2:1–4); other related textual clues, such as the prohibitions against grumbling and arguing (2:14); and Timothy's example of looking out for the interests of others (2:21; cf. 2:4). While it can be too easy to infer something meaningful

---

25. The omission is present only in the Western textual tradition. The SBLGNT includes *kai* in its text.

26. This may also be the meaning of the verse without the *kai*. 'Perhaps there is in the end little difference either in grammar or in practice: Paul's point certainly is not self-neglect or self-loathing but a genuinely unselfish investment of ourselves for the good of other people' (Bockmuehl, p. 113).

about a letter's audience from each exhortation or prohibition (i.e. 'mirror-reading'), in this case there is adequate textual evidence to infer an issue of disunity in the Philippian church that Paul addresses (see examples of more tenuous mirror-readings at 2:14 and 3:15).

*Theology*
As Paul turns to exhortations in this letter, his goal is to shape the Philippian church in profoundly countercultural ways. The Roman colony of Philippi was saturated with images and messages of the primacy of Roman power, of the emperor and his family, of the gods who had blessed Roman endeavours, and of the values that were integral to Roman prosperity. Into this context, Paul enjoins his brothers and sisters to a singular loyalty to Christ and to the gospel. As I have suggested, Paul uses the language of *politeuomai* (1:27; and *politeuma* at 3:20) intentionally to 'underline the political significance of the gospel' and to advocate for wholehearted allegiance to Christ.[27] Contrary to some interpretations, Paul is not recommending a mindset of dual allegiance that gives equal loyalty to God and to country. The Lordship of Jesus and the centrality of the gospel preclude any such compromise of the church's ultimate commitments.

What this might look like in any particular cultural context is not yet clear from the exhortation itself. In Philippi, this exhortation would have ruled out some religiously focused cultural practices and allowed for other angles of cultural engagement (see comments on 4:8–9). In specific contemporary contexts, singular allegiance to Christ will press for particular countercultural stances and practices and will rule out some activities altogether, while allowing for areas where faith and culture engage each other and lead in fruitful directions.[28] As Fowl suggests,

> While Christians will need to discuss and discern together the concrete shape of a common life worthy of the gospel in light of the particular

---

27. Smith, *Good Life*, p. 48.
28. Smith understands Paul in 1:27a to be intimating a 'larger *telos*, the well-being of the *polis*' or state (*Good Life*, 50).

secular orders they find themselves under, they must avoid thinking of themselves as holding dual citizenship. They have one Lord and serve only one master.[29]

This perspective may be an uncomfortable one to hold if we find ourselves in a sociopolitical context that has fostered a close connection between faith and political adherence. The church ought to take stock of how it understands its identity and mission in the world, seeking to be true to the New Testament vision of the church as a people made up of those from every 'tribe and language and people and nation' (Rev. 5:9) and not tethered to any particular political or national entity.

As we seek to live out allegiance to Christ alone in our own political and cultural settings, Paul helps us along in his continued exhortations (2:1–4). His vision for the Philippian church is a compelling vision for the church today as well. Central to this vision is the community of believers unified around a common mindset that has, as its hallmark, the surprising virtue of humility.[30] It was certainly surprising to Paul's Philippian audience, as Becker notes.

> When Paul, probably from a Roman imprisonment, writes to the Philippians – as the community that has been shaped to the greatest extent by Roman culture – to campaign for [*tapeinophrosynē* or humility], he . . . effects at least a cognitive dissonance among his addressees. Paul propagates a biblical ethos, which turns Greco-Roman orientation metaphors on their head.[31]

---

29. Fowl, p. 62. Fowl goes on to suggest, 'The world (particularly nation states), being the sort of place it is, is threatened by the presence of those who find their security in God and give their allegiance to God alone' (p. 69).

30. Becker connects Paul's call to humility more closely to Graeco-Roman political philosophy than to moral philosophy, highlighting the political dynamics of this ethic (*Humility*, pp. 62–65) – an observation that helps contemporary readers hear the inherent connection between 1:27a and 2:1–4.

31. Becker, *Humility*, p. 62.

I expect true humility continues to be a surprising virtue today. In spite of the opportunity over two millennia to acclimatize to the centrality of humility for a Christian ethic, the church has often found itself enamoured with and enmeshed in power, status and prestige. And, even as concepts such as servant leadership are widely circulated in the contemporary church, the realities in church leadership of abuses of power and exploitation of privilege and status remain far too common.

Part of the problem may be that we have relegated humility to an internal attitude about ourselves in relation to God (e.g. 1 Pet. 5:6), with little or no external manifestation towards others expected. Yet in Philippians 2:1-4, humility is defined by distinctive conduct towards others in the community of faith, and specifically by an attitude and by actions that put the needs and concerns of others over our own. The humility that Paul references also has significant status connotations, with the implication that self-promotion and status preoccupation have no place in the church. And this vision of a community where members divest themselves of status and do so in service to the other will always be compelling and countercultural.

# 4. JESUS AS EXEMPLAR: THE ULTIMATE SERVANT (2:5–11)

*Context*

To ground his exhortations to communal unity and humility focused on the needs of others (1:27 – 2:4), Paul now provides the ultimate exemplar. Christ himself, in his 'emptying' and exaltation, is the central example for all of his followers. Paul's pattern in the letter of moving from exhortations to examples and back again can be seen at this turn: exhortations (1:27 – 2:4); Jesus as exemplar (2:5–11); exhortations (2:12–18); Timothy and Epaphroditus as exemplars (2:19–30).

A key theme that Paul highlights in this passage is the proper 'mindset' his audience is to pursue: Jesus becomes the example par excellence (2:5). Paul reiterates the language of *phroneō* for the mindset of Christ that the Philippians are to emulate (2:5), the term used at 2:2 to call them to a shared 'mindset' (2:2). Thematic connections with other parts of the letter include the metaphor of being a slave (used of Christ at 2:7 and Paul and Timothy at 1:1) and the corresponding affirmation of Jesus' Lordship, set out as a confession at 2:11 (see 3:8) and affirmed by title across the letter (e.g. 1:2; 2:19; 3:20; 4:23).

Given the prominent rhythmic and even poetic characteristics of 2:6–11, traditionally called the 'Christ hymn', the form and source of this passage have been a matter of much scholarly debate. The genre proposals run the gamut, from elevated prose to prominent poetic characteristics to full-blown poetry, with corresponding metre and stanzas. For some, the lack of consensus on versification argues against identifying it as a fully developed poem. Yet the inability of contemporary, non-native Greek speakers, working on a text that was not initially laid out in poetic (or any kind of) lines, to reconstruct its poetic particulars would be unremarkable. And such exacting reconstruction is not a prerequisite for identifying significant poetic features in 2:6–11, as well as drawing on its poetic genre to guide interpretive work on the text.[1] For example, the use of a cluster of closely related terms, rather than simple repetition of the same word, is a feature of poetry. This can be helpful in sorting out the relationships among the terms translated 'nature' (or 'form', *morphē*), 'likeness' (*homoiōma*) and 'appearance' (*schēma*) (2:6–8). Identifying this passage as poetry also focuses attention on the words that are repeated as potential cues to structure and versification (e.g. 'nature' in 2:6, 7; see comments).[2]

The source of this poem has been a point of continuing discussion, especially since the development of the form-critical method in biblical studies. Scholars who identify the poem as pre-Pauline often suggest it functioned in the early church as a hymn (cf. Eph. 5:19), sung to extol Christ (hence the nomenclature of 'Christ hymn'). In this view, Paul drew on this hymn and adapted it for particular use in the letter to the Philippians. Form-critical analysis has often suggested parts of the hymn that were added or modified by Paul. For example, the final line of 2:8 is frequently proposed to be a Pauline addition, both given the way it seems to interrupt the balancing of the lines and because of its characteristic Pauline

---

1. Silva refers to the poem's structural reconstruction, even if not precisely accurate, as 'exegetically useful' (p. 93).

2. The last 'stanza' (2:9–11) has additional prose features, including longer lines (as in the NIV's scansions) and more conjunctions introducing lines.

emphasis on Jesus' 'death on a cross' (cf. 3:18; 1 Cor. 1:17, 18; Gal. 5:11; 6:12, 14). Any number of scholars suggest that Paul himself is the author of this poem (as, e.g., 1 Corinthians 13); as such, they focus attention solely on his purposes for penning it in the context of his exhortations to the Philippians.[3] In the end, discerning how Paul uses this poem (whether it predates his writing or is his own creation) is not the most relevant issue for interpretation. As Flemming suggests, *'in the setting of the letter,* these are the apostle's words and thoughts'.[4] Given this hermeneutical assumption, I will refer to Paul as author in my discussion below, understanding that it is Paul's use of the poem that is relevant to its meaning in Philippians.

The poetic cast of 2:6–11, and especially 2:6–8, has interpretive importance (see below). For this reason, I refer to this section of Philippians as a 'poem' or 'the Christ poem' in my discussion. By this, I do not mean to imply a particular view of its source (e.g. as a Christian hymn). I use 'poem' only to highlight its poetic features, which in general follow Hebrew poetic parameters, such as line parallelism (vv. 7c/8a), careful arrangement of ideas and lines (e.g. *morphē,* 'very nature', used as a frame) and use of sound devices (repetition of sounds).[5] To find Jewish poetic conventions in Greek texts is unsurprising.[6] For example, Wisdom of Solomon, thought to be originally written in Greek, includes a number of features of Jewish (Hebrew poetry), including parallelism and minimal use of subordinate conjunctions (e.g. Wis. 9:9–18).

*Paul's rhetorical emphases in Philippians 2:5–11:* As he moves from prose to a poetic register in 2:6–11, Paul uses logos – specifically a narrative logic – combined with the emotive pathos intrinsic to poetry. He tells the story of Christ's descent and subsequent glorification to motivate the Philippians towards a shared mindset of

---

3. For example, Fee, pp. 192–194; Thielman, pp. 110–112.

4. Flemming, p. 10. Or as Gorman puts it, 'Whether or not Paul wrote it . . . he clearly owned it' ('Cruciform Way', p. 68).

5. Martin (*Carmen Christi*, pp. 12–13) lists these kinds of poetic features in 2:6–11. See also Hansen, p. 128.

6. Fowl, *Story*, p. 23 n. 2, who references as examples Sir. 51; Jdt. 16; and the Greek additions to Daniel.

humility (2:3–4). Paul narrates Christ's story from its heights of 'equality with God' (2:6) to the depths of embracing the status of a slave (2:7), in his incarnation and, at the final turn, in a shameful death by crucifixion (2:8), a fate most often reserved for slaves. This downward descent *by choice* (2:6) could presumably heighten the audience's emotions towards Christ, as he is portrayed as the epitome of self-giving.[7] The second half of the poem draws the reader into Jesus' ascent 'to the highest place' (2:9), as God grants him authority and Lordship (2:10–11), with an expected audience response of worship and allegiance.

*Comment*
## A. Jesus as model for believers' mindset (2:5)

**5.** Paul introduces the poem (2:6–11) with an exhortation to communal imitation of Christ (2:5). This introduction is quite densely packed, with some words or phrases standing in for more expansive concepts. The initial verb and its object, *touto phroneite*, provides an exhortation to 'have this mindset' or 'consider this' and recalls the unified mindset that is to typify the Philippian community (2:2). The brief phrase *en hymin*, which can be rendered 'among you', identifies the community being addressed and shaped. The NIV helpfully fills this out with *in your relationships with one another*.

The second half of 2:5 is a relative clause modifying 'this': *ho kai en Christō Iēsou*, rendered woodenly 'which also in Christ Jesus'. This clause has either a kerygmatic (i.e. a theological, and specifically Christological) function or an ethical focus, a much-debated point among scholars. On the kerygmatic reading, the 'also' (*kai*) connects the desired mindset to what believers already possess 'in Christ Jesus': 'have this mindset, which *you also have* in Christ Jesus'. Given that Paul uses the language of *en Christō*, which signals believers' participation with Christ in his experience and benefits, this reading would emphasize that a part of this participation includes the gifting of Christ's mindset to believers.

---

7. As deSilva notes, pathos has to do with 'arousing strategic emotions in the hearers' ('Appeals', p. 258).

The ethical reading, however, seems more likely. In this reading, the word 'also' connects the mindset to be pursued with the example of Christ's own mindset: 'have this mindset, which *Christ Jesus also had*'. This makes more sense in context, with 2:5 acting as a bridge between Paul's exhortation for the Philippians to have a unified and humble mindset (2:2) and the Christ poem that actively illustrates Christ's self-giving, status-divesting mindset (2:6–11). Paul illustrates how Christ's mindset (2:5) is fundamentally shaped by renunciation of status (2:6–7) and self-humbling (2:8). The purpose of the Christ poem, then, is to provide an example for the Philippians on which to pattern their common life. Christ's mindset provides the ideal model, as 'Christ . . . becomes the narrative paradigm of low-disposition' – of humility.[8]

## B. Jesus' descent in humility (2:6–8)

*Context*
The 'Christ poem' (as I will refer to 2:6–11) begins with a relative pronoun ('who') which connects the introduction (2:5) with the poem itself (2:6; cf. Col. 1:15, which begins in Greek with a relative pronoun). Although the poem itself, in its present form in the letter, does not reference Christ until 2:10–11, the pronoun makes it clear that he is the subject, as the last words of 2:5 are 'Christ Jesus'.

The poem itself is usually visualized in three or four stanzas, with 2:9–11 making up the final stanza. This leaves 2:6–8 as the most-discussed section of the poem, for reasons both structural and semantic. This part of the poem, while it functions together to express Christ's descent from the divine heights to the depths of the human condition, can be divided into two or three stanzas, with both options having solid support and numerous adherents. Although the three-stanza option for 2:6–8 is probably the most popular among contemporary commentators,[9] an analysis focused on the poetic qualities and features of these three verses suggests the two-stanza pattern (formatted here in my own translation):

---

8. Becker, *Humility*, 26.

9. For a visual representation, along with its strengths, see Cohick, p. 116.

6a Who, though being in the form of God,

  6b did not consider equality with God as something to be exploited;

7a rather, he emptied himself

  7b by taking the form of a slave.

7c Being made in the likeness of human beings[10]

  8a and being found in appearance as a human being,

8b he humbled himself

  8c by becoming obedient to death,

  8d all the way to death on a cross.[11]

A number of formal observations suggest this particular structure:[12] (1) *morphē* ('form' or 'nature') frames the first stanza (6a/7b) and the participle *genomenos* ('being made'/'becoming') frames the second stanza (7c/8c);[13] (2) the twofold repetition of *theos* ('God') in the first stanza corresponds to the dual use of *anthrōpos* ('human being') in the second stanza; (3) both stanzas (6a/7c) begin with a preposition phrase beginning with *en* ('in the form'/'in the likeness'); and (4) the finite verbs in the third line of each stanza ('emptied'/'humbled') have the same object (*heauton*, 'himself') and are both followed by a line featuring a participle showing the way the action is accomplished (7b: 'by taking' / 8c: 'by becoming'). This structural analysis also preserves the clear parallelism between adjacent lines 7c and 8a, with its repetition of *anthrōpos/oi* ('human being/s'), synonymous nouns in the dative ('in the likeness'/'in appearance') and dual participles ('being made'/'being found').[14]

---

10. This line begins v. 8 in many translations.

11. This line reproduces Bockmuehl's phrasing (p. 139).

12. See Jeremias, 'Zu Phil 2:7', pp. 186–188.

13. In this analysis, 8d is an extension of that final, fourth line. For those who conceive of the poem as a pre-Pauline hymn, 8d is routinely understood as a Pauline addition to that hymn.

14. For further alignments and structural cues, see Jeremias, 'Zu Phil 2:7', especially pp. 186–187. See also Silva (pp. 98–99), who argues for this two-stanza structure and notes, 'Whether or not such an arrangement

The first stanza portrays the movement from Christ enjoying divine status and prerogatives, to Christ taking on human status.[15] As part of the figurative language of the poem, Paul portrays Christ moving to the place of lowest human status, that of a slave. The point of this metaphor is to show the great descent of Christ, from the heights to the depths.[16] If the language of 'Christ' retains some level of messianic connotation,[17] then a reader might assume Christ would move from divine status to a kingly human status (i.e. messianic status). But that is not the status embodied by Christ. Instead, in his incarnation he took 'the form of a slave'. As Oakes describes the distanced travelled in 2:6–7b, 'Between being like God and being like a slave, there is the widest status gap imaginable by Paul's readers.'[18]

If the first stanza shows, generally and in broad strokes, the great 'distance' in status travelled by Christ in his incarnation, the second stanza provides a more granular view of what occurred in Christ's embodiment, from his identification with humanity to his obedient death on a cross, the form of execution used for slaves and criminals. In this stanza, the poem echoes the creation narrative (and Gen. 1:26 specifically) to show that Christ's incarnation, in a sense, enacts the *imago Dei* in reverse. As humanity (Gen. 1:26; LXX: *anthrōpos*) is made in the image of God (in God's *homoiōsis* or 'likeness'), so in the incarnation Christ is made in 'the likeness [*homoiōma*] of human beings [*anthrōpoi*]' (2:7). As Eastman suggests, by taking on humanity's likeness Christ 'repeats, replicates, and reverses Adam's story'.[19]

---

(note 14 *cont.*) puts us in touch with the original structure of the hymn, it is certainly suggestive and may have a bearing on exegesis' (p. 99).

15. For the status associations in the Christ poem in the light of Roman culture, see Hellerman, pp. 105–107.

16. Fee (p. 204) rightly emphasizes the metaphorical use of 'the form of a slave'.

17. Novenson, *Christ*, p. 91.

18. Oakes, *Philippians*, p. 196.

19. Eastman, 'Imitating Christ', p. 445.

*Comment*

**6.** There are three key exegetical issues to address. The first involves the Greek term *morphē*, *very nature* (or 'form', as in the NIV footnote), which begins the first line (6a) and the last line of the stanza (7b). In line 6a, the phrase *en morphē* ('in the form') immediately follows the relative pronoun (*who*), showing a marked emphasis. Much ink has been spilled to determine the meaning of this word in the context of the poem, especially since these are the only instances of *morphē* in the Pauline letters and the term occurs elsewhere in the New Testament only at Mark 16:12 and less than a handful of times in the Septuagint. This minimal amount of corroborating biblical evidence, coupled with its Christological significance in Philippians 2, accounts for the significant amount of space devoted to the term.

It is important to consider the two occurrences of *morphē* together, since they are used by Paul in parallel fashion: Christ, who was in the *morphē* of God, took on the *morphē* of a slave (2:6–7). As Fee notes, it is the twofold use of the term that helps us understand its meaning in context.[20] Key to the debate is whether this term, which regularly denotes the outward, visible appearance or 'form' of something or someone (BDAG, p. 659), has the added connotation of ontology (concerning essence) in the poem. If so, then the NIV's *very nature* is an appropriate translation.[21] Others, such as Fowl and Bockmuehl, propose a close connection between 'the form of God' and manifestations of divine glory (e.g. Exod. 16:10; 40:34–38; LXX), so that Paul uses *morphē* to indicate that Christ shared in God's glory.[22] I am persuaded by Hellerman, who understands Christ's movement from 'being in the form of God'

---

20. Fee, p. 204 (and n. 47).

21. In this vein, Fee (p. 204) defines *morphē* as *'that which truly characterizes a given reality'* and so speaks to the characteristics of something/someone and not just its/his or her external features. Fee suggests that, had Paul not wanted to use *morphē* in the second occurrence, he probably would have used 'something like . . . "being God in nature"' (*phusis*) in the first occurrence (p. 204 n. 47).

22. Fowl, pp. 91–94.

to 'taking the form of a slave' as a self-chosen descent in status. 'Paul's audience in Philippi would have heard both expressions as explicit references to Christ's social status' and his related power or lack of it.[23] This proposal fits well the pattern of 2:6–8, when conceived in two stanzas. This reading does not rule out hearing in *morphē* an ontological connotation, especially given the language of *equality with God* that follows the first occurrence.[24] It does, however, place emphasis on how this term fits the status concerns Paul has already evoked in 2:2–4.

Addressing a second key issue, there is an implicit contrast in lines 6a and 6b between the status that Christ shared with God and Christ's attitude or mindset towards it, which did not take advantage of or exploit that equality. Given this implied contrast, it makes most sense to read the participle 'being [in the form of God]' concessively ('though being . . .'). Christ did not have the mindset of pursuing all the advantages of his 'equality with God', *even though* he was in the form of God, sharing divine status and power. While the participle is sometimes read causally ('because he was in the form of God, he did not consider equality with God as something to be exploited'), this reading is less likely since it assumes the audience would presuppose self-giving as a divine quality. Paul, in this passage, most certainly portrays Christ in his Godlikeness as the epitome of self-giving. But he does not presuppose that portrait or assume his audience will do so. Instead, he argues against convention and expectation for such a portrait in 2:6–8.

The third major exegetical question of 2:6 involves the unusual term *harpagmos* ('something to be exploited'), which occurs only here in all of biblical Greek (LXX and NT). It can indicate the act of seizing something (negatively, as in 'robbery'), or it can be read passively, referring to something seized, claimed or grasped

---

23. Hellerman, 'Social Status', p. 781.
24. Cohick, pp. 111–114. Given that I read 'taking the form of a slave' as a metaphor, hearing an ontological connotation in *morphē* in this occurrence would not require understanding Christ to have become a literal slave.

(BDAG, p. 133). Most commentators understand the term passively: 'something to be [exploited]'. Another interpretive question relates to whether Paul couples this term with the phrase *equality with God* to indicate that Christ had this equality and did not want to exploit it, or to indicate that Christ did not have this equality and did not aspire to it (i.e. he refused to 'steal' it).[25] The former seems more likely and is the preferred reading of most commentators.[26]

Having discussed in some detail a number of exegetical facets of 2:6, we can now address the import of these opening lines of the Christ poem. Christ is portrayed as sharing in divine status and power, while having a mindset about this status that is surprising. The verb, *hēgeomai* (*consider*), is used regularly in Philippians (2:3, 6, 25; 3:7–8) to indicate a particular mindset and so corresponds to the similar term *phroneō* ('mindset') in Philippians and specifically at 2:5 ('the same mindset'). Christ *did not* consider his divine status 'something to be exploited', *something to be used to his own advantage*. Instead, Christ released it and began his descent, or what has been called his 'downward mobility' (described in 2:6–8).[27]

**7a–b.** The poem continues by moving from the negative (Christ 'did *not* consider . . .') to the positive action of Christ ('he emptied himself'). This language (Gk *kenoō*, 'to empty') has generated rich theological reflection on Christ's *kenosis*, or self-emptying. Especially on the minds of later theologians was the question of what it was that Christ emptied himself of, and specifically what divine qualities Christ might have divested himself of in his incarnation. In its use here, two observations prove fruitful. First, this verb is closely connected to the negative statement of 2:6: Christ did not 'consider equality with God as something to be exploited; rather, he emptied himself'. Second, the subsequent line makes

---

25. This reading usually sees an Adam comparison being made in 2:6: while Adam aspired to Godlikeness beyond his created status, Christ did not do so. One problem with this reading is that allusions to Adam via Gen. 1 do not occur until 7c/8a. There are no such allusions in 2:6 to confirm this reading (Fee, p. 209).

26. For an extended discussion, see Wright, '*Harpagmos*', pp. 321–352.

27. Brackley, 'Downward Mobility', p. 3; see Eastman, 'Incarnation', p. 17.

clear that Christ's emptying is also closely tied to his 'taking the form of a slave', a downward movement in status, with the participle indicating how Christ emptied himself. His emptying (*kenoō*) involved 'divestiture of position or prestige' (BDAG, p. 539) instead of laying claim to his divine status. This fits well Paul's use of a related term, *kenodoxia* ('vain conceit'), in 2:3 to address an inordinate focus on status and self-interest. Christ's story provides the antidote for such vain grasping at status.

The reference to Christ making himself 'of no reputation' (GNV for *kenoō*) fits exceptionally well the flow of the first stanza of the poem (2:6–7b), which portrays the steep descent of Christ in status from 'the form of God' to the 'form of a slave'. The most relevant backdrop for *doulos*, 'slave', is the practice of slavery in antiquity, when slaves occupied the lowest rung of society.[28] Even though the experience and position of a slave could vary significantly (with some slaves occupying important administrative positions in the household or state), the reminder from Aristotle is telling: a slave is a 'living tool', owned by his or her master. This metaphorical image of Christ taking the form of a slave would have provided a jarring juxtaposition to his starting point: 'being in the form of God'.[29]

There is some debate about the referent of Christ's descent to 'the form of a slave' – does it refer to the incarnation or the cross? Those who suggest that the cross is in view rightly highlight the close connection between slavery and crucifixion (see comment on 2:8) and often see Isaiah 53 at work, with its key point of

---

28. Some have seen the relevant backdrop for *doulos* as the Isaianic suffering servant. While there are potential echoes of Isa. 52:13 – 53:12 (the fourth 'servant song') in Phil. 2:6–11, they are rather faint (terms for 'humbled', 'death', 'exalted'), and the relevant term in the Septuagint for 'servant' in Isa. 52:13 is *pais*, not *doulos* (though *doulos* is used at Isa. 49:3, 5). For more connections in Aquila's Greek translation of Isaiah, see Bockmuehl, p. 135.

29. In 1:1, Paul has identified himself and Timothy as 'slaves of Christ Jesus' (*doulos*; NIV: 'servants'), potentially for the resonance his audience would hear in its repetition in the Christ poem.

emphasis on the Servant's death (53:11–12). I follow the former interpreters who understand 'taking the form of a slave' as a reference to Christ's incarnation, especially given the subsequent lines referring to Christ's humanity and not yet to his death. In this reading, Christ taking 'the form of a slave' provides a more general nod to his incarnation, which will be fleshed out (pun intended) in lines 7c/8a. And importantly, this phrase concludes the first stanza with its significant movement from 'form of God' to 'form of a slave'.

**7c–8a.** The last line of verse 7 (7c) and the first line of verse 8 (8a, in the NIV)[30] are closely parallel in form and meaning, and so should be treated together.[31]

7c Being made in the likeness of human beings
8a and being found in appearance as a human being

Parallelism is first apparent in the dative that begins each line in the Greek (*homoiōmati* and *schēmati*), translated as 'in the likeness' and 'in appearance'. The two aorist participles translated 'being made' and 'being found' are also similar in meaning and so parallel in form and substance. Finally, parallelism is clear in the repetition of *anthrōpos*, first in the plural, then in the singular. This change provides the clue to the nature of the relationship between these two lines. They are not simply synonymous; rather the relationship is one of progression and particularization.

To understand this relationship, it is important to hear the allusion to Genesis 1:26 (LXX) in the first line, as Paul connects

---

30. Some translations follow the major Greek editions and set the NIV's 8a as 7d; e.g. CEB, NET.

31. Fee argues that the 'and' (*kai*) more naturally signals a movement between the larger sections (rather than joining closely these two parallel lines) (pp. 214–215 n. 3). Fee's argument makes sense if 2:6–8 is more prose than poem and if the two lines are essentially redundant. I suggest the conjunction *kai* makes a great deal of sense in *poetry* to connect two parallel lines (e.g. Ps. 1:1–3, LXX); and, as I argue, the two lines are not simply redundant.

Christ's incarnation to humanity's creation in the image of God (my translations).

Phil. 2:7c   Being made in the likeness [*homoiōma*] of human
             beings [*anthrōpoi*]
Gen. 1:26a   Let us create humanity [*anthrōpos*] according to . . .
             our likeness [*homoiōsis*][32]

In his incarnation, Christ is made in the likeness of humanity, as humanity was created in the likeness of God. As Eastman comments, Christ 'assimilat[ed] to Adamic humanity in a mirror reversal of Adam's creation in the likeness of God'.[33] The second line goes further by particularizing Christ's human experience: he is found 'in appearance as a human being', or as Eastman suggests, 'in the trappings of a singular human being' (7c).[34] The singular form ('human being' rather than the plural) extends the idea from Christ's incarnation in solidarity with humanity to the particular expression his humanity took – that is, a Jewish man born into a world shaped by Roman power and might.[35] Though the poem does not specify these particulars, the first half does conclude with a reference to crucifixion (2:8), a specifically Roman form of execution. So these two lines affirm that Christ became human and appeared in all his human particularity, leading into the affirmation that Christ humbled himself.

**8b–d.** In this reading, lines 7c/8a, with their adverbial participles, anticipate and modify the independent clause *he humbled himself*, the third finite (independent) verb of the poem. In the circumstances of his incarnation – both representative and individual – Christ humbled himself through obedience. Christ's act of humbling

---

32. The two cognate nouns, *homoiōsis* and *homoiōma*, both denote 'likeness'.

33. Eastman, *Paul*, p. 137.

34. And in reference to theatrical performance, which Eastman argues forms the backdrop of the poem ('Incarnation', p. 2).

35. Bockmuehl understands the verb used here ('found' or 'appeared') to indicate 'the way a person's circumstances turn out in the event, rather than what is the case in principle' (p. 138).

himself provides the central point of connection between the example of Christ (2:5–11) and the exhortations that have preceded it (1:27 – 2:4). Specifically, Paul's exhortation to humility (*tapeinophrosynē*, 2:3) finds its ultimate example in Christ's action of self-humbling (*tapeinoō*). Here, we arrive at the centrepiece of the (Christ) mindset referenced at 2:5 and extolled at 2:3. And we should be careful to hear the status connotations of this terminology. Paul affirms that Christ willingly let go of divine status for a human life of obedience to God. And we should hear this action, especially on the part of one with the highest status, as starkly countercultural. Additionally, unlike the first (disobedient) Adam, the second Adam perfected obedience by being faithful to God even to death, with the preposition *mechri* indicating extent, even '*to the point of* death'. In Romans 5:19, Paul contrasts the 'disobedience of the one man', Adam, with the obedience of Christ, focusing specifically on his obedient death (5:18: the 'one righteous act'). We hear in the poem this close association of obedience with death, even though Christ's death is only the culminating moment in an entire life of obedience (cf. Heb. 5:8).

The final line of this first half of the Christ poem falls outside of either proposal regarding stanzas for 2:6–8, being an additional line for either the three-stanza or the two-stanza proposal. For those who understand this to be a pre-Pauline hymn or poem, this specific line is typically attributed to Paul himself. In either proposal, 2:8d provides a significant point of emphasis: 'all the way to death on a cross'.[36] Paul emphasizes the full measure of Christ's willing obedience to God's mission to go to the greatest of lengths – even to crucifixion. The implicit associations of crucifixion with slavery in this part of the Christ poem further connect the two stanzas, as Paul has referenced Christ 'taking the form of a slave' (2:7) in the first stanza. Although slaves were not the only persons subjected to crucifixion, it was a form of execution closely associated with slavery, so much so that 'the expression *servile supplicum* ("slaves' punishment") came to be used as a technical expression for death by crucifixion'.[37] Crucifixion was understood to be a shameful way

---

36. Bockmuehl, p. 139.
37. Hellerman, p. 118.

to die, setting up the stark contrast of Christ's divine exaltation in the stanza that follows (2:9–11).

## C. Jesus' glorification to Lordship (2:9–11)

The rehearsal of Christ's story now turns from shameful cruci-fixion to glorious exaltation. With this turn, the poetic elements are somewhat muted, as subordinating conjunctions, which have been absent from the flow of thought in 2:6–8, now appear.[38] Yet the NIV rightly sets out these lines poetically, not least because of the quotation drawn from an Old Testament text, itself composed in poetic parallelism (Isa. 45:23, with borrowing shown in italics below). Philippians 2:9–11 reads:

> 9a Therefore God exalted him to the highest place
> 9b and gave him the name that is above every name,
> 10a that at the name of Jesus *every knee should bow*,
> 10b in heaven and on earth and under the earth,
> 11a *and every tongue acknowledge* that Jesus Christ is Lord,
> 11b to the glory of God the Father.

**9.** With the conjunction pair *dio kai* (*therefore*), Paul makes it clear that it is because of Christ's action of self-humbling (and all that accompanies it in 2:6–8) that he is exalted by God.[39] The two lines of verse 9 are parallel to each other in their subjects (God), their objects (Christ) and the similarity of their verbal ideas (exaltation to the highest place and the bestowal of the highest name). The first verb, *hyperypsoō*, signals an exaltation to a high place of honour or to the highest place (BDAG, p. 1032). Because of Christ's

---

38. Subordinating conjunctions: *hina*, 'that' of 10a; *hoti*, 'that' of 11a. Note also the coordinating conjunction *dio* ('therefore'; 9a), which is more at home in prose than in poetry.

39. The *kai* (often 'and' or 'also') could simply intensify the sense of *dio* (*therefore*), or it may suggest an implied comparison between Christ's humbling to the lowest place and God's exaltation of him to the highest ('likewise'; BDAG, p. 495).

self-emptying and self-humbling to the greatest extent (to death even on a cross), God, in like fashion but opposite direction, has exalted Christ to the greatest extent possible. This supreme exaltation is explained in the parallel phrase, *and [God] gave him the name that is above every name*. The verb, *charizomai* (*gave*), denotes an act of gracious giving, often used 'in honorific documents lauding officials and civic-minded persons for their beneficence' (BDAG, p. 1078). God freely bestows on Christ the highest name in response to Christ's humble obedience.

The name granted Christ by God must be understood within the fuller context of 2:9–11, and especially in the light of the use of Isaiah 45:23, where it is the divine name (Yahweh) that is connected to the exalted status in view.[40] The highest (*hyper*) name resonates lexically with the earlier verb *hyperypsoō* (*exalted . . . to the highest place*), contributing to the poetic feel of the verse by repetition of sound.

**10–11.** The divine act of exalting Christ results in his universal Lordship; that is, the granting of universal authority. The introductory conjunction of 2:10 (*hina, that*) can indicate either purpose or result, but in this particular case the difference is negligible, given that exaltation to the highest place and universal Lordship are so similar conceptually.

The use of Isaiah 45:23 at this climactic moment of the Christ story provides clarity about the 'name . . . above every name' (2:9) and about the universal Lordship of Christ. The larger context of Isaiah 45 offers an extended argument against all would-be contenders to Yahweh, Israel's God. Across the chapter, a monotheistic refrain resounds: 'I am the LORD, and there is no other' (45:5, 6, 18; cf. 21–22). As we narrow to look at the more immediate context and turn specifically to the Septuagint, the Lord (the divine name, expressed in the LXX as *kyrios*) is affirmed as the only god who speaks the truth (45:19); and idolatry is denounced (45:20). The *kyrios* of the whole earth invites all peoples to turn to

---

40. Although the Greek article is missing from some Greek manuscripts, it likely was original (having strong external support) but omitted by scribes who did not catch the allusion to the divine name of Isa. 45 (i.e. *the* name).

the one true God (45:22). In the crescendo leading up to Isaiah
45:23, the same phrase is re-emphasized: 'I am God, and there is no
other' (45:21, 22, LXX). At 45:23b, the Lord speaks as the rightful
recipient of universal worship and acknowledgment: 'to me every
knee will bow and every tongue will acknowledge God' (LXX).

Paul, surely aware of the intensity of expression of monotheism
in this Scripture text, draws from it to affirm worship and acknowledgment of *Jesus* by all creation. The emphasis on the scope of
Christ's authority comes from the twice-repeated *pas* (*every*), as well
as the insertion within the alluded text: *in heaven and on earth and
under the earth*. This conclusion to the Christ poem places Jesus
squarely within the place of Yahweh in the Isaiah text. Isaiah's
affirmation of the one true God as the recipient of universal
acknowledgment is transposed in the Christ poem to affirm that
*Jesus Christ is Lord* (Phil. 2:11). As Bauckham suggests, this use of
Isaiah

> is no unconsidered echo of an Old Testament text, but a claim that it is
> in the exaltation of Jesus, his identification as YHWH in YHWH's
> universal sovereignty, that the unique deity of the God of Israel comes
> to be acknowledged as such by all creation.[41]

The end result is *glory* to *God the Father* (2:11). We can hear in this
verse an expression of binitarian worship, in which Jesus as Messiah
and now Lord shares in the divine identity, without collapsing the
persons of 'God [the] Father and the Lord Jesus Christ' (1:2; see
comment there).

The Isaiah allusion also clarifies what is meant by 'the name that
is above every name' (2:9). Yahweh (LORD) is the divine name that
echoes across Isaiah 45 and is expressed as *kyrios* in the Septuagint
(e.g. 'I am, I am the Lord [*kyrios*]' in Isa. 45:19, LXX). The Lord
(*kyrios*) God is the one to whom every knee will bow. As such, Jesus
shares in the divine name itself (i.e. sharing in the identity of God,
manifested in universal Lordship), having been granted the divine
name by God (Phil. 2:9). While some suggest that the superlative

---

41. Bauckham, *Jesus*, p. 38.

name is Jesus (2:10; versus Lord/Yahweh), this makes less sense in conversation with Isaiah 45 and in the light of the emphasis on Jesus Christ as *Lord* (with *kyrios* placed at the front of the Greek phrase for emphasis). 'Jesus is Lord' is the quintessential Christian confession (see Rom. 10:9), which has both the Jewish resonance we have been discussing here, as well as significant purchase in the Roman context of Philippi. In a sociopolitical context where Caesar was regarded as Lord (*kyrios*), the confession that Jesus is Lord has significant political overtones. The proclamation of Christ as Lord, at the very least, implies that Caesar is not.[42] And it also means that the church is not to replicate the Roman social world built on jockeying for social status.[43]

## Theology

Describing Philippians 2:5–11, Flemming writes that it 'is one of the lofty peaks, not only of this letter, but of the entire [New Testament]'.[44] This is no hyperbole, as the realities conveyed in this text – what Gorman refers to as Paul's 'master story'[45] – reverberate across his letters and also resonate deeply with the portrait the Gospel writers paint of Messiah Jesus.[46] Although Paul uses the Christ story to provide the best possible example for his Philippian family to follow, the shape of the story is in no way incidental to Paul's Christology. Christ's act of self-humbling not only speaks of

---

42. While I do not think Paul is writing primarily (and in coded language) for anti-imperial purposes, I do, with Heilig, hear 'critical connotations' here and elsewhere in the letter (i.e. critical of Rome). As Heilig concludes, 'Maybe it was not Paul's *primary* intention to say something about Caesar, but rather to say something about the Messiah and God, although he was perfectly aware of the critical *implications* these statements had for other competing worldviews' (Heilig, 'Counter-Imperial', p. 90).

43. Oakes, *Philippians*, p. 206.

44. Flemming, p. 105.

45. Gorman, 'Cruciform Way', p. 68.

46. E.g. Matt. 20:28, discussed in Brown and Roberts, *Matthew*, pp. 187–188.

how Christians are to live. It also reveals something about Christology and so something about who God is.

The Christ poem illumines the one who is both divine and human. In his incarnation, Christ identified with humanity fully, becoming our representative (2:7c) and becoming a singular human being with the particulars that entailed (see discussion at 2:8a). The poem emphasizes the full extent of Christ's descent: 'taking the form of a slave' and humbling himself in complete obedience 'all the way to death on a cross' (2:8b–d). There is no part of our humanity Christ refused to embrace. As the writer to the Hebrews penned,

> For this reason he had to be made like them, fully human in every way, in order that he might become a merciful and faithful high priest in service to God, and that he might make atonement for the sins of the people.
> (Heb. 2:17)

He also writes, 'For we do not have a high priest who is unable to feel sympathy for our weaknesses, but we have one who has been tempted in every way, just as we are – yet he did not sin' (Heb. 4:15; cf. 2 Cor. 5:21). As Gregory of Nazianzus would later affirm, 'what has not been assumed [by Christ] has not been healed'.[47]

The exaltation and Lordship of Messiah Jesus (2:9–11) receives equal space with Christ's descent in this Pauline poem. Yet I would suggest the part of the poem that is most needed in contemporary reflection (and addressing my own cultural context particularly) is the story of Christ's 'downward mobility': his choice to divest himself of status rather than exploit it for his own benefit. Such a counter-intuitive act would have been striking for all those in Philippi. 'Paul's point is that although "normal" deities in the pagan world might be expected to [exploit their status for self-serving benefit], Jesus the Messiah's equality with the one true God, the God known in Israel's Scriptures and history, was displayed in radical self-giving.'[48]

---

47. A statement Gregory attributes to Origen, in his letter to Cledonius (Daley, *Gregory*, p. 14 n. 73).
48. Gorman, 'Cruciform Way', p. 70.

Christ's self-humbling, I suspect, is counter-intuitive to many popular views of Jesus in our contemporary contexts. If I am drawn to the portrait of Jesus as the powerful Lord more than to images of him as the self-giving human one who willingly took the form of a slave and was executed on a cross, I might need to hear an invitation to meditate on Philippians 2:6–8. For those of us in the USA, commonplace hyper-masculine images of Jesus as a tough guy or as a maverick are more cultural than biblical and probably speak to our own projection of cultural values on to our Christology.[49]

Finally, this text speaks not only to Christology but also to theology proper. John's Gospel asserts that Jesus shows us in the flesh what the unseen God is like (1:18). Likewise, the Christ poem of Philippians 'suggests that what Christ did . . . is a manifestation of Godlikeness'.[50] What a startling claim – that in Christ on the cross God is most fully revealed. And that, if true, has the power to reorient the ways we think about God and to transform the way we live.

---

49. See Du Mez, *Jesus*. She adds quite a number of descriptions to the list of popular images, including 'Warrior Leader, an Ultimate Fighter, a knight in shining armor, a William Wallace, a General Patton' (p. 295).
50. Gorman, 'Cruciform Way', p. 70.

## 5. EXHORTATIONS: TO OBEDIENCE, UNITY, MISSION AND JOY (2:12–18)

### Context

In 2:12–18, Paul turns from Jesus as the ultimate example for Christians to a set of exhortations for their life together, continuing the alternating pattern between exhortations and exemplars. Much as the exhortations for a communally centred mindset in 1:27 – 2:4 lead naturally into Jesus as exemplar of that mindset, the exhortations towards faithfulness and mission in 2:12–18 are embodied in the examples of Timothy and Epaphroditus in 2:19–30. For instance, Paul describes ministry in terms associated with work or labour across 2:12–30 (2:16, 25, 30; cf. 2:12–13).

Although Paul's exhortations here are distinct from those in 1:27 – 2:4, they share some themes with the earlier instructions. The prohibition against 'grumbling or arguing' correlates with the identification of self-promotion and status preoccupation as detrimental to the unity of the believing community (2:3a) and provides a negative counterpoint to the humble, other-centred mindset exhorted at 2:2–3. Paul also reiterates that the Philippians should stay the course, whether he is absent from them or present with them (1:27; 2:12). Paul presses the community in their outward witness in both passages, though mission to outsiders receives greater emphasis in 2:15–16a (cf. 1:27–28). The gospel is the centrepiece of the church and its witness in both texts (1:27; 2:16: 'the word of life'). Finally, Paul's call for rejoicing reappears at 2:17b–18, a strong emphasis across the letter (e.g. 1:18; 3:1; 4:4).

Paul draws from his audience's experiences of temple (cultic) sacrifice and service in 2:17 to describe the fruits of the Philippians' partnership with Paul, language that will reappear later in this chapter and at the conclusion of the letter (2:25, 30; 4:18). It is likely that these images find their source in both Jewish and Graeco-Roman cultic sacrifices associated with thanksgiving (see comment on 2:17).

Paul also evokes Old Testament texts and images in this passage (2:14–16; cf. Deut. 32:5), a feature not all that prominent in other parts of the letter (though see comments at 1:19; 2:7–8, 9–11; 3:2; and 4:5). The allusions to and echoes of Deuteronomy 32 may indicate that Paul is not targeting a specific and significant problem in the Philippian church with his call to avoid grumbling and arguing (i.e. we should be cautious about mirror-reading this exhortation). Rather, he seems to be highlighting behaviour – blameworthy and laudable – that arises from his focus on this covenantal text from Deuteronomy to guide the church to embrace their identity as 'children of God' (2:15; cf. 1 Cor. 10:10).

*Paul's rhetorical emphases in Philippians 2:12–18:* Paul leans into logos in this passage, grounding his exhortations to obedience, unity and mission in the prior and pervasive work of God (2:13) and in identity formation drawn from Deuteronomy 32 (Phil. 2:14–16a). Paul taps into his own ethos as he shares his desire to boast in the fruit of his ministry among the Philippians in the final day (2:16b). This personal sharing also seems intended to draw the Philippian believers to respond positively to the instructions he has just given, so that they can participate faithfully in Paul's labours (a move towards pathos). The metaphor Paul paints of the commingling of his temple offering and theirs has a similar dual effect – to strengthen even further their partnership with Paul and to motivate their continued faithfulness. Finally, Paul draws directly on pathos as he indicates his own joy over them and encourages them to rejoice with him.

*Comment*
## A. The work of salvation (2:12–13)

**12.** Paul transitions from the exalted language at the conclusion of the Christ poem to another set of exhortations, which build on and extend his exhortations given in 1:27 – 2:4. The initial conjunction (*therefore, hōstē*) provides the inference from what has preceded. The Philippians' obedience rightly grows out of what Christ has done in his path of humility and exaltation (2:6–11) and his mindset which they are to emulate (2:5). Christ provides the model of cruciformity that is to mark their lives. Paul will also ground their obedience, or the 'working out' of their salvation, in God's initiating work in them (2:13).

Although Paul regularly calls the Philippian church his 'brothers and sisters' in the faith (1:12; 3:1, 13, 17; 4:1, 8), here he deepens his address further to speak of them as his *dear friends* or 'beloved ones' (*agapētoi*; also twice in 4:1). This personal tone continues in the extended comparative clause (*as [kathōs] you have always obeyed . . . my absence*), in which Paul reminds them of his prior presence among them and his current absence (cf. 1:27). Paul connects his absence from them to the necessity for even greater attention to obedience (*much more*).

12a *Therefore, my dear friends,*
12b *as you have always obeyed*                [12b/c: comparison with 12d]
12c *– not only in my presence, but now much more in my absence –*
                                              [comparison with 12b]
12d *continue to work out your salvation with fear and trembling . . .*

The text set off by dashes in the NIV is also a comparative, a comparative phrase set within the longer comparative clause and introduced by *mē hōs* ('not [as]'). This suggests that the set-off text modifies the verb *obeyed* (an indicative verb) rather than the subsequent verb *work out* (an imperative verb), in spite of the widespread use of *mē* (*not*) with non-indicative moods.[1] This reading is also the more natural one in terms of the Greek word order and is closely replicated in most English translations.

The relationship of the comparative clause to the main verb is one of continuity. Paul attests that the Philippians have *always obeyed*, affirming their past faithfulness in connection with his present exhortation to them to *work out [their] salvation*. Paul is encouraging them to continued obedience (hence the NIV's <u>*continue to work*</u> for the present-tense verb) and will specify at least part of what this obedience entails in 2:14–16.

Paul frames his exhortation to continuing obedience in terms of work: *continue to work out your salvation*. The verb *katergazomai* fits a composite of terms Paul draws on across the letter to reference both divine and human work: God's (salvific) work (1:6; 2:13); Christ's work specifically (2:30; 3:21); and Paul's own work of ministry (1:22; 2:16: 'labour'). Paul also refers to his co-workers in ministry (2:25; 4:3), and he affirms Epaphroditus's ministry as 'the work of Christ' (2:30). Paul's exhortation to *work out your salvation* should be heard in the light of this integrated pattern of divine and human cooperation. Paul does not shy away from describing Christian ministry as work and labour. Yet he does not suggest that what God has done in Christ is inadequate for salvation. Instead, he expresses in no uncertain terms that God is involved throughout the process of salvation, as the one who begins it and completes it (1:6). God is also the one who instils in believers 'the working' – empowering them in their faith (see comment at 2:13). In the light of these insights, we can speak of 'working out your salvation' as the Philippians cooperating in their salvation, but it must be understood as a quite uneven cooperation. Human obedience in response to God's work in Christ is always that – a response. And for Paul, it is a response that is covered from beginning to end by the continuing divine work of salvation (see Theology below). We should also note that the verb for *work out* is a plural imperative in

---

1. Since there is no verb in the comparative phrase set off by dashes, Paul might intend the *mē* as negation of an implied verb within that clause conceived as a (non-indicative) participle (cf. Phlm. 14).

the Greek; Paul calls the Philippian church to work out its (corporate) salvation (cf. the communal image in Eph. 4:11–16).

The manner in which the Philippians are to *work out [their] salvation* is captured by the idiom *with fear and trembling*. This word pairing (*phobos* and *tromos*) occurs elsewhere in Paul (1 Cor. 2:3; 2 Cor. 7:15; Eph. 6:5) and finds its origins in the Old Testament. In the Septuagint, the word pair occurs frequently enough, and in a number of instances it refers to the fear and trembling non-Israelites will experience because of God's work in Israel (Exod. 15:16; Deut. 2:25; 11:25; Isa. 19:16). In other words, *fear and trembling* is the appropriate stance for Gentiles when encountering the work of God (also Jdt. 2:28; 15:2). The two terms are also used in parallelism in Psalm 2:11 (LXX) to highlight a proper response to God: 'Serve the Lord in fear [*phobos*] / And rejoice over him in trembling [*tromos*].'

Given its stock use in Jewish literature, Paul may not be evoking any particular text, although if he is, Psalm 2:11 is a likely contender given its positive use of these terms (in a call to serve and rejoice) and the psalm's enthronement theme (2:2, 6–10).[2] Paul may be using the commonplace word pair because the terms are particularly appropriate to the humble posture of believers for collaborating with God in their own salvation, recognizing God's overwhelmingly prominent and gracious role in that collaboration.

**13.** Having landed on the exhortation for the Philippians to work out their salvation (as the final word of 2:12 in the Greek), Paul immediately grounds that exhortation in the work of God: *for it is God who works in* [or *among*] *you*. God's work is primary and makes possible human collaboration, as Paul has already made clear (1:6). The phrase *en hymin* probably indicates a corporate sense given the plural pronoun: 'among [all of] you'. Paul is affirming that God is at work in the Philippian congregation to lead them to final salvation.

The particular work of God in the community of believers provides them with the resolve and the capability to join in the divine work of salvation on their behalf. The two infinitives (*to will* and *to act*) function as nouns, but with a verbal or active quality.

---

2. McAuley, *Scripture*, pp. 178–192.

The Greek term rendered *to act* is *energeō*, and is initially used in this verse to describe God's work in the Philippians. The term shares the same root with *katergazomai* ('work out'), further interlocking divine and human efforts in 2:12–13. The picture is one of God inspiring and empowering believers to grow more fully into the salvation that God has already begun in them (1:6).

The final phrase of the verse indicates the advantage or purpose coming from God's salvific work, which surrounds the Philippians' work in response to divine grace: *in order to fulfil his good purpose*.³ Fee calls the Greek phrase 'perfectly ambiguous'.⁴ First, the Greek prepositional phrase does not include a pronoun (woodenly, 'for the good purpose/pleasure'), so it is possible grammatically to connect the noun to either the Philippians or God. Earlier, in 1:15, Paul has used the same term (*eudokia*) to refer to the 'goodwill' of some of his fellow believers towards him. In the present context, however, given that God is the primary actor in view (and the subject of the sentence), it is more likely that it is God's good purpose or pleasure that Paul highlights as a goal of God's work among the Philippians.

Second, there are two primary senses of *eudokia*, either 'being kindly disposed' or 'being favored' (BDAG, p. 404). The first results in a translation of 'goodwill' or 'good purpose', the second is often translated 'good pleasure'. Does Paul affirm that the divine work of salvation in people brings about God's 'benevolent purpose'?⁵ Or is he affirming that God's pleasure or happiness is the goal of the divine work of salvation? Most commentators take the latter course, though with differing conclusions about it. It is possible to read this phrase as indicating that God is the primary beneficiary of the divine work of salvation – it is 'on behalf of God's good pleasure'. Yet since, in 2:12–13, God's pleasure is

---

3. Although some translations imply that this final phrase is the object of the Philippians' willing and working (e.g. 'the desire and the power to do *what pleases him*', NLT [emphasis added]), the preposition that begins the phrase, *hyper* ('for' or *in order to fulfil*), works against this reading.

4. Fee, p. 239.

5. Lightfoot, p. 116.

intimately connected to the salvation of people, there is probably no definitive distinction between the two ideas. As Fowl suggests, 'God's work in the lives of the Philippians is God's good pleasure . . . God's deepest desire.'[6]

## B. God's holy children on mission (2:14–16)

**14.** In 2:14–16, Paul fleshes out something of what it means for the Philippians to 'work out [their] salvation'. He does so by drawing from Israel's ancient story to remind the Philippian believers of their identity as God's children and their need to shape their behaviour in line with that identity. Paul alludes to Deuteronomy 32 and echoes a number of other scriptural texts focused on Israel's identity and conduct. Even if the Philippians would not have caught every Old Testament connection, Paul could well have echoed these intentionally for shaping the core values of his audience; and such shaping could have happened whether or not each and every echo was identified. Yet the Philippians, including Gentiles who had responded to Paul's preaching of the gospel, would have held Israel's Scriptures as their own and 'so would have been schooled in the stories and messages of [the] Old Testament', at least in their broad contours.[7] I suggest that this meta-story of God's redemptive work in Israel would have been part of Paul's preaching of the good news of Jesus, Israel's Messiah. As such, the plotline of Israel's wilderness disobedience prior to entering the Promised Land could very well have been known to these primarily Gentile Christians. And any Jews or proselytes in the Philippian church, even if fewer in number, would have been able to highlight relevant allusions and educate the rest of the community in these formational narratives.[8] We should recall as well that Epaphroditus would have been on both ends of the conversation – with Paul when the letter was being written and with the Philippians when it was being read (or when he read it to them). His

---

6. Fowl, p. 121.

7. Brown, *Gospels as Stories*, p. 110.

8. Green, *1 Peter*, p. 5.

commentary would have been a natural place for the Philippians to hear more about these allusions and echoes.[9]

The clear and potential echoes of the Old Testament (LXX) in 2:14–16 (17) include the following:

- 'grumbling' (*gongysmos*): characteristic response of Israel in the wilderness;
- 'children of God' (*tekna theou*) 'in a warped and crooked generation' (*genea skolia kai diestrammenē*): allusion to Deuteronomy 32:5 (cf. 32:20);
- 'without fault' (*amōmos*): echo of and contrast to the 'blemished [*mōmētos*] children' of Deuteronomy 32:5;
- 'shine . . . like stars' (*phainō hōs phōtēres*): echo of Daniel 12:3;
- 'word of life' (*logos zōēs*): possible echo of 'this word . . . is your life' of Deuteronomy 32:47;
- 'labour in vain' (*eis kenon ekopiasa*): echo of Isaiah 65:23 (or 49:4);
- images of a 'drink offering' (*spendō*) and 'sacrifice and service' (*thysia kai leitourgia*): see comment on 2:17.

The clearest allusion to Israel's story in this passage, Deuteronomy 32:5 at Philippians 2:15, is anticipated by Paul's opening exhortation to *Do everything without grumbling or arguing*. The reference to grumbling (*gongysmos*) appears to echo a memorable narrative moment from Israel's time in the wilderness – their grumbling during their time of wandering. This motif occurs across Exodus and Numbers (e.g. Exod. 16:6–12; 17:3; Num. 11:1) and is recapitulated in the opening chapter of Deuteronomy as Moses rehearses the Israelites' disobedient refusal to enter the land (Deut. 1:19–26) and their grumbling (*diagongyzō*) against the Lord (1:27, LXX).

Paul uses this part of Israel's story as a counter-example for the Philippians. Unlike Israel in the wilderness, everything they do should be untainted by grumbling or arguing. This high calling fits Paul's earlier admonitions to unity and an other-centred mindset

---

9. Cohick, p. 145.

(1:27; 2:1–4). It seems very likely that Paul's choice of language here is drawn from Israel's story, especially given the other allusions to and echoes of Israel's narrative in this brief paragraph. Paul uses these allusions to shape the Philippians even more deeply into their identity as God's children (2:15).

**15.** Obeying the command to avoid all grumbling and arguing will lead to holiness. Paul has already set out the goal of holiness in related, though not identical, language in his prayer for the church: 'that you … may be pure and blameless' (1:10). Paul uses three adjectives in close succession to describe this aspirational goal of holiness: *blameless and pure … without fault.* The first term (*amemptos*) will reappear in Paul's rehearsal of his past (pre-Christ) pedigree; he was blameless in regard to the law (3:6; see comment there). In the Septuagint, this term is often paired with 'righteous' (*dikaios*) and is used in synonymous parallelism with *dikaios* at Job 9:20 to indicate a consistent faithfulness. The word *amōmos* (*without fault*) is commonly used in the Old Testament to describe the necessary quality for a sacrificial animal to be 'unblemished' or 'without defect' (e.g. Lev. 3:1, 6). The term is also used metaphorically to refer to a moral quality of blamelessness (e.g. Ps. 118:1, LXX [119:1, Eng.]), as it is here in Philippians. Given its prevalence in the Old Testament in contexts related to sacrifice, *amōma* resonates with Paul's sacrificial images in 2:17 (see comment there). Paul uses these two terms, along with *akeraioi*, as synonyms to reflect an abiding moral purity and righteousness, without corruption or fault. Paul piles up this language with poetic flourish (the synonyms alliterate as well: *amemptoi, akeraioi, amōma*) to emphasize the divine design for the Philippians to be holy. The central image for understanding this call to holiness is the portrait of the Philippians as *children of God*, a phrase which is situated within the list of adjectives that designate holiness. As the people of Israel were to embody their identity as God's children by living distinctively – being holy – among the nations, so the Philippians are called to live out their identity as God's holy children in their own setting of Philippi.

Paul's reference to the Philippians as *children of God* grounds their identity theologically, by drawing on Deuteronomy 32:5 (LXX). Deuteronomy 32 relates the song of Moses, which narrates in poetic form the story of God's faithfulness to Israel, even when they were unfaithful during their wilderness wanderings, and tells of the consequences God will bring upon them for their disobedience. Yet it concludes with a promise that God will relent and will, in the end, vindicate Israel and make atonement for them. In Deuteronomy 32:5, Israel is described as 'blemished children' and even 'not [God's children]' (although across the chapter, Israel will continue to be called God's people; 32:6, 9, 36, 43). The second, parallel line (32:5b) further describes Israel and is repeated virtually verbatim in Philippians: *genea skolia kai diestrammenē*, 'a generation, warped and crooked'.[10]

Paul uses this language to encourage the Philippians to live fully into their identity as God's children, in continuity with Israel as God's people. He encourages this identity formation, even though many of them are Gentiles and so have come to this identity not by birth, but upon their reception of the gospel and of Christ Jesus. Their obedience (2:12, 14) will demonstrate that they are truly *children of God without fault* ('without blemish'). Paul contrasts the portrait of Israel's disobedience in the wilderness – they are 'blemished [*mōmētos*] children' (cf. 32:5) – with the Philippians, who will be 'without blemish' as they 'work out [their] salvation', obediently and 'without grumbling or arguing' (2:12, 14). In an interesting twist, the words from Deuteronomy 32:5b that describe Israel's wilderness generation – 'a warped and crooked generation' – are instead used by Paul to characterize the surrounding Philippian society with its allegiances that run counter to the church's loyalty to Christ.

Paul's use of Deuteronomy provides a contrasting portrait – a negative example – for the Philippian believers. They are to, in effect, steer clear of the example of ancient Israel in the time of wilderness disobedience, while living into Israel's identity as the people of God and their mission to be a light to the nations. Paul captures this missional motif by alluding to Daniel 12:3 (LXX): *Then you will shine among them like stars in the sky.* This Danielic text refers to the day of resurrection when the wise will 'shine like stars' (*phainō hōs phōteres*) in the heavens. Paul captures the rhetorical alliteration (the repeated *ph* sound) using the same three Greek words, *shine . . .*

---

10. The only difference is the case of the phrase.

*like stars*, for the Philippians as they live as obedient children. Through their faithfulness to Christ, they will shine brightly – they will be distinctive – to the world (*kosmos*) around them. The NIV's *sky* understands *kosmos* to continue the metaphor (*shine . . . like stars in the sky*; i.e. 'universe'). While this reading is possible, it seems more likely that Paul is playing on the language from Daniel (as he has with Deuteronomy), where those who are wise will, in that final day, 'shine like stars in heaven' (*ouranos*). Paul shifts the imagery to describe the Philippians, in their obedience and loyalty, as 'shining like stars in the world' – in their present time and place.

**16.** Paul adds a final phrase to the long (Greek) purpose clause he has begun in 2:15: *as you hold firmly to the word of life*. As the Philippians pursue faithful obedience (2:12–14), they will become increasingly holy, leaning into their identity as God's children within a disobedient generation, among whom their distinctiveness is apparent, *as [they] hold firmly to the word of life*. To refer to the 'gospel' (*euangelion*), Paul can readily use *logos* (*word*) as a synonym, as he does here (and in 1:14, with *logos* there being translated 'gospel' [NIV]; see also 2 Cor. 2:17; cf. Eph. 1:13).

The meaning of the verb *epechō*, rendered either 'holding out' or 'holding firmly', is vigorously debated. Some scholars on both sides of this debate argue from the relevant lexical evidence (most of it outside the New Testament) that the other meaning is unfounded. But such conclusions are overdrawn. Evidence exists for both meanings when there is a direct object (as here), so that the word can indicate holding something (i.e. *hold[ing] firmly to the word of life*) or offering something ('holding out the word of life').[11] Both make sense in the context of Philippians. Paul certainly affirms the importance of the church's continuing steadfastness in relation to the gospel, whether by highlighting God's continuing work in them (1:6; 2:13) or the need for their accompanying endurance (1:27; 2:12; 4:1). So his desire for them to *hold firmly* to the gospel fits well the letter's emphases. And in the immediate context (2:15), an intention for them to offer the gospel to others fits the implicit missional emphasis already begun in the reference

---

11. See Keown's extended discussion, I, pp. 488–492.

to their illuminating distinctiveness in society (*shining like stars* in the world).

The phrase *word of life* occurs nowhere else in Paul's letters (cf. 1 John 1:1). As already noted, *word* (*logos*) here is synonymous with the gospel. The additional descriptor, *life* (*zōē*), indicates either that the gospel *brings* life (genitive of result) or that the gospel *is* life (genitive of apposition). It may be that, with this phrasing, Paul provides an additional allusion from Deuteronomy 32. Later in that chapter, after the song of Moses concludes and the narrative resumes, the author emphasizes the importance of Israel obeying 'all the words [*logoi*] of this law' (32:46) and provides the rationale for their obedience: 'because for you this is not an empty word, since it is your life' (32:47, LXX, using *logos* for 'word' and *zōē* for 'life'). The law or Torah is referred to as Israel's very life (cf. 32:47b). If Paul has this text in view, he analogously identifies the gospel as the lifeblood of these Jews and Gentiles who believe in Jesus, the Jewish Messiah. The gospel will also prove to be life-giving for any among the present generation who respond positively to the Philippians' distinctive witness (2:15b–16a).

The faithfulness and obedience of the Philippians will bear fruit for Paul as well. Paul points to his desire to boast about the Philippians *on the day of Christ*. He has already referred to the 'day of Christ [Jesus]' in his opening thanksgiving and prayer (1:6, 10) to signal what the Scriptures called 'the day of the Lord' – the eschatological horizon when Israel's God would enact ultimate restoration and justice. Paul's end expectation centres on Christ and his divinely granted authority (2:10–11) and involves the vindication and perfection of Christ's followers (1:28; 3:14, 21).

Language of boasting (*kauchēma*) reappears here, having been introduced in 1:26. In that earlier context, Paul references boasting in Christ (also at 3:3). Such boasting is eminently appropriate as Christ is the centre of the believer's hope and life. Yet here Paul speaks of his own end-time boast or celebration because of the Philippians.[12] Paul considers boasting in the fruit of his God-given

---

12. For more on the ancient convention of boasting, see Cohick, pp. 143–144.

ministry acceptable, given that it falls within the sphere of the work to which God has called him. We hear this line of reasoning explained in 2 Corinthians, a letter that frequently uses the language of boasting in fellow believers (*kauchēma* and its cognates). In 2 Corinthians 10:12–18, Paul defines proper boasting to include only the fruits of ministry accomplished among the people 'assigned' to him by God (10:13). He continues by insisting, 'we do not want to boast about work already done in someone else's territory' (10:16). The conclusion of his argument intimates that appropriate boasting in those people who are within one's God-given charge falls within the category of 'boasting in the Lord', since it is the Lord's work being done and the Lord who commends the workers (10:17–18). In line with this perspective, we hear of Paul's boast in his churches in other letters (e.g. 1 Cor. 15:31), and perhaps most poignantly in 1 Thessalonians: 'For what is our hope or our joy or our crown of boasting – is it not you? – before our Lord Jesus at his coming' (2:19, my translation).

The particular content of Paul's boast is framed negatively: *that I did not run or labour in vain*. Positively stated, the enduring faithfulness of the Philippian church will be the proof that his ministry among them was successful – that it bore the ultimate fruit of salvation, multiplication and holiness. For Paul, this will be cause for utmost celebration, with 'boasting' overlapping in semantic range with 'joy', 'glory' and the like. Paul commonly compares his ministry to the activities of labour or running, with the latter evoking the image of a race in an athletic game (e.g. Phil. 3:12–14; cf. 1 Cor. 9:24–27; Gal. 2:2).[13] The phrase *labour in vain* occurs a number of times in the Septuagint, and Paul may be borrowing it from there (whether intentionally or unintentionally). If the echo is intentional, it may be that Isaiah 65:23 is in mind, given its similar eschatological context. In Isaiah 65, we hear the idyllic description of the time of 'the new heaven and the new earth' (65:17, LXX). In that new time, 'the days of [God's] people' will be like 'the days of the tree of life' (65:22, LXX), evoking Genesis 2 in its Edenic perfection. In the last days, God's 'chosen ones will

---

13. Flemming, p. 136.

not *labour in vain*' (*kopiaō eis kenon*; 65:23, LXX [emphasis added]). If Paul has this text in mind, he desires the results of his own missional labour to match the Isaianic vision of God's people enjoying the fruit of their work (65:21–23).

## C. Joy over commingled service (2:17–18)

**17.** In 2:17–18, Paul turns to reflect on his relationship with the Philippian believers in line with the communal vision he has provided in 2:14–16. Echoes from Old Testament texts and images continue to enrich his discourse. And Paul continues envisioning a celebration at the final day, when he hopes to boast that his work among the Philippians has resulted in their ultimate salvation. He moves into metaphor to describe his ministry among them and their own service in response: *But even if I am being poured out like a drink offering on the sacrifice and service coming from your faith* ... The initial combination of conjunctions (*alla ei kai, but even if*) suggests that Paul considers his own *being poured out* as the ultimate result of his ministry to the Philippians. The meaning of this image, however, is not immediately apparent. Does *being poured out* reference Paul's death in ultimate service to Christ? Or is the entire scope of his ministry among the Philippians in view? And how does this image fit with the double metaphor of the *sacrifice and service* attributed to the Philippians?

Paul's core metaphor features a temple setting and portrays a liquid offering (a libation) being poured on to a sacrifice of some kind. For Paul, this picture would have resonated with his own Jewish context, and the Jerusalem temple specifically. For example, in Leviticus we read of the use of a libation of olive oil poured over a grain offering (Lev. 2:1). This image would also have resonated with the Philippians in their own setting, as drink offerings were a part of sacrificial practices in Greek and Roman temples. The particular kind of sacrifice in view may have been the 'commensal' sacrifice, which was followed by a common meal characterized by rejoicing.[14] This would certainly fit the letter's context, where Paul

---

14. Patterson, *Metaphors*, pp. 36–41, 87.

expressly highlights the mutual rejoicing that should typify his relationship with the Philippian believers (2:17b–18).

Patterson suggests that, on the Jewish side of the equation, the thanksgiving offering or *šĕlāmîm* (sometimes translated as the fellowship or peace offering) forms the backdrop for Paul's imagery (see Lev. 3:1–17; 7:11–34).[15] This offering included, as an integral part, the thanksgiving of the worshipper (Lev. 7:12–13, 15) and concluded with a meal of joy (cf. Deut. 12:7).[16] The thanksgiving offering was accompanied by a grain and drink offering (Lev. 7:12; Num. 6:17). Again, this would cohere nicely with the motif of rejoicing in Philippians 2:17–18.

This backdrop of cultic sacrifice clarifies the various parts of the metaphor cluster.[17] Paul's ministry is the drink offering that is poured over a sacrifice (*thysia*), which represents the Philippians' faith (with *faith* probably functioning as a genitive of apposition used to clarify the metaphor).[18] This dual image portrays a commingling of Pauline ministry and Philippian faith offered to God, with 'the actions of the Philippians as the primary offering'.[19] Yet Paul's metaphor menagerie is not yet complete. He layers in one more image tied to temple sacrifice: the *service* (*leitourgia*) that a priest would render in offering the sacrifice on behalf of a worshipper. This complexifies the composite image, by creating a picture of the Philippians as both the sacrifice offered on the altar and the agents of priestly service offering it. While such a portrait is not literally possible, it has great figurative potential. The Philippians' faith – that is, the whole-life response they give to Christ – is analogous to a sacrifice offered to God; and it corresponds to the priestly service performed at a temple. Their life of faith

---

15. Patterson, *Metaphors*, pp. 47–48, 110.

16. Wenham, *Leviticus*, pp. 74–75.

17. 'Sacrifice was a familiar action, a familiar complex of actions, to everyone in Paul's context, pagan or Jew' (Patterson, *Metaphors*, p. 86).

18. Their faith viewed broadly as trust and faithfulness is the sacrifice and service of the metaphor. Alternatively, the NIV's *coming from your faith* suggests a genitive of source.

19. Patterson, *Metaphors*, p. 92.

involves both a yielding attitude to divine initiative (1:6; 3:9) *and* active engagement (2:12).

Having explored Paul's rich set of metaphors, we can return to the question of whether Paul's role as *drink offering* refers to his sacrifice to the point of death. While *being poured out* certainly allows for the possibility of Paul's death as his final act of self-giving, the image is more expansive than this. The phrase metaphorically evokes his entire life in ministry and mission – his 'unstinting Christian practice'[20] – commingled with the whole-life faith of the Philippians, all in service to God. Even if Paul spends himself fully in this endeavour, he reports that he is *glad* and he 'rejoices' with the Philippians. Paul's inclusive *all of you* seems to be an intentional embrace of the whole church community. Even as there is some amount of division in the Philippian community (2:1–4; 4:2–3), Paul is not taking sides (see 4:2 and comment).[21] Instead, he addresses all members of the church.

**18.** Paul invites his Philippian sisters and brothers into the same stance of rejoicing: *So you too should be glad [chairō] and rejoice [synchairō] with me.* For Paul, sacrifice and self-offering are in no way contradictory to the disposition of joy, especially when life and ministry carried out for the good of the other (2:4) are done in partnership with the whole body. As Paul and the Philippians share together in gospel-centred ministry, service and mission, there is a shared experience of joy.

*Theology*
Paul's exhortation for the Philippians to work out their salvation raises the issue of the interaction of divine and human activity in salvation. As already suggested, Paul regularly describes Christian living and ministry as work in this letter. And this work is compatible with, and seen as a response to, the overarching and encompassing divine work of redemption. In 2:12–18, Paul also envisions the community's working out of their salvation as flowing from their identity as God's children, an identity that is, by

---

20. Patterson, *Metaphors*, p. 92.
21. Keown I, p. 509.

nature of the analogy, given and not earned. The image of believers in Jesus as children of God is a relational, covenantal image, drawn from Israel's covenantal experience with Yahweh.

This image is an important one for theological reflection, not least because it steers away from a transactional understanding of salvation towards a more relational one. The Old Testament portrays God as relational and intent on spreading light, life and blessing to all humanity through Israel. While Israel's frequent waywardness at times seems to thwart God's plan, through the incarnation God takes on flesh to be and represent fully faithful Israel in Jesus the Messiah. This relational portrait of the God who pursues human redemption frames all human activity pointed towards salvation as derivative – as a response to God's prior initiative.[22]

In 2:12–13, Paul highlights the Philippians' *present response* to God's work. As Hunsinger reflects, 'Paul writes here about the present tense of salvation. Its past and future tenses are presupposed but not explicated. In its future tense God will be all in all … In its past tense … salvation is a finished and perfect work.'[23] He goes on to affirm, 'In the present tense, while there is only one Saving Agent, there is more than one acting subject. God operates in the faithful, even as they also "cooperate" with [God's] saving work.'[24]

As we consider how Paul draws on Israel's story for his primarily Gentile audience, it is important to affirm clearly what Paul is *not* saying. Paul's purpose in tapping into Deuteronomy is not to propose a replacement theology, as if Israel were being replaced by Gentiles as God's children. The first point against such a reading is Paul's own Jewish identity, an identity he will soon describe in detail (3:4–6). While Paul's frame of reference for contemplating the particulars of his Jewish lineage and experience has undergone a profound transformation in the light of the arrival of

---

22. Paul elsewhere has no problem describing his mission as calling
    Gentiles to 'the obedience that comes from faith' (Rom. 1:5; 16:26).

23. Hunsinger, p. 70.

24. Hunsinger, p. 71.

the Messiah (3:7–8), he does not indicate that his Jewish identity
has been altered or eliminated (e.g. the first three descriptions of
3:5). And, given that the Philippian congregation is primarily
Gentile, we do not hear in this letter Paul's perspective on how
Jewish believers should live out the particulars of their Jewish
identity in the light of Christ's arrival, other than his warning
against pressuring Gentile Christians to observe the Torah (3:2;
cf. Gal. 2:14). Elsewhere, Paul allows for differences of practice
between Jewish and Gentile Christians, with the understanding
that a deep sense of welcome is to characterize their relationship
(Rom. 14:1 – 15:13).

A second argument against hearing a replacement theology at
2:13–16 follows from consideration of what seems to be Paul's
careful use of Israel's history. He alludes to *a particular point* in
Israel's history – their time in the wilderness and their disobedience
to Yahweh during those years. It is unfair to generalize this
historical moment, especially given that the unfaithfulness of the
wilderness generation is already a stock image in later Old Testament writings (e.g. Hos. 13:5–6; Amos 5:25–26). It is certainly
beyond Paul's intention with the Deuteronomy allusion to provide
a generalized anti-Jewish portrait of his own people.

In a contemporary context, it is important to grapple with the
tendency for the (now primarily Gentile) church to misread ancient
and modern Judaism, as well as to recognize how Gentile Christianity has historically used certain New Testament texts to
misrepresent Judaism and even to harm Jewish people. An ethical
reading of Philippians should take such historical patterns into
account.[25]

What Paul exhibits in Philippians, even if not as clearly as he
does in other letters where Scripture is used more transparently and
extensively, is reliance on the Old Testament – its stories, images

---

25. See Brown and Roberts, 'Reading Judaism Ethically in the Post-
     Holocaust Era', in *Matthew*, pp. 506–522, with the goal of that chapter
     'to suggest there are better ways of reading Judaism in Matthew that
     are truer to the realities of its historical setting and more sensitive to
     avoiding any potentially harmful effects today' (p. 522).

and texts. It seems clear that Paul finds the Hebrew Scriptures 'God-breathed' and 'useful for teaching, rebuking, correcting and training in righteousness' (2 Tim. 3:16).

# 6. TIMOTHY AND EPAPHRODITUS AS EXEMPLARS: SERVICE TO OTHERS (2:19–30)

*Context*

Continuing the alternation between exhortations and exemplars, Paul turns from encouraging his audience to live out their salvation in ways that illuminate the gospel, to highlighting two exemplars known to the Philippian believers – Timothy and Epaphroditus – who are models for the Philippians to emulate. Paul's inclusion of these commendations at this point in the letter, rather than at its conclusion where such 'news' items would normally be included, emphasizes these two people as exemplars for the Philippian congregation.[1] Precisely because of the practical nature of this section of the letter (i.e. Paul outlining his actions and plans in relation to these two co-workers), it can be easy to overlook its insights for better understanding the relationship between Paul and the Philippians, and with these two individuals. In these practical ruminations, Paul recommends the exemplary

---

1. Bird and Gupta, p. 98.

patterns set by Timothy and Epaphroditus, since they live out the calling to prioritize the other that Paul has commended earlier (2:2–4) in their behaviour both towards Paul and towards the Philippian congregation.

Timothy (2:19–24) has already been mentioned in 1:1, identified along with Paul as an originator of the letter. Paul's reflections on Timothy in the third person in 2:19–24 clarify that Timothy is a co-sponsor of the letter rather than co-author (see Introduction 2a), a role (co-sponsor) attributed to him more than once in the Pauline correspondence (2 Cor. 1:1; Col. 1:1; 1 Thess. 1:1; 2 Thess. 1:1). Paul's description of Timothy as one who looks out for the interests of the Philippians and so those of Christ (2:20–21) echoes Paul's earlier exhortation to look out for the interests of others (2:4). In this passage, Paul also reiterates his confidence (*peithō*) that he himself will be able to return and see the Philippians soon (2:24; cf. 1:25–26).

Paul first mentions Epaphroditus here in the letter, although it can be inferred from his discussion that Epaphroditus, as he returns to their community, has brought the letter itself to the congregation (2:25, 29). For present-day readers of Philippians, this section (2:25–30), along with 4:18, helps us reconstruct the occasion of the letter (see Introduction 2e). Given the length of this passage and Paul's energetic commendation of Epaphroditus in it, some scholars have suggested that the Philippians may have needed convincing to welcome back Epaphroditus with open arms. This suggestion has then generated a few distinct reconstructed scenarios that might account for a need for such a strong recommendation (for examples, see comment on 2:25).

The way Paul describes Timothy and Epaphroditus – as co-workers with Paul for the sake of the gospel (2:22, 25) – resonates with similar language he will use to describe Euodia and Syntyche, co-workers who 'contended at [Paul's] side in the cause of the gospel' (4:2–3). Paul will also reference a larger group of co-workers (which includes Clement) at 4:3, signalling his solidarity with believers in Philippi in the ministry of the gospel.

*Paul's rhetorical emphases in Philippians 2:19–30:* In this part of the letter Paul moves away from logos, or argument (cf. 2:12–18), and relies heavily on ethos and pathos. Contributing to ethos, he demonstrates his own concern for his Philippian sisters and brothers in the faith by communicating his desire soon to send Timothy in his stead to care for their needs and, upon his return, to hear from Timothy that they are doing well (2:19–20). He also heightens ethos by sharing his concern for their well-being, a concern that propels him to return Epaphroditus to Philippi (2:28). All of this also works to prompt a sense of pathos in his audience – to stir their affections for him (and for Timothy and Epaphroditus) and, potentially, to cause them to breathe a sigh of relief at Epaphroditus's safe return after his serious illness. Paul's reliance on ethos and pathos in this section not only has the potential to strengthen the already solid relationship he shares with the Philippians; it also invites these believers in a personal and compelling way into emulation of Timothy and Epaphroditus as role models of other-focused living.

## Comment
### A. The model provided by Timothy (2:19–24)

**19.** Paul begins a new subsection of the letter, engaging with practical, logistical matters – in the first case related to his co-worker Timothy. Paul expresses his expectation to send Timothy, who is with Paul as he writes (1:1), in his stead to encourage the Philippian church. Timothy's relationship with the Philippian church is assumed in the letter (here and at 1:1), so it can be helpful to review what we know about that relationship from other sources. In Paul's earlier or contemporaneous letters, we gain hints of Timothy playing a regular and important role in Paul's itinerant ministry. He is a co-sponsor of 1 and 2 Thessalonians, 2 Corinthians and Colossians (indicated in the opening of each), and Paul refers to him as his co-worker (*synergos*) in the greetings of Romans 16 (v. 21). He has an important role in the Thessalonian and Corinthian congregations, travelling to these cities to encourage the believers there and to carry news from and to Paul (1 Thess. 3:2, 6; 1 Cor. 4:17; 16:10).[2] Turning to Acts, Luke

---

2. While some suggest that Paul's commendation of Timothy in Phil. 2:19–24 reveals an underlying tension between the Philippians and

narrates Timothy's conversion and circumcision (as Timothy's mother was Jewish) in the paragraph before Paul and his company turn towards the region of Macedonia (in Greece) and to Philippi more particularly (Acts 16). Although Paul and Silas are the primary persons in the account of the founding of the Philippian church (e.g. 16:19, 25, 29), Timothy and the author of Acts are also part of the entourage – part of the 'we' who travel with Paul in Acts 16:10 (cf. 16:3–4). And Timothy is expressly mentioned again at Acts 17:14–15. Although not named and highlighted in the account about Philippi, there is no indication that he would have been in any way out of favour with or inconsequential to the church at Philippi.[3] For the purposes of Acts, Paul and Silas are the important protagonists of Acts 16 since they are both Roman citizens, a key facet of the plot twist in the chapter (16:37–39). Additionally, Timothy presumably interacts with the Philippian believers more than once after this initial engagement (Acts 19:21–22; 20:1–6) and so quite probably was well known to them.

Even in the practical matter of whether to send Timothy to Philippi (Phil. 2:19), we can hear Paul's theological point of view. He *hope[s] in the Lord Jesus* that he might send Timothy, framing his plans in the light of the Lordship of Jesus. While we could hear *kyrios* (*Lord*) as merely a title here, it is likely that Paul means more by the phrase (*en kyriō, in the Lord*), given its use as a frame for 2:19–24, with its repetition at 2:24 signalling Paul's confidence in his own arrival in Philippi after not too long: 'I am confident *in the Lord* that I myself will come soon' (emphasis added). Additionally, Paul has, just prior to this passage, identified 'Jesus Christ is Lord' as the central confession of allegiance for Christians (2:11), so it would not be far-fetched for the reader to hear the language of *kyrios* in 2:19 and 24 evoking that central confession expressed in the Christ poem.[4]

---

(note 2 *cont.*) Timothy, Paul's commendations of Timothy at 1 Thess. 3:2 and 1 Cor. 4:17 suggest that Phil. 2:19–24 fits a pattern of commendation.

3. *Pace* Hawthorne, pp. 153–154.

4. Note Hawthorne's translation: 'I hope, under the Lordship of Jesus, to send Timothy . . .' (p. 151).

Timothy's assignment, when he is able to leave Paul and travel to Philippi, seems to be twofold. Mentioned in this verse, his role would be liaison between Paul and the Philippian church, providing news of these believers upon his return to Paul. In this way, Paul would *be cheered* (*eupsycheō*), a term that includes the idea of being relieved of anxiety (BDAG, p. 417). Beginning with this term, and across this section, Paul will utilize language related to anxiety and relief from it to express the depth of the relationships that exist among the Philippians and Timothy, Epaphroditus and Paul himself (see comments on 2:20 and 26–28, and Theology below). In the final words of the verse (*news about you*), Paul draws on a compact grammatical pattern he has used before to reference his own or the Philippians' situation.[5] This phrase will be repeated in the next verse as the object of Timothy's concern, rendered helpfully in the NIV as 'your welfare'.[6]

**20.** Timothy, if he travelled to Philippi, would also function as a stand-in for Paul, ministering to the Philippian church by caring for their needs and growth. Paul makes this role clear in his high commendation of Timothy: *I have no one else like him, who will show genuine concern for your welfare.* The first phrase, in which Paul says he has no-one *like* Timothy, includes the term *isopsychos* (*like him*), a synonym of *sympsychos* ('one in spirit') already commended in 2:2, with the idea in both cases of being like-minded or sharing the same attitude (L&N, p. 322). In his unity with Paul, Timothy demonstrates the communal posture Paul commends for the entire church. The term Paul uses to signal Timothy's concern for the Philippian church is *merimnaō*, which has the sense of being apprehensive to the point of significant anxiety or showing care or

---

5. Consisting of a plural article + preposition + pronoun (as at 1:27; cf. 2:23); here, woodenly, 'the [things] about you' (*ta peri hymōn*). See comment on 1:12.

6. A result of using this compact construction is that it allows the reader to supply for the phrase the nuance appropriate from context. In 2:19, Paul hopes to be cheered by receiving 'news about you' (the Philippian church). In 2:20, Timothy is a person who shows genuine concern 'for your welfare'.

concern for something or someone (BDAG, p. 632). The latter sense fits best here, although it is intriguing that Paul will guide the Philippians away from being anxious about anything, using the same term (*merimnaō*) at 4:6. In 2:20, Timothy's disposition towards the Philippians is one of being rightly concerned about and invested in the Philippian church.

**21.** Paul moves to explaining why no-one else is like Timothy in caring for the Philippians on Paul's behalf, and he does so by borrowing language from earlier in the chapter: *For everyone looks out for their own interests, not those of Jesus Christ.* Paul has used the same construction (*ta heatōn*: 'own interests') at 2:4, where he has discouraged the Philippians from focusing on their own interests over the interests of others (see comment there). In 2:21, the contrast is between one's own interests and the interests of Christ, implicitly aligning Christ's interests with the interests of the other and providing a compelling vision of Jesus' identification with his people.

The reference to *everyone* in contrast to Timothy may be generic, as Paul accents Timothy's exemplary, even rare, other-centred mindset. Alternatively, Paul may be obliquely indicting those in his arena who pursue their own interests fuelled by a selfish mindset. In the letter itself, we have heard about some who fit this description in 1:15–17: those who compete with Paul in the environs of his imprisonment as they preach the gospel 'out of selfish ambition' (1:17; cf. 2:3). Timothy provides a contrasting example to this selfish mindset and so can be a trustworthy guide for living out the exhortations Paul has outlined in 2:1–4.

**22.** Paul calls on the Philippians as witnesses to his assessment of Timothy's character: *you know that Timothy has proved himself.* Paul's evidence for this claim taps into Timothy's qualifications, both functional and relational. Timothy has served with Paul *in the work of the gospel* (*euangelion*), and Timothy has been to Paul like a son – like his own child (*teknon*) – in that work (also in 1 Cor. 4:17). Paul has referred to himself and Timothy in the very first line of the letter as 'slaves of Christ Jesus' (*doulos*); now he refers to Timothy as one who has served (*douleuō*) with him, the verbal cognate of the noun used at 1:1, indicating total service to a cause (BDAG, p. 259) – in this case, to the gospel.

**23–24.** Following Paul's tribute to Timothy, he repeats his hope that he might dispatch Timothy to Philippi in his stead. What keeps him from doing so, it seems, is the uncertainty of Paul's imminent trial and its outcome. As soon as Paul has a better sense of what lies ahead,[7] it appears that he will send Timothy to update the Philippians on the particulars of his situation. It may be that Paul desires Timothy's counsel on matters related to his trial or that he simply needs Timothy's presence with him until there is more clarity about Paul's future. If Paul is, as seems likely, in military custody shackled to one or more soldiers, Timothy would provide him with needed resources, physical and spiritual, for his well-being (see Introduction 2c).

These two verses (23–24) are connected by a *men* ... *de* construction in Greek that signals a correlation, and some type of a contrast, between the ideas of the two verses (having the sense of 'on the one hand ... and on the other ...'). In this specific instance, it is the initial verbs that form a contrast of sorts: Paul 'hopes' (*elpizō*; also in 2:19) to send Timothy, while he is *confident* (*peithō*) that he will be able to rejoin the Philippians soon. This confidence echoes Paul's earlier affirmation of the same: 'convinced' (*peithō*) that his release is necessary for the Philippians, Paul 'knows' (*oida*) he will have opportunity to return to the Philippians (1:25). Paul continues to assure the Philippians that God will work in his situation for their benefit. He qualifies his statement of confidence with the phrase *in the Lord*. His confidence is grounded in his trust in Christ (the referent of *the Lord*), as is his hope to send Timothy (2:19). In both cases, Paul frames his hopes and plans under the direction of Jesus as his Lord.

## B. The model provided by Epaphroditus (2:25–30)

**25.** In 2:25–30, Paul turns from Timothy to the example of Epaphroditus, who is returning to Philippi and the church there, presumably delivering the letter itself as he returns (see Intro-

---

7. Using the same grammatical construction (article + preposition + pronoun); see comment on 2:19.

duction 2e). Because Paul has no need to introduce Epaphroditus to his own home congregation, commentators have suggested that the sheer length of space Paul devotes to him in the letter (2:25–30; cf. 4:18) signals some problem or issue between the Philippians and Epaphroditus. One proposal is that Epaphroditus needed to return home, unable to complete the service to Paul for which the Philippians commissioned him (2:25b). Evidence for this view includes not only the length of Paul's explanation but also the 'almost apologetic' sound of Paul's opening, *I think it is necessary.*[8] Another proposal, offered tentatively by Silva, is that the Philippians were expecting Timothy – that is, an apostolic visit – not Epaphroditus. But since the latter was unable to stay with Paul, Paul needed Timothy to remain with him at a precarious time. So Paul sent Epaphroditus back home, along with his commendation.[9] While these are possible scenarios, it is just as likely that Paul's focus on Epaphroditus, like his words about Timothy, is meant to do double duty: it both offers important details of explanation about Paul's decisions related to his co-workers, and provides the example of Epaphroditus for the Philippians to follow.[10]

While Paul has indicated that he hopes to send Timothy to Philippi (2:19, 23), he considers it *necessary to send back* Epaphroditus. Paul has used this strong language (*anankaios*, a 'necessity' versus a hope or a desire) already at 1:24, where he talks of his possible release from prison as (more) 'necessary' (*anankaioteron*) for the Philippians' benefit. As we will see, Epaphroditus's illness and the potential depth of the Philippians' concern about him apparently provide at least a part of this 'necessity' (2:26).

Paul describes Epaphroditus in glowing terms, with a number of descriptors. The two consecutive pronouns (*mou, my*, and *hymōn, your*) clearly divide the verse into Epaphroditus's roles related to Paul and his role related to the Philippians. On Paul's side, Epaphroditus has functioned as *brother, co-worker and fellow soldier.*

---

8. Bockmuehl, p. 170; also Thielman, p. 153.

9. Silva, p. 136.

10. Fee argues that 'this profession of commendation is part of [the] affection' that is apparent in every part of the letter (p. 273).

While *brother* (*adelphos*) is the expected term for a fellow believer, it is instructive to compare it with Paul's description of Timothy as his 'son' (*teknon*) in the previous paragraph. It may be that Paul intentionally places Epaphroditus on equal terms with himself with this word, while still retaining the familial connection and warmth common to both terms. The descriptors *co-worker and fellow soldier* (for the latter, cf. Phlm. 2) highlight Epaphroditus's role sharing with Paul in the ministry of the gospel, or as Paul will frame it, 'the work of Christ' (2:30). Epaphroditus, as *co-worker* (*synergos*) with Paul, belongs to a larger group of co-workers Paul mentions later in the letter – a group that comprises Euodia, Syntyche, Clement and 'the rest of [Paul's] co-workers [*synergoi*]' (4:2–3).

In relationship to the Philippians, Epaphroditus is described as their *messenger* (*apostolos*). While most occurrences of this term in the Pauline literature carry a more narrow, semi-technical sense (e.g. Rom. 1:1; 11:13; 16:7; 1 Cor. 9:2, 5; 15:7, 9; Gal. 1:1, 17, 19), this use, along with that in 2 Corinthians 8:23, probably conveys the general sense of 'messenger' or 'emissary' – one who stands in as representative for the sender(s).[11] In these latter two cases, the *apostolos* functions in relationship to a specific church (e.g. Epaphroditus as *the Philippians'* messenger, sent out from them). Some scholars suggest the more technical meaning is being used by Paul here to indicate that Epaphroditus had attempted a stint as an apostle in his time with Paul but did not succeed.[12]

The Philippians have sent Epaphroditus in a particular role as their messenger and stand-in to *take care of [Paul's] needs*. Paul will describe in more detail how the Philippians have provided for him in 4:16–18, where Paul refers to 'the gifts' they sent to him through Epaphroditus to attend to his needs. The language for *needs* (*chreia*) is the same here as at 4:16 ('when I was in need'), a connection which highlights Epaphroditus's role in service to Paul. Epaphroditus's service is described by the Greek term *leitourgos*, a word that indicates a person who serves, often in relation to cultic or temple service – for example, a priest. The more specific and

---

11. Brown, 'Apostle', p. 472.
12. Osiek, p. 79.

elevated sense can carry over in non-cultic contexts (BDAG, p. 591) and seems to be applicable here, especially since Paul will use the cognate, *leitourgia* ('service' or 'help'), in close proximity (2:30; cf. 2:17 with its cultic use). By describing Epaphroditus with this term, Paul stresses the significance of his service for Paul, which included his delivery of financial support but also involved his presence with Paul. This dual service provided by Epaphroditus – messenger and also stand-in for the Philippians' presence – makes the most sense in context given Paul's need to explain at the outset why he has sent Epaphroditus back to Philippi. If his only mission was to deliver the church's gift to Paul, he would not have been expected to stay with Paul for any length of time. Epaphroditus was also, it seems, meant to stay with Paul to help and encourage him (see comment on 2:23–24). And Epaphroditus's presence and personal service while Paul was in prison functioned as a service performed as if by the Philippians themselves. The service Epaphroditus rendered to Paul stood in for their service (with 'help' rendering *leitourgia*): 'the help you yourselves could not give me' (2:30).

**26.** Paul turns in 2:26–28 to provide the rationale (*for*) for his sense of necessity in sending Epaphroditus home. At the centre of that rationale is Epaphroditus's unanticipated and serious illness (2:26–27). Paul begins in 2:26 by speaking of Epaphroditus's longing and distress while he was with Paul. Epaphroditus was longing for his spiritual family at home in Philippi. This term (*epipotheō*) has been used earlier by Paul to express his own longing for the Philippians – a longing grounded in 'the affection of Christ Jesus' (1:8). Similar language will reappear at 4:1, where Paul refers to the Philippians as those 'whom I ... long for' (*epipothētos*). Epaphroditus was also distressed, knowing his Philippian siblings in Christ (*all of you*) would have learned that he was ill. Paul uses *adēmoneō*, a term that denotes being distressed, anxious, troubled (BDAG, p. 19). This potent language is used elsewhere in the New Testament only to describe Jesus' deep distress in Gethsemane on the eve of his crucifixion (Matt. 26:37; Mark 14:33). This is the second time in 2:19–30 that Paul describes a kind of relational anxiety that exists among his co-workers, himself and the Philippians (see comment on 2:20). Epaphroditus, exhibiting a concern for others over self (e.g. 2:4), cares about how his spiritual family would be receiving word of his illness, worrying because they might worry (see Theology below).

Paul does not make clear the nature of Epaphroditus's illness and would not have needed to do so, as Epaphroditus could have filled in details for his fellow believers upon his return to Philippi, with letter in hand. The language used is quite general (*astheneō*), indicating a debilitating illness or, even more broadly, a weakness of some kind (BDAG, p. 142). We glean from context that it was serious enough to bring him to the brink of death (2:27, 30). Although nothing is said about when Epaphroditus contracted his illness, he would have done so either while he was travelling to Paul or sometime after he arrived at Paul's location.

Scholars often deliberate about when and how the Philippians heard of Epaphroditus's illness, although such determinations contribute more to the question of the letter's provenance (where Paul writes from) than to the meaning of the passage itself. A great part of this interest has to do with reconstructing the number of communications and/or treks that occurred between Paul and the Philippian church related to the letter and its contents. The greater the number of trips, the less likely it is that Paul is imprisoned in Rome – a good 800-mile (*c*.1,300-km) journey from Philippi – and the more likely that Paul writes from a closer destination like Ephesus, about a 300-mile trip (*c*.500 km) from Philippi (see Introduction 2c). Relevant to that discussion, we can note that the language *you heard he was ill* does not require that Paul has received word (by letter or person) that news of Epaphroditus's illness had been delivered to the Philippians. It only requires that this news had been sent to the Philippian church and time enough had elapsed for Paul and Epaphroditus to be fairly certain the Philippians now knew of the illness.[13] Wondering if the Philippians had already received this news and how they might be responding could have actually increased Epaphroditus's worries. A papyrus letter from the second or third century AD (from a soldier to his

---

13. To put it another way, the verb *heard* applies to the Philippians hearing news of the illness and not to Paul and Epaphroditus hearing news of the Philippians having received the news.

mother) provides an interesting parallel of familial concern: 'I was much grieved [*lypeō*; cf. *lypē*, 2:27] to hear that you had heard about me, for I was not seriously ill' (MM, p. 382).

**27.** Paul repeats that Epaphroditus was ill (using the same Greek term) and includes that he was 'near death', indicating a physical and serious malady of some kind.[14] In the same breath as he describes the direness of the situation, Paul heralds God's intervention: *But God had mercy on him*. Paul uses language of mercy most often in relation to the granting of salvation. But in this case, he highlights God's compassionate healing of Epaphroditus and the extension of mercy to Paul as well – to spare him *sorrow upon sorrow* (*lypēn epi lypēn*). Here, Paul indicates the depth of grief he would have experienced if Epaphroditus had died. It is possible to hear this phrase, with its double use of 'sorrow' connected with the preposition, signalling an 'even greater sorrow'. In this case, interpreters seek to identity the first sorrow Paul has in mind (e.g. Paul's current imprisonment). More likely, *sorrow upon sorrow* is a figurative expression, with the piling up of sorrow used to indicate the deep sorrow Paul was anticipating had he lost Epaphroditus to an untimely death.

**28.** Having explained Epaphroditus's near-death illness and the ensuing relational and emotional impact, Paul continues to discuss his decision to return Epaphroditus to Philippi and to the church there. He indicates his eagerness to send Epaphroditus back home as springing from the joy the Philippians will experience upon seeing Epaphroditus once again, intimating that they too would have been grief-stricken if they had lost him (*when you see him again you may be glad*). This glad reunion will also have an impact on Paul, in spite of his physical distance from them. Paul speaks of having *less anxiety* upon the congregation being reunited with their spiritual brother and messenger. Paul's use of *alypos* (in comparative form: 'less anxious') echoes his description of being spared 'sorrow upon sorrow' (using *lypē*, 2:27). Fee argues against 'free from anxiety' as a definition for *alypos* by suggesting that the first letter, alpha, in

---

14. And almost assuredly ruling out homesickness or emotional instability as the issue (Hawthorne's view, p. 165).

*alypos* simply negates the stem *lypē* ('sorrow' or 'affliction') and results in 'free from sorrow'.[15] Even if he is correct about the formal relationship between the two terms, *lypē* can denote anxiety (BDAG, p. 605), and so *alypos* can mean 'free from anxiety'. Regarding this connection, ancient writers 'often spoke of grief in terms of anxiety'.[16] That Paul could express a sense of anxiety about the well-being of his fellow believers is clear from 2 Corinthians 11:28, where Paul notes his 'anxiety [*merimna*] for all the churches' (NRSV).

Knowing that Epaphroditus is out of harm's way has kept Paul from deep sorrow or anxiety (*lypē*, 2:27) and made possible a reunion of his dear friends that will alleviate much of his present anxiety (*alypoteros*, 2:28). The relational angst of these verses turns into a renewed possibility of joy because of divine mercy. The pervasive theme of joy (*be glad*) in the letter reappears here (cf. 1:25; 2:2, 17–18).

**29.** From descriptions of Epaphroditus's situation and anticipated return, Paul turns to commendation. He encourages the Philippians to welcome Epaphroditus, as he returns and as he delivers Paul's letter. While an array of terms could be used for 'welcoming' someone, Paul uses *prosdechomai*, which he uses similarly at Romans 16:2 to encourage the Romans to welcome Phoebe, the carrier of that letter (16:1–2). Paul modifies the verb with two prepositional phrases, *in the Lord* and *with great joy*, both thematic in the letter. On the theme of joy, Paul has just written that he anticipates that the Philippians will rejoice (*chairō*) when they see Epaphroditus; and now he exhorts them to welcome him with *great joy* (*pas* + *chara*). The other modifier, *in the Lord* (*en kyriō*), forms a pervasive refrain in this part of Philippians (2:19, 24, 29; 3:1), potentially stemming from the climactic confession of 2:11 – 'Jesus Christ is Lord' (see comment at 2:19). In addition to welcome, Paul calls the Philippian congregation to *honour people like him*, including Epaphroditus in this distinction but also pointing

---

15. Fee, p. 281 n. 40.

16. Holloway, p. 183 (see his references to Seneca, Plutarch and Cassius Dio).

to him as an exemplar: a standard for admirable behaviour and commitments.

The exhortation to honour (*entimous*) Epaphroditus taps into discussions of honour and practices promoting honour that were prominent in Roman society, but Paul inverts expectations by exhorting honour of those who focus their energies on the 'work of Christ' (2:30) – that is, a Messiah who humbled himself to the point of crucifixion (2:8).[17] By calling for honour to be bestowed on *people like him*, Paul both highlights that Epaphroditus is worthy of honour and demonstrates his service as exemplary for others. The scope of those in view is not limited to Christian leaders but includes all who commit themselves to 'the work of Christ'. Although *tous toioutous* (*people like him*) is a masculine pronoun, it very probably functions here as a generic (with the masculine linguistic gender filling this role in ancient Greek): not 'such men' (e.g. ESV) but 'such ones', to include any persons who are like Epaphroditus in their faithful service.

**30.** Paul concludes by providing the reason for such welcome and honour of Epaphroditus: *because he almost died for the work of Christ*. Paul reaffirms the serious nature of Epaphroditus's illness, using the same language used to describe Christ at 2:8 – *mechri thanatou* ('to the point of death') – and almost certainly echoing intentionally that part of the Christ poem with this distinctive phrasing. Epaphroditus is imitating Christ, who became obedient to the point of death. Epaphroditus has come near to death because of his loyalty to *the work of Christ*. This way of expressing the ministry of the gospel is unique within the Pauline epistles, and it seems some scribes found the phrase, which has strong manuscript support, unusual enough that they reverted in their copying to 'the work of the Lord' (as Paul writes in 1 Cor. 15:58; 16:10) or 'the work of God' (see Rom. 14:20), or by dropping the modifier altogether.

Paul describes Epaphroditus as having *risked his life*, which provides a general reference to his serious illness, whether contracted while travelling to Paul or when with him. Paul highlights the courage of Epaphroditus in putting the interests of

---

17. Hellerman, p. 163.

spiritual kin: Timothy as a son to him (2:22), Epaphroditus so dear
that his death would have been a 'sorrow upon sorrow' (2:27), and
with news of his Philippian brothers and sisters having the capacity
to cheer him or cause him anxiety (2:19, 28). On Epaphroditus's
part, he has felt distress anticipating how his home congregation
would be responding to his illness (2:26), and Paul describes their
reunion upon Epaphroditus's return as making the believers there
glad (2:28).[19] The 'language of emotional interconnectedness' is
palpable in this part of the letter.[20]

Although we may not be used to considering reflection on such
'mundane' features of the biblical text as rising to the level of
theology, I believe we would lose much by ignoring these rich
relational moments in Philippians. Fredrickson observes that
modern commentators on Paul often overlook the theological
import of Paul's suffering that comes from 'feeling [Christ's]
absence . . . or missing his beloved friends'.[21] Instead, Fredrickson
references the 'possibility of thinking about God, Christ, the
church, and the world from the experience of loss and grief'.[22]

To consider anxiety theologically in conversation with Philippians involves hearing what the social sciences have discovered
about anxiety. By tapping into this area of human knowledge (a
part of general revelation), we are able to sidestep hasty assessments
of the oft-quoted verse from later in Philippians: 'Do not be
anxious about anything . . .' (4:6). Such quickly formed assessments
may judge all anxiety to be sin or assume anxiety to be simply a
matter of choice. In their book on relational spirituality, Sandage
et al. distinguish between depth and surface views of anxiety.
From a depth perspective, anxiety 'can be problematic but can also

---

19. Even if the church has some hesitation regarding Epaphroditus's
    accomplishment of the tasks to which he was commissioned and
    needed Paul's encouragement to welcome him (2:29–30), Paul seems to
    tap into an existing relationship strong enough to weather whatever
    breach had occurred.
20. Bird and Gupta, p. 99.
21. Fredrickson, *Christology*, p. 37.
22. Fredrickson, *Christology*, p. 39.

others before his own (2:4) in service to Paul. The way Pa
describes Epaphroditus's service emphasizes again his role as
stand-in for the Philippian church: *to make up for the help [leitourgi*
*you yourselves could not give me.*

Paul illuminates the service that the Philippians were unable to
provide themselves (but did provide through Epaphroditus) with
a pair of related terms that indicate a lack (*hysterēma*: *could not give*)
that is filled (*anaplēroō*: *make up for*).[18] The same word pair is used in
1 Corinthians 16:17, where Paul refers to three believers from the
Corinthian church who, by their arrival, have 'supplied what was
lacking from you. For they refreshed my spirit' (1 Cor. 16:17–18a;
cf. 2 Cor. 9:12). These similar contexts demonstrate that this
language is not used by Paul negatively to point out a deficiency in
or an intentional withholding by his audience. Instead, the word
pair appears to signal that what the whole community simply could
not do (travel to be present with Paul in prison), one or more emis-
saries could accomplish, thereby ministering effectively to Paul in
his need.

*Theology*
The writing of this commentary coincided with a worldwide
pandemic, with all the relational angst that goes along with caring
deeply for family and friends in such a precarious time. So many
across our world have lost loved ones to the disease, experiencing
the deep grief that such loss entails. Paul's letter addresses death and
loss at a number of turns and so can offer guidance and hope for
those who trust in Christ, as it has for me and my family in the face
of devastating loss. Paul provides perspective on his own death,
which he frames in the light of his relationship with Christ (1:21–22).
In this passage (2:19–30), with all the relational warmth and concern
threaded through it, Paul had anticipated losing his dear friend
Epaphroditus to illness and was relieved when God spared his life.

In my own grief over the loss of my father, I have found comfort
in the ways Paul describes the web of relationships among his

---

18. Paul will return to these terms in his thanks for the Philippian gift
(4:10–20), using *hysterēma* at 4:11–12 and *plēroō* at 4:18–19.

serve an important activating function in the discovery and construction of meaning related to ultimate concerns about life and death'.[23] From this perspective, some level of anxiety is understood as a given of human existence.[24] The goal is not to eliminate all anxiety but to move towards a productive 'holding' of anxiety within the context of 'supportive attachments and well-differentiated relationships'.[25]

This kind of supportive web of relationships, I would suggest, is what we hear in Philippians and are especially privy to in 2:19-30, with language of anxiety woven together with expressions of warm attachment. There is no need to dismiss the presence of relational angst or assume that it is problematic. As Sandage, Jensen and Jass counsel, 'Even positive relational experiences, such as feeling known, understood, or loved, can provoke crucibles of anxiety as the existential shadow of possible loss looms.'[26] Although Paul holds a profound eschatological conviction that assuages fear of his own death (1:21; 3:11, 20-21), as he considered the possibility of the death of his dear brother Epaphroditus, Paul, it seems, faced an existential loss – one he can describe as a 'sorrow upon sorrow'. As Fee frames it,

> Without being maudlin or saccharine one may rightly note that Paul lived as a believer in a world surrounded by friends, that those friends brought him joy, and that the untimely death of such friends would have been for him immeasurable grief.[27]

It seems no accident that the section of Philippians in which Paul addresses personal and practical matters as well as various comings and goings also has a high proportion of language related

---

23. Sandage et al., *Spirituality*, p. 82.
24. Bird and Gupta suggest that, 'In some ways, to be human is to be anxious and feel unease', as they note Paul's use of the same verb for 'being anxious/concerned' in 2:20 (for Timothy) and 4:6 (p. 176).
25. Brown and Sandage, 'Relational Integration', p. 184.
26. Sandage, Jensen and Jass, 'Transformation', p. 195.
27. Fee, p. 284.

to what we could call 'relational anxiety'. Those we care about most deeply have the power and potential to move us into higher levels of concern for their well-being.

# 7. PAUL AS EXEMPLAR: A CONTRAST TO OPPONENTS OF THE GOSPEL AND THE CROSS (3:1 – 4:1)

In Philippians 3, Paul warns the Philippians about two groups of people who provide a vivid contrast to right ways of living in Christ (3:2, 18–19). Paul offers himself as a counter-example to these groups, as someone who has prioritized identifying with and knowing Christ (3:7–10) and whose mindset is shaped by what is still to come: resurrection and the arrival in this world of Jesus Christ and the heavenly commonwealth (3:11, 20–21).

## A. Paul's experience of prioritizing Christ (3:1–11)

*Context*
There is a change in topic and tone at the juncture of Philippians 2 and 3. Paul moves from commendation of Timothy and Epaphroditus and discussion of the matter of sending Epaphroditus home, to a warning about what seems to be an external threat to the Philippian congregation (3:1b–2). Given this seemingly abrupt shift – along with the introductory adverbial phrase, rendered 'further' (NIV) but which can also indicate a final turn in a letter

('finally'; see comment on 3:1), a number of commentators have argued that the shift illuminates a seam where two letters of Paul have been 'stitched' together. In this view, Philippians shows signs of being a composite of two or three shorter Pauline letters (see Introduction 3c). Reumann is representative in his identification of 4:10–20 as the first letter sent by Paul (a thank you for their gift), with 1:1 – 3:1 and potentially early parts of chapter 4 constituting a second letter. Philippians 3:2–21 would then make up the third letter received by the Philippians, with its warnings against various opponents.[1] Yet an increasing number of commentators argue for the integrity of the letter; that is, Philippians hangs together as a single letter. Part of the argument for the integrity of Philippians involves an allowance for Paul to address details about the dispatch of the letter prior to its conclusion (2:25–30) and a recognition that Paul's brief descriptions of opponents (3:2, 18–19) are intermingled with more detailed descriptions of his own example (3:4–14, 17). The latter is consistent with his offering of exemplars across Philippians 2, tying these two chapters more closely together than previously thought.

As Paul has been drawing on exemplars across the letter (Jesus, Timothy, Epaphroditus), he now points to himself as an example for the Philippians. His own mindset centred on the gospel leads him to put 'no confidence in the flesh' (3:3) and instead to consider everything a loss compared to 'the surpassing worth of knowing Christ' (3:8). Paul's deep desire to pattern his life after Jesus connects his expression of identification with Christ in 3:10–11 with the story of Christ narrated in 2:6–11. In 3:17, Paul explicitly exhorts the Philippian believers to 'join together in following [his] example' – a point on which he elaborates at 4:9.

Other themes from the letter woven into 3:1–11 include rejoicing (3:1; cf. 1:4, 18; 2:17–18; 4:4, 10) and the need to consider all things from a gospel mindset (3:7–8; cf. 2:2, 5; 3:13, 15; 4:2). Paul's eschatology is on display across this chapter as he considers his own final-day resurrection (3:11) and Christ's return and transformation of believers through resurrection (3:20–21).

---

1. Reumann, p. 3.

The 'opponents' Paul mentions at 3:2 may be the same group he references at 3:18–19, or they might be a distinct group. The brevity of Paul's comments makes it difficult to identify these groups 'with any precision', yet their function in the chapter as a counterpoint to Paul's positive example is clear enough.[2] I will argue that these two references identify distinct groups, with 3:2 referring to Christ-followers whose goal is to influence fellow believers who are Gentiles to become Jewish proselytes and take on circumcision and Torah-observance. A related issue is to determine whether this set of opponents is a current, active threat to the Philippian church (see comment at 3:2).

*Paul's rhetorical emphases in Philippians 3:1–11:* Paul leans heavily on ethos in this section of Philippians, as he provides his own example of assessing life before and after Christ (3:4–6 and 7–11, respectively). His intent is that the Philippians emulate his mindset, as they consider their own 'before Christ' and 'after Christ' experiences. Paul also uses logos, as he argues for the identity of Christ-followers as 'the circumcision' (3:3) and recounts that *where* he places his confidence has radically shifted in the light of the gospel, namely, the story of the death and resurrection of the Messiah.

## Comment

### i. Warning against confidence 'in the flesh' (3:1–3)

1. Paul changes topic at 3:1, moving from commendation of Epaphroditus and his service to both Paul and the Philippians (2:25–30) to a warning against putting confidence in anything but Christ (3:1–11). Yet the movement at 3:1 is not as abrupt as has often been claimed. One thread unifying the two sections is the use of exemplars for the Philippians to emulate. Having highlighted Christ and then Timothy and Epaphroditus (2:5–30), Paul now offers his own example. Other connecting motifs include service (*leitourgia*, 'help' in 2:30; *latreuō*, 'serve' or 'worship' in 3:3) and rejoicing (2:29; 3:1). Additionally, the conjunction that begins the chapter (*to loipon*, *further*) does not always signal a conclusion, as it clearly does in 2 Corinthians 13:11. For example, this term is used

---

2. Holloway, *Consolation*, p. 135.

for a transition and so translated 'As for other matters' at 2 Thessalonians 3:1 (*to loipon*) and 1 Thessalonians 4:1 (*loipon*). Given the aural reception of Philippians, Paul's use of terms 'expressing closure', such as *to loipon*, is quite natural. As such, 'in a text shaped for the ear', this term 'would have alerted the listener that one topic had ended and another was about to begin'.[3]

Paul's exhortation for his spiritual siblings to rejoice (3:1a) is followed by what seems to be a change of tone towards warning (3:1b). Paul indicates he is writing *the same things* (*ta auta*), although he does not make the referent clear. By *the same things* does he mean his exhortation to rejoice, which is repeated from 2:18 and 2:29? Or does Paul's use of the plural have a wider referent, including multiple exhortations and reminders already included in chapters 1–2? Alternatively, does *ta auta* point forward to his warnings of 3:2, with the implication that he has previously warned them about these people in earlier correspondence? Those who suggest the latter draw their conclusion, in part, from Paul's twofold observation about *the same things*: it is *no trouble* for him to raise again these warnings, and it provides *a safeguard* for the Philippians.

Yet there are other ways to understand and so translate these two terms: *oknēros* (*trouble*) and *asphalēs* (*safeguard*). Through comparison with many ancient letters, Reed has demonstrated that *oknēros* (or cognates) combined with 'to write' (*graphein*) is a common formula for indicating hesitation.[4] The use of this 'hesitation formula' communicates that an author is not being negligent but is fulfilling his or her duty to the audience.[5] For the Philippians' part, Paul's writing *the same things* provides a solid foundation for them (*sphalēs*; BDAG, p. 147). Thus, 3:1b could be rendered expansively, 'I do not hesitate to write the same things to you, and I do so to provide you with a solid foundation.'[6]

---

3. Achtemeier, 'Oral Environment', p. 26.

4. Or, with a negative (as here), a lack of hesitation.

5. Reed, *Discourse Analysis*, p. 238. His conclusion is embraced by Fowl (pp. 143–144) and Keown (II, pp. 96–97).

6. Cf. Fowl, p. 143.

Returning to the question of the referent for *the same things*, Paul is probably referring to the exhortation to rejoice that he has just written (3:1) and which provides the third such entreaty in the letter (2:18, 28–29). Paul, in line with letter-writing convention, assures the Philippians that he is not at all hesitant to reiterate his call to rejoice; he is, in fact, being faithful to them in repeating this exhortation, as it will put them on solid ground. Rejoicing is not simply Christian window dressing, but is a bedrock mindset and practice, especially for those in the throes of significant cultural pressure and even suffering (1:29–30) and in the light of other potential threats (3:2).

**2.** Having assured the Philippians that a stance of rejoicing in the Lord will give them a firm foundation, Paul turns to warn them about a potential threat to their allegiance to Christ. His warning comes in three staccato lines, each beginning with the same verb, *watch [out]* (*blepō*). The verb on its own does not have a negative cast, but in the context of its use here (with three negative objects) we rightly hear these as warnings. These descriptions are framed alliteratively, each beginning with a kappa sound: *watch out for those dogs* [*kynas*], *those evildoers* [*kakous ergatas*], *those mutilators of the flesh* [*katatomēn*]. Paul may be drawing on language and ideas from the three lines of Psalm 22:16 (Ps. 21:17, LXX) to frame his warning in the context of potential suffering faced by the Philippians as they stand against this threat, given that the early church aligned this psalm with Christ's sufferings at his crucifixion (see Matt. 27:46 and context).[7]

With this threefold description of those posing some kind of threat to the Philippian church, there is a shift in the letter's tone. While it may be tempting to consider Paul's use of this potent language as unnecessarily inflammatory, it can be helpful to note a few contextual features. First, the letter of friendship genre, with which Philippians shares at least some features, often employed warnings against 'enemies' as a stock feature.[8] Second, if Paul draws from Psalm 22 for these images and language, we could

---

7. Henderson, 'Overlooked Allusions'.

8. Stowers, 'Friends', pp. 115–117.

describe Paul's tone as 'impassioned but measured'.[9] Finally, Paul's audience is not those he describes in 3:2. Instead, he wants to warn *the Philippians*, and uses strong language to make that warning as effective as possible.

The three descriptions identify a single group, with Paul piling up forceful terms to signal the potential danger they pose to the Philippian church. The first term, *dogs*, was a 'general slur' in the ancient world, given that dogs were, for the most part, undomesticated or semi-domesticated, were associated with scavenging and, in both Jewish and Gentile contexts, were ritually impure.[10] The second term is equally vague in terms of referent: *evildoers* or 'evil workers'. It is only with the third term that the group's identity is clarified, especially against the wider backdrop of the Pauline letters.

The description *those mutilators of the flesh* captures the idea of *katatomē*, a noun referring to physical mutilation ('watch out for the mutilation'). This term plays on the word 'circumcision' (*peritomē*), used in 3:3. Paul is in all likelihood referring to attempts by certain Jewish believers in Jesus to compel Gentile believers to 'Judaize' – to become proselytes or converts to Judaism (*ioudaizō*; Gal. 2:14). These 'Judaizers', as they are often called, would have worked from the conviction that Gentiles were not yet full participants in God's community unless they converted. Paul was adamant that, because of the arrival of the Messiah, Gentile believers did not need to become members of Israel to be fully incorporated into God's eschatological, messianic community. In fact, if Gentile believers pursued circumcision and other distinctives of Jewish proselytism, they would be 'turning back' to what had previously enslaved them (Gal. 4:8–11). Paul's strong language in Philippians 3:2 frames such conversion as enacting not circumcision (the central sign of conversion to Judaism) but 'mutilation'.

In Galatians, Paul references attempts to 'Judaize' Gentile believers (Gal. 2:11 – 3:29), and most commentators see a similar

---

9. Holloway, *Consolation*, p. 133.
10. Zoccali, *Philippians*, p. 87, who agrees with Nanos that this was not well-established Jewish slang for Gentiles when Paul wrote (see Nanos, 'Dog').

issue as the backdrop for Philippians 3:2. Yet, given that Paul's warning here is fleeting and comes more than halfway through the letter, any challenge from 'Judaizers' seems only potential at this point and not an immediate threat. Especially given the way Paul includes this warning within his own counter-example, this group functions, at least in part, to highlight that comparison.

The Philippian church seems to have been primarily Gentile, made up of Greeks (e.g. Macedonians and others) and Romans, with other ethnicities from Philippi's slave population also probably represented (see Introduction 2b[ii]). The Jewish population of Philippi itself appears to have been fairly small, and this ratio would seem to apply to the make-up of the Philippian church as well. It is quite possible that, if there was pressure exerted on Gentile believers to become Jewish proselytes, it could have come from Christians outside their local fellowship as much as from within (cf. Gal. 2:12–13). Pressure towards Jewish conversion could also have arisen from existing social realities, one of which was Rome's allowance for Jewish people to provide offerings for the emperor instead of directly worshipping at the imperial cult. In this sociopolitical context, for Gentile believers to convert to Judaism would protect them from the prospect of civic pressure and potential persecution for refusing to participate in imperial worship.[11] If so, Paul's warning of 3:2 would encourage the Philippian church to hold fast to their identity in Christ (3:3, 8–9), which had already ushered them fully into God's covenantal community.

**3.** Paul concludes his forceful warning by affirming the Philippians' covenantal identity. The central reason (signalled by *for*) why the Philippians need not capitulate to pressure to 'Judaize' is that they are already full members of God's family: *it is we who are the circumcision* (*peritomē*; cf. *katatomēn*, 'mutilation', in 3:2). Paul focuses on circumcision since it is the central sign of Jewish identity for both ethnic Jews and proselytes – that is, Gentiles who had converted to Judaism. In this way, circumcision evoked covenant. Paul's emphasis on *we* (dually present in verb and pronoun) shows

---

he envisions the community of faith as inclusive of both Jew and
Gentile, since Paul is quite able to delineate 'you' for Gentiles and
'we' for Jews (e.g. Gal. 2:15–18; 3:23–29; 4:8–11). Gentiles alone are
not the 'true circumcision' (3:3, NASB). Believers in Jesus, both
Gentile and Jewish, have this identity and belong to God's people
in the time of Jesus the Messiah. The sentiments here resonate with
Paul's reference to 'circumcision of the heart' (Rom. 2:29; cf. Jer.
4:4; 9:26; also Deut. 10:16). Paul gives no hint of replacement
theology, in spite of the strong rhetoric of 3:2.

Paul further defines this covenantal identity with three phrases
that highlight key stances and practices characterizing followers
of Jesus. A defining characteristic is religious service offered to
God (*latreuō*) – a term indicating the 'perform[ing of] religious
rites as a part of worship' (L&N, p. 533).[12] The object of worship
is implicit within the Greek term and in context: *we who serve God*
(NIV).[13] This practice connects the church closely with its Jewish
roots. It is worship of the one true God (Yahweh) that Paul
implicitly references. Although Paul has not asked (or wanted) his
Gentile converts to take on Jewish identity markers such as circumcision, he has expected them to turn from their gods to the
one true God of Israel (1 Thess. 1:9). In the Graeco-Roman
context in which ancestral 'gods ran in the blood',[14] Paul has
called Gentiles to a distinctively Jewish, monotheistic posture.
Yet Paul combines this affirmation of identity with an eschatological reminder. Christian service is empowered by the promised
'Spirit of God' (NASB; *pneumati theou*), whose arrival in fullness
functions as an important sign of God's final-day redemption
(Ezek. 36:24–27; Joel 2:28–29). God, through the Spirit, works in
and among the Philippian believers, empowering them 'to will
and to act' (2:13).

---

12. This term is related to *leitourgia* (2:17, 30; see L&N, p. 546 n. 3).
13. This verb takes its direct object in the dative case, and it is likely that
    the presence of the dative *theō* ('God') in some manuscripts, instead of
    the well-attested possessive genitive ('God's' or 'his', as in NIV), was a
    scribal clarification, providing explicitly the object of Christian service.
14. Fredriksen, 'Apostle', p. 640.

'Boasting in Christ Jesus' is another practice that is to characterize the church – Jew and Gentile. Paul uses the verb *kauchaomai*
to signal the activity of boasting, exalting or celebrating – a term
he most often uses with Christ as object (see comment on 1:26). It
is boasting in Jesus as their Messiah that is eminently appropriate
for those who are the beneficiaries of his work and have come to
know him (3:7–8). This specific community characteristic of
boasting in Christ complements the final description: *who put no
confidence in the flesh*. These two ideas elaborate on each other:
boasting in Christ gives the positive side of not putting confidence
in the flesh.[15] The key distinction is the object of believers' confidence and, as a result, of their boasting: is it the Messiah or the
flesh? Paul seems to use the term *sarx* (*flesh*) in this context to evoke
a perspective of one's identity and status that is at odds with God's
perspective (cf. comment on 1:23–24).[16] It is the believer's identity
in and relationship with the Messiah that counts, as Paul will make
clear in 3:4–11. While Paul draws on his own Jewish identity and
status as an example of placing confidence in the flesh (3:4–6), the
concept of putting *no confidence in the flesh* is more general, and can
be understood to refer to 'one's ethnic status, whether Jewish or
Gentile' (e.g. Greek or Roman).[17]

### ii. Paul's former confidence in his Jewish identity (3:4–6)

**4.** Paul turns to illustrating how confidence in the flesh is
contrary to celebrating and boasting in the Messiah by drawing
from his own life experience. He qualifies this contrast by noting
that, if anyone is able to place confidence in his or her identity and

---

15. Silva notes that *kauchaomai* ('boast') and *peithō* ('put confidence')
    'occupy the same semantic field' (p. 149).

16. Fowl, p. 149. Holloway suggests that *sarx* is 'more evocative than
    descriptive' here (p. 152) and encourages caution to avoid over-
    interpreting the term in this context – e.g. as specifically about
    circumcision (p. 153).

17. Zoccali, 'Rhetoric', p. 29. These identities are certainly more than
    ethnic alone, since they also include important religious and social
    dimensions (e.g. *sarx* as 'human credentials' [NET]).

status when viewed from a merely human perspective, it would be Paul himself. Although the first half of 3:4 continues the sentence of 3:3 and a new sentence begins at 3:4b (both in Greek and NIV), the topic of Paul's own example and experience along with significant verbal repetition join closely the two halves of the verse.

Paul states in bold terms that he himself has *confidence in the flesh*. Although it will become unmistakable that he no longer places his confidence in his own identity and status (3:7–8), here Paul frames his confidence *in the flesh* in an unqualified way: 'I myself have confidence.' The NIV's inclusion of *reasons* clarifies that Paul has had a change of perspective about his former confidence in his identity and status. Paul repeats the phrase *confidence in the flesh* three times (3:3, 4a, 4b) to emphasize what should no longer characterize those in the messianic community and to introduce how he of all people has reasons for 'confidence in the flesh' (*if someone else . . . I have more*).

**5–6.** In 3:5–6, Paul elaborates his 'reasons for . . . confidence' in his Jewish identity and the elevated status he had attained through it (referred to as his 'gains' at 3:7). He provides seven emblems of his Jewish ethnic and religious identity and experience, with two groupings distinguishable by the grammatical markers, and specifically the Greek *kata* introducing each description in the second grouping.

> Group 1 (3:5a–d)
> > *circumcised on the eighth day,*
> > *of the people of Israel,*
> > *of the tribe of Benjamin,*
> > *a Hebrew of Hebrews;*
> Group 2 (3:5e–6)
> > *in regard to the law, a Pharisee;*
> > *as for zeal, persecuting the church;*
> > *as for righteousness based on the law, faultless.*

The items in the first group (at least the first three) are characteristics of Paul's Jewish identity that marked him from birth and his earliest days. He was circumcised when he was eight days old, in line with the scriptural command (Gen. 17:9–14; Lev. 12:3). And he was ethnically an Israelite, a descendant of Abraham, Isaac and

Jacob, and not a proselyte. These first two descriptions highlight that Paul already enjoyed what was being held up as the ideal for Gentile Christ-followers, an ideal only possible through conversion to Judaism. Paul was, also by birth, from the tribe of Benjamin, one of the two tribes (with Judah) that remained faithful to David's royal line (1 Kgs 12:20–21) and which was favoured as 'the one the LORD loves' within the Mosaic blessing on the tribes (Deut. 33:12).

The final description in this first set is more ambiguous: *a Hebrew of Hebrews* (with the Greek term *Hebraios* repeated). This phrase very probably functions as a summation of the previous three, indicating that Paul is the epitome of Jewish identity and practice. Since Paul was born and raised in the diaspora, this phrase could signal that his parents were fully loyal to their Jewish faith and practice. It may have an additional connotation of someone who knew Hebrew (or Aramaic), as seems to be the case in Acts 6:1 in its reference to the 'Hellenistic Jews' complaining to the 'Hebraic Jews' (*Hebraios*) that their widows were being neglected in food distribution. While there may be other cultural factors involved, a language barrier seems a primary reason for such inattention. A number of translations signal this linguistic focus by rendering *Hebraios* in Acts 6:1 as 'Hebrew-speaking' (NLT; cf. CJB) or 'Aramaic-speaking' Jews (CEB), with *Hebraios* used to refer to Aramaic in some cases (BDAG, p. 270). Philo seems to use the term with the same sense in his reference to Jews who were able to translate the law or Torah into Greek during the time of Ptolemy II (*On the Life of Moses* 2.32).[18] If Paul uses the term with this sense, then he is indicating his knowledge of Hebrew as a sign of his particular adherence to his heritage.[19]

Paul's self-descriptions in the second grouping (3:5e–6) locate him within specific sectors of first-century Judaism. He belonged to the Pharisees (cf. Acts 23:6; 26:5), a non-priestly group within Judaism with popularist support and known for its expertise in and

---

18. For additional discussion, see Bockmuehl, pp. 196–197.

19. According to Osiek, the term could indicate that Paul's 'first, household language was Hebrew or Aramaic, even in the Diaspora' (p. 88).

attentiveness to the Torah, and especially to the law's purity regulations.[20] Paul emphasizes this Pharisaic focus on God's law by calling himself a Pharisee *in regard to the law* (*kata nomon*). In contrast to modern negative views of Pharisees (e.g. 'pharisaic' as 'hypocritical'), Pharisees had earned the admiration of their fellow Jews for their faithfulness to God's law.

Paul also characterizes himself as *persecuting the church*, using this descriptor as a gauge of his level of zeal for Israel's God. Paul as persecutor of the church fits the portrait in Acts of his actions before encountering the risen Christ (Acts 7:58 – 8:3; 9:1–2). In Galatians 1:13–14, Paul closely connects his persecution of the church with his zeal for 'the traditions of [the] fathers', illustrating how he 'was advancing in Judaism' beyond many of his peers. This portrait suggests that *persecuting the church* is closely tied to Paul's commitment to the law, especially if we understand at least part of Paul's former concern about the church to be tied to a perceived laxness related to the Torah.[21] In the context of Philippians 3:5–6, Paul as persecutor is not a negative trait (cf. his lament in 1 Cor. 15:9) but contributes to the portrait of his complete commitment to his Jewish faith.

The last and longest descriptor provides the pinnacle of the entire inventory: *as for righteousness based on the law, faultless.* Paul describes himself as 'being blameless' or *faultless*, language he has already used to describe the aspirational goal for the Philippian community to be blameless (*amemptos*, 2:15). As noted there, this adjective often occurs in close proximity to *dikaios* ('righteous' or 'faithful') in the Septuagint (e.g. Job 9:20).[22] As such, the term does not indicate perfection, which was not a Jewish expectation, evident in the Torah's own provisions for forgiveness of sin in its sacrificial stipulations. Instead, *amemptos* denotes an abiding faithfulness to God, and here to God's law. Paul places this description of his covenant faithfulness in the context of a

---

20. Mason, 'Pharisees', pp. 784, 786. See Brown, 'Pharisees'.

21. Bird and Gupta, pp. 129–130.

22. *TLNT* (p. 322) notes that *dikaios* in the LXX can be understood as 'faithful' to God's commands.

*righteousness based on the law*, the standard to which he had himself held in his conduct.

Yet Paul will soon make it clear that, because of the arrival of the Messiah, he aspires no longer to 'a righteousness . . . that comes from the law', but to 'the righteousness that comes from God' (3:9). Elsewhere, Paul affirms that righteousness does not, in the end, come through the law (Gal. 2:21; cf. 3:21). And in an extended discussion of this question (Rom. 9:30 – 10:10), he suggests that historically Israel (and presumably himself with his people) pursued the 'Torah that offers righteousness [*nomon dikaiosynēs*], [but] did not reach what the Torah offers' (Rom. 9:31, CJB; cf. 10:3–5).

In this litany of his covenant heritage, status and commitments (Phil. 3:4–6), Paul places his own covenant faithfulness to God and God's law as the culmination of the list. Paul is not being ironic, although some have assumed so. And he betrays no sign that the law functioned to produce in him a guilty conscience to drive him to Christ. Instead, he shows what he has set out to demonstrate: that if anyone could put their 'confidence in the flesh' it would be Paul himself (3:4). 'Paul's problem was not that he couldn't make the grade; it was that he *did* make it, only to find out that it was the wrong standard of assessment.'[23]

### iii. Paul's Christ identity and identification (3:7–11)

**7.** The change in Paul's mindset effected by Christ is nothing short of remarkable: *whatever were gains to [Paul]* are now assessed as losses. Paul compares his former perspective on his Jewish heritage, status and commitments with how he now evaluates all of life in the light of the arrival of the Messiah. And he affirms that it is 'because of the Messiah' (*for the sake of Christ*) that the locus of his confidence has shifted, so much so that he can no longer place his confidence in his Jewish heritage and its markers.

It is crucial to hear the apocalyptic nature of this shift. It is not only that knowing Christ exceeds all other values, although Paul affirms this most vigorously (3:8). It is that, in the arrival of Jesus the Messiah, 'the culmination of the ages has come' (1 Cor. 10:11).

---

23. Flemming, p. 165.

In this new messianic age, God's covenant people are no longer distinguished by central Jewish markers, such as Torah and circumcision. The prophetic, eschatological vision of Israel's restoration, precipitating the ingathering of the nations, has begun (e.g. Isa. 2:1–5). This new community is marked and identified by the person of the Messiah and by the Spirit (3:3), rather than by specific indicators identifying Jew, Greek, Roman or any other ethnicity. As Zoccali suggests, 'Rather than replacing existing ethnicities, "in Christ" identity represents ... a superordinate identity that significantly *reorients* the worldview and praxis of both Jews and gentiles.'[24]

This eschatological and Christological transformation of the people of God from ethnic Israel to a multi-ethnic community (Israel with the nations) produces a transformed mindset. Paul uses *hēgeomai* ('consider') three times in a brief span (3:7–8) to reinforce this eschatological mindset. Paul has already used *hēgeomai* ('value' or 'consider' in 2:3, 6) along with *phroneō* (2:2) to express a gospel way of viewing the world and other people, a humble mindset epitomized by Christ (2:5–6). Here, the term is used to indicate Paul's revised point of reference for viewing his past. Because of Christ, he 'considers' what was gain to be loss. This language comes from financial accounting and its attention to 'gains' and 'losses' (*kerdos* and *zēmia*, respectively, and their cognates), with this imagery having interpretive significance.

> Paul's wholesale rejection applies not to the qualities and achievements listed but the *value* he had attached to them. In and of themselves he might now regard them as good, bad or indifferent ... Christ as the supreme gain has become the overriding concern of Paul's life.[25]

**8.** Paul repeats and intensifies his perspective on his past basis for confidence. Not only does he now view his past gains as losses in the light of Christ, he considers *everything a loss* when compared with knowing Christ. Here again, Paul indicates that compared

---

24. Zoccali, *Philippians*, p. 134.
25. Bockmuehl, pp. 204–205.

with *the surpassing worth of knowing Christ Jesus* everything else is viewed as loss. The vantage point for comparison has altogether shifted. Paul is focused with laser-like intensity on the gift of knowing *Christ Jesus my Lord, for whose sake I have lost all things*. In the relative clause, Paul moves from his changed perspective on life to his actual experience of loss of *all things*. He has paid a price for following Christ,[26] and he may be obliquely referencing the kinds of experiences he details in 2 Corinthians 11:21–28, which resulted from his change of status within Judaism (11:24). In the final and climactic affirmation of Paul's change of perspective, he considers everything as *garbage* (*skybalon*). This term can refer to refuse or dung – a crass term emphasizing the utter worthlessness of anything when compared with Christ.

Paul has expressed his altered perspective by moving from considering his past heritage and status as loss ('whatever were gains' to him previously), to considering all things a loss, to considering them *garbage* – all for the sake of knowing Christ. The believer's 'in Christ' identity is the one that matters, since it is 'the category that has soteriological significance'.[27] This highly rhetorical pathway highlights the supreme value of knowing and gaining Christ. Paul concludes this crescendo of loss and gain with his deepest desire: *that I may gain Christ*. Christ is the gift and prize that makes all else pale in comparison.

**9.** At this pinnacle of expression, Paul changes mode from 'gaining Christ' (an active verb) to *be found in him* (a passive verb). He shifts from his own part in counting relationship with Christ as his highest gain to God's part in incorporating believers (here Paul specifically) into Christ. The language of 'being found in Christ' occurs only here in Paul, yet it fits conceptually with Paul's understanding of the incorporation of believers into Christ (*en Christō*, 1:1; 2:1).[28] Paul wants to do all he can to participate in God's

---

26. Hawthorne (p. 192) translates, 'For him, I did in fact lose everything.'

27. Sumney, 'Paul', p. 71.

28. And provides an interesting comparison with Christ 'being found in appearance as a human being' (2:8, my translation). As Silva suggests, 'Jesus, through his humiliation, appeared in our human form . . . and

work of salvation (cf. 2:12; 3:12–14), although the part he plays is subordinate and responsive to the divine initiative of grace. Paul makes this clear in the rest of the verse, as he expresses the way that he is found in Christ.

Paul has already introduced the idea of a Torah-based righteousness, where he described himself as 'faultless' in relation to 'righteousness based on the law' (3:6). Now, he introduces the notion of a Messiah-based righteousness that grounds his participation in Christ. For Pauline readers who are deeply familiar with Galatians and Romans, Philippians 3:9 is reminiscent of the language and ideas of these letters. Yet in Philippians Paul offers no sustained argument, as he does in those letters, for Gentiles being incorporated into the people of God on the basis of faith, not Torah adherence, although this theme is implicit in his discussion at 3:2–3 (cf. 1:11). In his autobiographical reflections here, he makes it clear that he no longer relies on his own Torah adherence, with the implication that the Gentile Philippians should not pursue that route now that the Messiah has come. Paul has come to know Jesus the Messiah and he relies on the work and faithfulness of Jesus for a *righteousness that comes from God* rather than *a righteousness of my own that comes from the law* (Torah).

Paul no longer places his confidence in his own righteousness derived from Torah adherence. While elsewhere Paul clarifies that the problem with the Torah was a 'problem of empowerment' (e.g. Rom. 8:3; also 3:20; 7:7–8),[29] in Philippians we hear that, with the arrival of the Messiah, any righteousness derived from the Torah cannot compare to the gift of God's righteousness through the Messiah's faithfulness. This contrast fits the wider comparison Paul has offered between his former reasons for confidence derived from his ethnic and religious 'gains' and his present singular goal of knowing Christ Jesus. At its heart, this is an eschatological distinction.

---

(note 28 *cont.*) thus identified himself with us so that we might [be] united with him' (p. 162).

29. Holloway, p. 169.

While the people of God – the community of righteous ones – were in
the former dispensation demarcated on the basis of the ordinances of
Torah in total, that is, Jewish identity (3:6), in the dispensation of Christ
righteous status is found singularly in him.[30]

This contrast is at the core of the apocalyptic shift that has taken
place in the arrival of Christ. A righteousness from God is now
available to all people – Jewish and non-Jewish – 'through the
faithfulness of Christ'. The Greek term *pistis* can refer to 'faith' or
'faithfulness' (BDAG, p. 818), so the phrase *pistis Christou* can be
rendered either as *faith in Christ* or 'the faithfulness of Christ' (NIV
footnote reading). These two possibilities correspond to hearing
*Christou* as (respectively) an objective genitive ('Christ' as the
implied object of *pistis*) or a subjective genitive ('Christ' as its
subject). Since Paul uses this phrase (with or without 'Jesus') five
other times in his letters, the question of meaning is an issue of
Pauline theology (Rom. 3:22, 26; twice in Gal. 2:16; 3:22; cf. Gal.
2:20; Eph. 3:12).

While both readings have solid rationale and scholars are
divided on the issue, I favour the subjective genitive – 'the
faithfulness of Christ'. First, whenever Paul uses *pistis* with a
genitive referring to a person(s), the genitive is subjective (e.g. Rom.
4:5, 12, 16; cf. 3:3).[31] Second, scholars are essentially in agreement
that the phrase that concludes 3:9, *on the basis of faith*, refers to
human faith. If so, then *pistis Christou* is best read as 'the faith/
faithfulness of Christ', complementing rather than repeating the
role of human faith. Third, God's gift of righteousness comes to
people through the work of Christ – through his faithfulness or
obedience (2:8; cf. Rom. 5:19), rather than directly through human
faith. While human faith (*pistis*) as a response is crucial to receiving
God's gift of righteousness, this gift is only possible through
Christ's faithful mission to the cross. For Paul, his own righteous-

---

30. Zoccali, 'Rhetoric', p. 29.

31. Foster, 'Philippians', p. 96. This includes pronouns (e.g. Rom. 1:12; 2
    Cor. 10:15), where the subjective genitive (or possessive genitive) is
    natural.

ness based on the Torah could not compare to divine righteousness gifted through the faithfulness of the Messiah.

**10.** After a brief aside describing *how* he has come to 'be found in [Christ]' (3:9), Paul returns to his affirmation from 3:8 of his greatest value: knowing Christ. Here he purposes *to know Christ*, which for Paul involves participatory knowledge of Christ's central experiences of suffering and resurrection. Holloway describes these two facets of knowledge as a '"curriculum" for knowing Christ' (cf. 2 Cor. 4:8–10).[32] The ordering of these facets – resurrection and then suffering – suggests a chiastic structure for 3:10–11:[33]

A *the power of his resurrection*
    B *participation in his sufferings*
    B′ *becoming like him in his death*
A′ *attaining to the resurrection from the dead*

This ordering, with resurrection in first and last position, also highlights that for Christ-followers 'the resurrection is . . . both the first word and the last . . . The "fellowship of his sufferings" is always in light of [Christ's] past triumphant victory and our common glorious future'.[34]

Paul purposes to know Christ's resurrection power, a knowledge that has both present and future horizons. Paul will soon reference Christ's power to raise and transform Christians at the final day (3:21), and that future hope of 'knowing Christ's power' is certainly part of what Paul references here (cf. Rom. 8:11). But it is almost certain that Paul is indicating that he currently experiences 'resurrection power' (ISV) – God's power that raised Christ from the dead. This is intimated across the letter in Paul's references to God's effectual work in believers (1:6; 2:13; 4:13, 19) as the source of their own endurance and empowerment (1:6; 2:12). Elsewhere in Paul's letters, we hear that the divine power that raised Christ from the dead is at work at present in Christ-followers so that they might

---

32. Holloway, p. 169.
33. Cohick, p. 172.
34. Bockmuehl, p. 214.

be freed from sin's power (Rom. 6:1–14) and live fruitful lives (Col. 1:10–12; cf. Eph. 1:19–20).

Paul also purposes to know what it means to participate in Christ's sufferings. Paul has already referenced the suffering that has been 'granted' to the Philippian believers, a suffering that they share in common with Paul – a suffering 'on behalf of Christ' (1:29–30). Now Paul makes it clear that his own suffering on Christ's behalf is a *participation* (*koinōnia*) in the sufferings of Christ, signalling the relational unity of believers with Christ and so with one another (see comments on 1:5; 2:1). With this language, Paul does not baptize all suffering that believers may experience, since it is quite possible (taking a page from 1 Peter) for believers to suffer for doing wrong rather than for doing good (e.g. 1 Pet. 2:12, 20–21; 3:15–17). When believers suffer for their *allegiance to Jesus*, they are participating in the sufferings of Christ. For Paul, suffering for loyalty to Christ is not a sign of divine abandonment but of the reality of the believer's relational bond with Christ.

Closely connected to suffering with Christ is the goal of *becoming like him in his death*, a phrase which indicates how Paul participates in Christ's sufferings. This could refer to the Pauline sentiment that believers have already joined Christ sacramentally (in baptism) in his death (and resurrection) and have died to sin's power (Rom. 6:6–7). And given that the participle (*becoming like*) is present tense, Paul is also addressing his own present way of life in which he pursues Christlikeness (*symmorphizō*, 'conforming' to Christ). In this description, Paul probably echoes the Christ poem, which narrates the story of Christ's self-emptying and humbling to the point of death (2:6–8). Becoming like Christ in his death involves taking on his mindset of caring more for others than for self and renouncing the benefits and honour of high status. This mindset of Christ is the pattern that the Philippian believers are to follow (2:2, 5) and is the paradigm that Paul himself emulates.

**11.** Paul's desire to know Christ by patterning his life after his Messiah culminates in an expression of eagerness to reach *the resurrection from the dead*. This is the true, final goal of Jewish people in the first century who believed in life after death (e.g. the Pharisee sect and its many supporters; cf. Acts 26:6–8). Bodily renewal at the final-day general resurrection was the divine promise and the intense hope of the Jewish people (e.g. Dan. 12:1–3; 2 Macc. 7:9). In Paul's eschatology, Jesus' resurrection had come ahead of the general resurrection of the faithful and was itself the promise of the resurrection of believers still to come (1 Cor. 15:20–23). Here, Paul's desire to know the power of Christ's resurrection includes experiencing God's power to raise Paul and other believers at the final day, as 3:20–21 will make clear. The translation *attaining* for the Greek *katantaō* indicates that Paul aspires to reach the goal of final resurrection (though not in any way to earn it).

The aspirational tone of the language in 3:8–11 helps us to make sense of the *somehow* (*ei pōs*) Paul uses to introduce resurrection as his crowning goal. Paul has expressed multiple purposes in relation to Christ: he desires to gain Christ, to be found in Christ, to know Christ, and to know Christ in his suffering and resurrection. The intensifying cadence of these pursuits in 3:8–10, each of which includes a present component, leads him to frame that final, still-future goal in more aspirational language – 'if, somehow, to arrive at the final-day resurrection of those who have died' (my translation). There is no need to assume that Paul was quite unsure of his final status before God, especially as he has grounded that status in a God-given righteousness that has come through Christ's faithfulness. Instead, the tentative quality of his language emphasizes that Paul can think of no higher goal than resurrection, which will usher believers into the presence of Christ for ever.

*Theology*

Philippians 3:1–11 provides much food for theological thought. Paul's mindset, so influenced by his awareness that he and his fellow believers have experienced the turning of the ages in the arrival of the Messiah, is no longer focused on any human-based privileges. Instead, he considers knowing Christ as the ultimate gain. Paul highlights his Jewish heritage and privileges in this passage, and he is led down this autobiographical path given his warning to Gentile believers against anyone or anything that would pressure them towards taking on Jewish identity, potentially to shield them from sociopolitical persecution (3:2).

It does not follow, however, that Paul has simply discarded his Jewish identity (cf. Rom. 9:1–5).[35] Instead, this text gives an example of someone with ethnic and religious privilege (in this case, within the dynamics of the early church) who acknowledges and defers that privilege in the light of the arrival of the Messiah. The situation seems analogous to the one in Galatia where Jewish believers enjoyed certain privileges within the wider church context that made their position and advantages enviable to their fellow believers who were not Jewish (e.g. Gal. 2:11–13). For the purpose of 'acting in line with the truth of the gospel' (Gal. 2:14), Paul refused to encourage non-Jews to become Jewish and, in our passage, relinquished advantage and privilege for the sake of knowing Christ.

Yet it is instructive to turn to Romans, where Paul addresses a different context – one in which the tables have been turned between Jewish and Gentile believers. Gentile Christ-followers seem to have a significant advantage within the Roman church and a disproportionate amount of privilege in relation to Jewish believers (e.g. Rom. 11:13–21; 14:1 – 15:13), with a tendency towards a sense of superiority (Rom. 11:18). As Wright suggests, 'What Paul faced as a serious possibility in Rome was the mirror image of the problem he had met in Antioch', where Jewish believers had greater influence (Acts 15:1). In the Roman context, 'there was always the danger . . . that local anti-Jewish sentiment would lead gentile Christians . . . to isolate Jews within the Christian fellowship'.[36] In that context, Paul calls Gentiles – aligned significantly with 'the strong' – to give up their privilege to serve Jewish believers (aligned significantly with 'the weak'; Rom. 14:1 – 15:13). Paul seems to expect those with more power and privilege to forego those benefits for the sake of those with less advantage (see also, e.g., Phlm. 17–19; the Pauline household codes).

This pattern is suggestive for those in our own contexts who have advantages and privilege, whether ethnic, religious, socio-

---

35. As Sumney reflects on Phil. 3:4–11 in the light of Rom. 9 – 11: 'the things [Paul] says he has given up in Philippians 3 are valuable' ('Paul', p. 71).

36. Wright, *Pauline Perspectives*, p. 97.

economic or other kinds. And we would do well to note that such
privilege is often most hidden from those who are its beneficiaries.
It can be illuminating to ask ourselves, *What kinds of privileges are we
tempted to put our confidence in or boast about?* Paul provides his own
example of 'divesting himself of his Jewish privileges' (3:4–11) in
line with the ultimate example in Jesus, who did not use 'to his own
advantage' his divine status (2:6).[37] These examples provide
believers today with needed guidance towards a Christlike mindset.

## B. Paul's exhortation to an eschatological mindset (3:12 – 4:1)

*Context*

As he has in 3:1–11, Paul continues writing with an autobiographical
focus (especially in 3:12–18). Having stretched towards the eschatological horizon by envisioning his goal of resurrection at the final
day (3:11), Paul steps back to concede that he has not yet reached it.
This 'almost but not yet' reality presses him to strive with even
more energy towards that goal (3:12–16). Paul, who has been
offering himself as an example for the Philippian church, now
makes an explicit point of their following his example and the
example of all 'who live as we do' (3:17; cf. 2:29). This theme of
imitation (see Introduction 4f) will recur at 4:9 and fits the pattern
of Paul's use of exemplars in Philippians 2 – 3: Christ (2:5–11);
Timothy (2:19–24); Epaphroditus (2:25–30); and Paul himself (3:1–
17). This theme is heightened by the counter-example of those
whom Paul refers to as 'enemies of the cross' (3:18–19), similar to
his use of counter-examples at 1:15, 17 and 3:2.

Paul also continues his eschatological focus from 3:1–11, highlighting the hope of final-day bodily resurrection at 3:20–21 (cf.
3:11) that should energize the Philippians' mindset (3:12–16). He
returns to a motif introduced at 1:27, where Paul used the term
*politeuomai* as his first exhortation of the letter. Now at 3:20, he uses
the cognate noun, *politeuma* ('citizenship'), to highlight that the
Philippian believers have a distinctive allegiance to the gospel of

---

37. Bird and Gupta, p. 132.

the kingdom and to Jesus as Lord. Paul also recapitulates language from 1:27 at 4:1 in his call for his audience to 'stand firm' in their loyalty to Christ.

Paul briefly references a group of 'opponents' (3:18–19) who function as a negative example to his own positive one. These people seem to be distinct from the group referenced at 3:2,[38] especially as none of the descriptors in 3:19 provides much specificity (cf. 'the mutilation' in 3:2). The phrase 'enemies of the cross' (3:18) may simply be a way of describing unbelievers, or, as I will argue, may refer to some from the Christian community who are capitulating to societal pressure to return to their former pagan practices.

*Paul's rhetorical emphases in Philippians 3:12 – 4:1:* Paul continues to draw on ethos to highlight his own example for the Philippians to follow (3:12–14, 17). He also taps into pathos, in his reference to his own response of grief ('with tears') to those who live as 'enemies of the cross', as well as in his warm, relational descriptions of the Philippians: 'you whom I love and long for' (4:1). Focusing on logos, Paul continues to argue for an eschatological mindset. This mindset is one that he himself models in his present mode of 'pressing on' and 'straining ahead' (3:12–14). The Philippians are to 'take such a view' (3:15), avoiding the negative example of those who set their mind 'on earthly things' (3:19), since the future course of believers has been set by Jesus who will enact their final-day resurrection (3:21; cf. 3:11).

## Comment
### i. Living with the final day and end goal in view (3:12–16)

**12.** The previous passage has culminated with Paul's expression of his deepest desire to reach the future day of resurrection (3:11). Now, Paul moves to reflect on the reality of his temporal location between the arrival of the Messiah and the consummation of all things at the time of resurrection (cf. 1 Cor. 15:20–28). In the present time of the 'already but not yet', Paul concedes that he has not yet arrived at his final goal, using two verbs (and negating

---

38. Though some argue they refer to the same group; e.g. Osiek, pp. 102–103; Smit, *Paradigms*, p. 75.

them) in the first part of this verse (*obtained* and *arrived at . . . goal*). Holloway draws attention to Paul's use of *epidiorthōsis* or 'self-correction' here (in 3:12–14), a common rhetorical device 'to highlight the claim [of 3:7–11] that for the Christ-believer the knowledge of Christ remains a relentless pursuit'.[39]

Although there is no explicit object for the first verb, 'obtain' (*lambanō*), the NIV clarifies that the object includes all of what Paul has been describing as his purposes in 3:7–11 (*all this*).[40] The second verb is *teleioō* – the singular use of this verb in Paul's letters. This term can indicate reaching perfection or completion (BDAG, p. 996), so that, in this context, it can point to 'arriving at a goal' (NIV). The verb is most likely a passive form (not middle) and specifically a divine passive, indicating that God is the one who will (someday) usher Paul to his goal. At present, however, the negation of *teleioō* indicates that Paul 'has not yet reached eschatological completion'.[41]

Given Paul's use of *teleioō*, some interpreters have suggested that Paul is countering a perfectionist group in 3:12–16. For example, Bockmuehl considers it possible that the Jewish opponents identified at 3:2 thought of themselves as 'perfected' or already in possession of the covenant blessings, similar to the use of *tāmîm* (Hebrew for 'perfect') within the Qumran community to refer to themselves.[42] Paul then opposes this assumption in his own admission that he has not yet been 'perfected' (*teleioō*, 3:12). Such reconstructions are unlikely, given the lack of any other indications of a 'perfectionist group' and the embedding of this term within the context of Paul's autobiographical experience of the 'already/not yet' dynamic.

---

39. Holloway, p. 172.

40. Some manuscripts include the verb *dikaioō* between *lambanō* (*obtained*) and *teleioō* (*arrived at my goal*): *ē ēdē dedikaiōmai* ('or already been justified'). While there is early evidence for this reading, it is probably a scribal addition to fill in an implied object ('righteousness'; cf. 3:9), since the other two Greek verbs are objectless. For a defence of the originality of this reading, see Bockmuehl, p. 220.

41. Keown II, p. 196.

42. Bockmuehl, p. 221.

Instead of presuming he has 'arrived', Paul continues to *press on* (*diōkō*), a term indicating decisive movement to a goal (BDAG, p. 254) and repeated at 3:14.[43] This language, along with the use of 'straining' (*epekteinomai*, 3:13), communicates the intensity of Paul's drive to reach the eschatological goal. Seeing that goal ahead propels him forward. His eschatological mindset concerning 'the already but not yet' takes on an 'almost there but not quite yet' feel in this part of Philippians, providing the driving force for Paul's present existence.

Paul's goal, only implied so far in the language used in 3:12, is expressed in the latter half of the verse: *to take hold of that for which Christ Jesus took hold of me.* Paul's use of the prepositional phrase *eph' hō* seems here to function as *that for which* (NIV) rather than as causal (e.g. 'because Christ Jesus has made me his own', NRSV), especially given its similar use at 4:10 to point back to and complete the idea of the previous clause.[44] Yet this description, while compellingly articulated (with its double use of 'take hold', *katalambanō*), remains somewhat enigmatic. Paul endeavours to take hold of something, but this 'something' is not given any specific contours. Instead, Paul uses quite open-ended language: *that for which Christ Jesus took hold of me.* Whether or not Paul here obliquely references his initial encounter with Christ (1 Cor. 9:1; cf. Acts 9:1–19), Christ's purposes for 'taking hold of' Paul cannot be easily narrowed down. Paul seems to want to keep the referent broad enough to include all of what God in Christ has in store for him – and for all believers. Here, as earlier in Philippians (e.g. 1:6; 2:12–13), it is God's prior work that enlivens believers' responsiveness.

**13–14.** Paul will now reinforce the point he has just made about not having yet arrived at his final goal (3:12). He introduces this repetition by referring to his audience once more as *brothers and sisters* (1:12; 3:1; cf. 4:1, 8). And he describes his mindset for understanding his current situation using *logizomai* – a synonym of *phroneō* and *hēgeomai* in Philippians (see Introduction 4d). Although this is the first occurrence of *logizomai* in Philippians (cf. 4:8), Paul in

---

43. Another sense of *diōkō* is 'persecute', a sense that Paul uses at 3:6.
44. Fee, p. 346 n. 31.

Philippians 3 frequently references his mindset (*phroneō*, 3:15 [2x], 19) or the way he considers or frames his experience (*hēgeomai*, 3:7, 8 [2x]). Paul uses these terms to signal that he intentionally takes on an eschatological frame of reference that locates his life and ministry between the arrival of the Messiah and final resurrection and consummation.

Paul continues by repeating the verb *katalambanō* from 3:12, conceding once more that, although he presses towards his goal, he does not view himself as yet having *taken hold of it*. His present reality of not yet reaching consummation only spurs him towards that end as his singular purpose (*one thing I do*). Paul highlights two actions that provide the means for 'pressing on' (*diōkō*, repeated from 3:12): *forgetting* the past and *straining* towards the future. In context, part of what sits in Paul's past are his privileges and commitments arising from his Jewish heritage (3:4–6). But Paul's referent is wider than this; it includes everything in his past, with that totality emphasized through use of the plural, *ta opisō* (*what is behind*). Similarly, Paul has already filled in something of *what is ahead* (also a plural) in his mention of future resurrection (3:11) and his quite general reference to 'that for which Christ Jesus' had taken hold of him (3:12). Now, as he expresses his goal more fully, he moves to metaphor and piles up phrases: *I press on towards the goal to win the prize for which God has called me heavenwards in Christ Jesus.* Paul's goal is *the prize* (*brabeion*), which evokes the image of a runner in a race straining towards the finish line for a coveted prize. Paul values above all else what lies ahead – the fullness of salvation still to come. Yet he avoids any connotation of *earning* this prize by further describing it as 'the prize of God's heavenly calling in Christ Jesus'.[45] The term *klēsis* ('calling') is almost always used of divine initiative in calling or in offering an invitation (BDAG, p. 549), and Pauline usage elsewhere bears this out (e.g. Rom. 11:29; Eph. 1:18; 4:1, 4; 2 Tim. 1:9). It is God who invites, and the invitation has come 'in Messiah Jesus', meaning it is

---

45. The Greek *anō* indicates an upward direction and is rendered *heavenwards* by the NIV, reflecting that the calling comes from God and/ or is a calling towards the realm of God, from which believers await their Saviour (3:20).

*in the Messiah* that God's invitation to salvation has been given and enacted, and will be fully accomplished.

In this paragraph (3:12–14), Paul has highlighted his singular preoccupation with the eschatological goal, but he has not added much detail to his description of that goal. It is 'that for which Christ Jesus took hold of' him (3:12), and metaphorically it is *the prize for which God has called* him (3:14). In 3:8–11, Paul has already rehearsed his deepest desires, his ultimate goals: to know Christ, to participate with Christ, and to reach final resurrection. In 3:12–14, he seems to have run out of words to describe with any specificity the final goal beyond knowing Christ in a resurrected existence. That is the goal and the prize for which Christ took hold of him and of all who trust in Christ. As Flemming writes, the prize is 'none other than knowing Christ in a full and ultimate sense . . . The prize is Christ himself'.[46]

**15.** Paul turns from his vision of eschatological salvation and the fullness of knowing Christ to exhort the Philippians to take on the same kind of future-facing mindset. To indicate the shared perspective he calls the Philippians to engage, Paul uses the term *phroneō*, 'mindset', a term used thematically across the letter (e.g. 2:2, 5; 4:2). He shapes his exhortation expressly towards *all of us . . . who are mature*, with the likely impact of pressing his audience to follow his lead and so show themselves to fit this category of 'the mature' (*teleios*). While this term can denote being perfect, complete or mature, perfection does not fit well in the context of Paul's concession that he has not yet 'arrived' (3:12–14). It is intriguing that he has used the cognate verb, *teleioō*, to communicate that he has not yet 'reached the goal' (3:12); he has potentially drawn on these two cognate terms for a (rather ironic) wordplay. Whether or not a wordplay is intended, Paul draws on a different sense in each occurrence to make his point that Christian maturity in the present correlates to maintaining an eschatological mindset, not presuming to have already reached the eschatological goal.

While Paul encourages a shared, mature mindset, he also addresses some in his audience who might *think differently* (*heterōs*

---

*phroneō*) from him. He suggests that God will bring clarity in these areas of difference. While the reference to God's role in changing the perspective of those who think differently from Paul could sound like a heavy-handed way of promoting 'group think',[47] two observations shed light on Paul's tone and purposes here. First, Paul uses *phroneō* in this letter to commend the practice of communal discernment towards a shared mindset (2:2; 4:2; see Introduction 4d). The importance of this shared mindset is clearest where it is in jeopardy, as here and in Philippians 4. At 4:2, Paul will implore two of his fellow workers 'to be of the same mind' (*to auto phronein*). Here, Paul recognizes the possibility that some of the Philippians may see from a vantage point different from his own, but he commends through his own example an eschatological mindset that has an impact on attitudes and actions. Through his example (3:10–11, 17), Paul is endorsing an eschatological perspective on Christian suffering and identification with Christ, rather than highlighting specific differences in doctrine or theology.[48]

Second, Paul could have turned to exhortation in 3:15b as he does with Euodia and Syntyche at 4:2. Instead, he brings God expressly into the equation. The reference to God bringing clarity (*apokalyptō*) suggests a compelling moment of 'patient waiting on God's providence'.[49] As Paul has already demonstrated in the letter (e.g. 1:6, 9–11; 2:13), God can be trusted to form the Philippians towards the likeness of Christ.

> Paul's patience in the face of those who think and act 'otherwise' reflects neither confidence in his own rhetorical power nor in the reasonable nature of those he is addressing. Rather, it reflects a confidence in God's promises in Christ to maintain the church, which is itself a gift from God, until that time when Christ will perfect it.[50]

---

47. See, e.g., Osiek's reading, p. 99.
48. Hawthorne, p. 212.
49. Fowl, p. 165.
50. Fowl, p. 165.

**16.** Paul concludes this section with a call to action: *let us live up to* (*stoicheō*). Paul wraps up his exhortation to a mature mindset (3:15) with this entreaty to a particular way of life, indicating that the mindset he envisions is by no means exclusively cognitive. The word *only* (*plēn*) that introduces this exhortation (and follows the call to a right mindset) also suggests that Paul's primary concern is whether they are *living* eschatologically. Their entire way of life is to be oriented towards what God has done in Christ and the promised consummation of that divine work at the final day of resurrection. Paul calls the Philippians to live up to what they have *already attained* – their life in Christ that is already a palpable reality (cf. 2:1; 3:8–10) – thereby signalling the importance of living into this already/not yet mindset. Emphasis is placed on what they have *already attained* by putting this object clause at the front of the Greek sentence.

Paul's choice of verb, *stoicheō* (*live up to*),[51] fits the idea of imitation (see Rom. 4:12; Gal. 5:25; 6:16), which Paul will make explicit in his next sentence but which is already implicit in his autobiographical portrait of 3:4–15. Paul calls the whole community, including himself (*let us*), to *live up to* what they have already received or attained. They are to continue on the path that God has set for them; they are to act in keeping with who they already are in Christ. This line of reasoning is quite Pauline, as in Galatians 5:25, where Paul enjoins the Galatian believers (and uses the verb *stoicheō* in the last clause): 'Since we live by the Spirit, let us keep in step with the Spirit.'

The clipped expression of this Greek sentence (3:16) seems to have led some scribes to fill out its ideas by adding language; for example, a noun as the object of *stoicheō*: 'let us live up to the same *rule*' (*kanoni*; as in Gal. 6:16). Given the weight of the manuscript evidence, as well as scribal tendencies to use additional language to fill in what was ambiguous or implicit, the shorter reading is much more likely to have been the earlier one.

---

51. The Greek infinitive functions imperatively, i.e. as a command (see discussion in Keown II, p. 217 n. 117). The *us* comes from the first-person-plural form of the verb for *we have already attained*.

## ii. Positive and negative examples of living eschatologically
## (3:17 – 4:1)

**17.** Paul has sketched out the example of his own life and mindset for his audience across Philippians 3, and now he explicitly admonishes the Philippians to 'follow' *my example*. He calls the Philippians – his spiritual *brothers and sisters* – to join one another in being 'imitators' (*symmimētoi*, with the *syn* prefix indicating 'together') of Paul himself: *Join together in following my example* (cf. 4:9). While some have viewed the term *symmimētoi* as indicating that Paul exhorts the Philippians to join with him in imitating Christ, the word order and grammar of the verse lean away from this view.[52] Yet it is clear from Philippians 2 – 3 that Paul himself imitates Christ's example of a mindset focused on the other (3:10–11 in the light of 2:5–8). Here at 3:17, Paul is calling the Philippians to join together as they imitate him, in line with Christ's example. In this communal exhortation, Paul is again fostering a sense of unity in a letter very much focused on that theme (1:27; 2:1–4, 14; 4:2–3).

After commending his own example, Paul expands the circle of influence to *those who live* as Paul does and so who, together with Paul, provide *a model* (*typos*) to contemplate and cultivate. Paul highlights the importance of contemplating such exemplars by using *skopeō*, here with the sense of paying careful attention (BDAG, p. 931). Already in chapter 2, Paul has offered Timothy and Epaphroditus as exemplars for the Philippians to contemplate and follow (2:19–24, 25–30). And, in his commendation of Epaphroditus, Paul has exhorted the Philippians to 'honour people like him' (2:29). Imitation forms a central practice of the Christian life, as those who are mature (3:15) set an example of how to follow their Lord Jesus, forging a pathway to guide other believers.

Paul's emphasis on imitation fits well in the context of ancient educational practices. Imitation (*mimesis*) was foundational within

---

52. Paul's reference to focusing on *those who live* 'in the same manner' points back to his self-reference (i.e. his own example) at the beginning of the verse, and, if Paul were using *symmimētoi* to join with the Philippians in imitation, a dative *(moi)* rather than the genitive *(mou: my)* would be likely (Fee, p. 364 n. 10).

Graeco-Roman education, in which the teacher (along with exemplars from history and literature) functioned as a model for the formation of students.[53] For example, the Roman philosopher Seneca writes, 'The way is long if one follows precepts, but short and helpful, if one follows patterns' (*Epistulae morales* 6.5). Eastman summarizes the contribution of Seneca and others on imitation: 'it was the relationship in which imitation occurred that both validated the subject matter and grounded the developing character of the student. For mimetic education to take hold, the student had to participate in the teacher's life.'[54]

**18.** Having enjoined the Philippians to imitate the positive examples of an eschatological mindset provided by himself and by others, Paul pivots to speak, quite emotively, of those whose lives provide a counterpoint to this mindset (3:18–19). The people Paul refers to – those who *live as enemies of the cross* – seem to be fellow believers, especially given Paul's poignant expression of emotion about them: *I have often told you before [about them] and now tell you again even with tears.* The path and behaviour that this group of believers has pursued seems to have been a matter of serious warning when Paul was in Philippi (having *told* them before) and is a continuing subject of sorrow for Paul. Another clue that these are believers whom Paul can call *enemies of the cross of Christ* is Paul's use of the same verb for them (*peripateō*: *live* or 'walk') as for the exemplars he has just mentioned: 'those who live as we do' (3:17). While Paul regularly uses *peripateō* in his letters, the only two occurrences in Philippians sit in close proximity in 3:17–18 and provide an unmistakable comparison between two distinct paths the Philippians could take.

Paul and other mature believers – both within the Philippian church and beyond – are exemplars for staying focused on the goal ahead and embracing whatever participation in Christ's sufferings proves necessary in the meanwhile (3:10). The other path – the one to avoid – is described as living as an enemy of *the cross of Christ*. The *many* Paul can describe this way probably comprise some outside

---

53. Eastman, 'Imitating Christ', pp. 430–433.

54. Eastman, 'Imitating Christ', p. 434.

the Philippian congregation along with some within it. Together, they provide an example to avoid.

It is important for understanding the phrase *enemies of the cross of Christ* to notice that Paul does not refer to 'enemies of the gospel' or 'enemies of Christ'. In that case, these negative examples could more easily be identified as non-believers. Instead, to be an enemy of the cross provides a different connotation. Paul has used the term *stauros* (*cross*) earlier, in the Christ poem. There, it signalled the point of Christ's deepest 'descent' into the human condition – a descent 'even [to] death on a cross' (2:8). In Paul's reflections on his own reoriented goals, he points to sharing in Christ's death as a central goal: 'to know . . . participation in his sufferings, becoming like him in his death' (3:10). This is what it looks like to be a 'friend of the cross'.[55] One who lives as an enemy of the cross presumably would be someone who avoids suffering that comes specifically from one's allegiance to Christ (see 1:27). It is a way of living the Christian life that embraces the idea of knowing 'the power of [Christ's] resurrection' without a corresponding participation in his sufferings (3:10).

Paul's reference to *many* who live antagonistically to the cross – to Christian suffering – can be understood as a broad brush that could comprise all who might seek a way out of suffering with Christ (3:10) brought on by staying loyal to Christ. For example, if part of the lure of Judaizing was a lessening of expectations related to the imperial cult (see comment on 3:2), then those drawn to this option of Jewish conversion could be included in the *many* whom Paul references.

**19.** While Paul fills in the picture of those who 'live as enemies of the cross' with four descriptions, they are sufficiently vague to lead interpreters of Philippians in different directions regarding the specific identity of these people. I will argue that these descriptors fit the portrait I have already sketched of those Paul refers to as 'enemies of the cross of Christ' (3:18).

With the first description, Paul references not who they are but their final destiny as *destruction* (*apōleia*). Paul's use of the same term

---

55. See Fowl, p. 164.

to speak of the destiny of opponents outside the church at 1:28 has led some to argue Paul is referring to unbelievers in 3:18–19 as well. Yet given the clues in 3:18 that these are believers being tempted to forsake the way of the cross, the reference to destruction would provide a compelling warning against their present course. This is especially likely given the way Paul frames his language: *their destiny is destruction*. In highlighting the final destination (*telos, destiny*) of such a way of life, Paul encourages any believers on this path to change course and pursue salvation instead of destruction (cf. 1:28).

The second description adds an intriguing element to the portrait: *their god is their stomach* (*koilia*). The sense here is similar to Paul's use of the term at Romans 16:18, where he describes some people in the Roman house churches who are serving their own 'appetites' (*koilia*) rather than Christ through divisiveness and deception (16:17). In both contexts, Paul alleges that the primary allegiance of such believers is compromised as they put their present cravings at the centre of their lives, since they have, in essence, installed their appetites as their true god. In the context of Philippians 3, this fits Paul's concern to commend an eschatological mindset rather than one that is focused only or primarily on the present (cf. 1 Cor. 15:32). In the Philippians' setting, there would have been continuing pressure for residents of Philippi to capitulate to norms and requirements related to civic and religious duties (including in the imperial cult; see comment at 1:28). In this setting, deciding to 'live for today' and bowing to such pressures would put believers at odds with an eschatological mindset focused on knowing Christ, being willing to suffer with him, and arriving at the day of resurrection. A right mindset and loyalty are so essential that Paul paints the opposite, earthly mindset with the imagery of idolatry.

Paul's third description – *their glory is in their shame* – is more closely connected to the second description (sharing an initial relative pronoun) and so should be understood as extending the idea of those making their appetites their god. Especially since *glory* in this letter has been something belonging to God (1:11; 2:11; cf. 4:19–20), it probably functions similarly here. Since these people have made their own stomach their god, it stands to reason that they have traded what was their glory (the true God) for something shameful.

These three descriptions all point to the essential problem with those about whom Paul warns and grieves: *their mind is set on earthly things.* In contrast to Paul's extended autobiographical example of having an eschatological mindset (3:4–17), these believers who are acting as 'enemies of the cross' have a mindset (*phroneō*) focused on what is *earthly.* They have not understood the immense value of knowing and gaining Christ, even as this relationship means that believers must be ready to follow Christ on the path of suffering (3:8–10). And they are not pressing forward with all their energies towards the final day when they will take hold of all that Christ has for them (3:12–14).

**20.** Paul moves to contrast having an earthly mindset with the true identity and perspective of faithful Christ-followers: *but our citizenship is in heaven.*[56] The most obvious contrast is between the 'earthly things' that preoccupy some and the heavenly focus that defines (and so should characterize) believers: theirs is a *heavenly* citizenship. We hear in the second half of 3:20 (*we . . . await a Saviour from there*) that this is not so much about the heavenly destination of believers as the heavenly origin of their Saviour and their allegiance to him.

Paul uses *politeuma*, a term used only here in the Pauline letters. It has the sense of a commonwealth (BDAG, p. 846); that is, a political realm requiring allegiance. So while *citizenship* (NIV) highlights the requisite loyalty believers owe to Christ as their king, it makes it less clear that Paul uses the term to refer to the realm of God's kingdom, including a sense of location. As Osiek suggests, Paul probably uses *politeuma* with the sense of 'a group of citizens of a city living together in another place' (i.e. a colony).[57] And, while God's reign has its origins in 'the heavens' (*ouranoi*, plural), the

---

56. The conjunction between 3:19 and 3:20 (*gar*) often provides an explanation of prior material. In this case, Paul's reminder of the Philippians' true citizenship explains further the appropriate eschatological mindset of 3:16–17. The intervening negative example of those with an earthly mindset provides a contrast to both 3:16–17 and 3:20.

57. Osiek, p. 103.

gospel message celebrates that, in Jesus, the kingdom has been inaugurated in *this* world. As Smith puts it, 'incipiently, the transcendent realm of God's authority now exists spatially on earth through the reign of the Messiah'.[58]

Paul uses the first-person-plural pronoun (*our*) to remind the Philippian congregation to whom they belong and owe allegiance. If some of the Philippians are in a struggle to remain loyal to Christ in the face of societal pressure towards divided loyalties, Paul voices an affirmation of their unified allegiance: 'ours is a heavenly kingdom'. The language reverberates back to Paul's first exhortation of the letter (1:27), where he used the verbal cognate of *politeuma* to press the Philippians towards 'singular loyalty to the gospel of Christ' (*politeuomai*; see comment at 1:27). As loyal to the gospel, Christians are to be 'responsible citizens of a different reign'.[59]

The chord of loyalty is also sounded in Paul's affirmation that believers *eagerly await a Saviour* from the heavenly realm, especially as *Saviour* (*sōtēr*) in the Philippians' context could have significant political associations.[60] Various caesars (in addition to many Graeco-Roman deities) were described as 'saviour', including Augustus and Claudius.[61] Paul's language describing an eagerly awaited Saviour could have pressed towards a comparison with the emperor.

> In 3.20, the [*sōtēr*] is an eagerly awaited figure who comes, from the state to which his people belong . . . to another state where they are living, in order to rescue them . . . In the first-century Graeco-Roman context, the only such leader likely to be thought of was the Emperor. In Philippi, this would be yet more likely.[62]

---

58. Smith, *Good Life*, p. 57.
59. Migliore, p. 148.
60. Paul uses this term sparingly; apart from the pastoral epistles, it occurs only here and at Eph. 5:23.
61. See textual and inscriptional examples in Oakes, *Philippians*, pp. 138–140.
62. Oakes, *Philippians*, p. 139.

Paul names their Saviour as *the Lord Jesus Christ*, language he uses in the opening and closing greetings of the letter (1:2; 4:23). Yet this language is anything but perfunctory, since *Lord* (*kyrios*) is the title routinely ascribed to Rome's emperor and is also the term used in the Greek Old Testament for Israel's God (translating the divine name). Paul's confession of Jesus Christ as 'Lord' (2:11; cf. 3:8) reverberates across the letter and informs his use here. For Paul and the Philippians, the true Lord is not the already present emperor, as claimed in Roman 'presentist' eschatology.[63] Instead, the true Lord is Jesus the Messiah, the crucified and risen one, whose coming believers earnestly anticipate.

**21.** In keeping with Paul's hope of reaching the day of resurrection (3:11), he now describes Jesus as the one who *will transform our lowly bodies so that they will be like his glorious body*. For Paul, the final state of believers is not some sort of heavenly disembodied existence but embodied, resurrection life in a renewed creation (cf. Rom. 8:19–23; Gal. 6:15). And Christ's resurrection body is the prototype, with Christ being the 'firstfruits' or guarantee of the future resurrection of believers (1 Cor. 15:20–23). Christ himself will effect this transformation (*metaschēmatizō*) of *our . . . bodies* to make them *like* (*symmorphos*) his body. Paul has used forms of these two terms earlier in contexts communicating the integral identification between believers and Christ. He has used the root of the word for *transform* to describe Christ's incarnation into human 'appearance' or 'form' (*schema*, 2:7), and has used the verbal cognate of *symmorphos* to refer to his own conformity to the likeness of Christ's death (*symmorphizō*, 3:10). Christ was made like humanity, and Christians seek to be like Jesus in his death, while embracing the promise of one day being transformed into the likeness of Christ's resurrected life.

Paul describes present life in the body with the term *tapeinōsis* (body 'of lowliness'), in contrast to Christ's *glorious body* (*sōma tēs doxēs*; woodenly, 'body of glory'). This contrast is very much a temporal one, between the present body in the present age and the body as it will be at the resurrection in the age to come. Christ

---

63. Smith, *Good Life*, p. 57.

alone is the 'firstfruits', whose resurrection has come, as it were, ahead of schedule – prior to the resurrection of the rest of humanity (1 Cor. 15:20–28). And so the church waits for that day of transformation of their *lowly bodies*. As Hawthorne explains this phrase, 'every person, this side of the Parousia, is marked by frailty, suffering, sorrow, vanity, death, and corruption'.[64]

Transforming believers at the resurrection is part of Christ's wider work of *bring[ing] everything under his control*. The power already granted Christ to subdue all things, including eventually death itself (cf. 1 Cor. 15:24–28), is the power he will exercise to resurrect those who believe in him. Paul's description of Christ's power contributes to a vision of Christ's Lordship over all creation and all contending powers. And it resonates with the portrait in the Christ poem of God's exaltation of Christ to the highest place – to the place of Lordship of all things 'in heaven and on earth and under the earth' (2:9–11). In fact, 3:20–21 shares any number of parallels with the Christ poem or hymn of 2:9–11, causing some to suggest that in this passage we can discern another Christological hymn that Paul incorporates into the letter.[65]

**4:1.** Paul concludes the discourse of Philippians 3 by exhorting the Philippians to *stand firm in the Lord in this way*. The comparative (*in this way*), along with the opening conjunction (*Therefore*), points directly back to Paul's extended autobiographical example of holding an eschatological mindset (3:1–21). Yet, given that he has issued an initial call to 'stand firm' (*stēkō*) at 1:27, the repetition at 4:1 could signal that *in this way* refers to all that Paul has commended to the Philippians in 1:27 – 4:1. They are to *stand firm in the Lord*, picking up on the recent reference to 'the Lord Jesus Christ' (3:20).

Paul piles up quite a number of descriptions to address the Philippians and to augment his exhortation to *stand firm*. Paul calls them his *brothers and sisters* (*adelphoi*), his most frequent way of addressing believers, in Philippians and in his other letters (e.g. 1:12; 3:1, 13, 17; 4:8). He also uses the language of *agapētoi*, repeating it at the beginning and end of the exhortation: *you whom I love . . . dear friends*

---

64. Hawthorne, p. 233.
65. For a listing of parallels, see Hawthorne, p. 229.

(also at 2:12).[66] Paul joins *agapētoi* with *epipothētoi* (those 'longed for') to deepen even further the warmth of expression: *you whom I love and long for* (cf. 1:8). Finally, Paul calls the Philippians his *joy and crown*, drawing on one of the letter's most pervasive themes to identify the Philippians as a central source of his joy. Paul also speaks of the Thessalonians as his joy and crown (and hope) in the final day (1 Thess. 2:19). For Paul, his future reward is all about people: it is found in believers who have responded to his offer of the gospel of Christ and been faithful to the end.

This effusive language reaffirms the depth of relationship that exists between Paul and the Philippian believers. It also signals a turning point in the letter by creating something of a pause in its pacing, as Paul directly addresses the Philippians personally and with deep affection. After refocusing attention on their relationship, Paul will move to identify and engage with two particular members of their fellowship (4:2–3).

### Theology

One can hardly read a single verse of Philippians 3 without hearing the eschatological tones and overtones Paul is sounding. Paul's eschatology is clear in his dual reference to the resurrection of the faithful (3:11 and 3:20–21), the quintessential Jewish and also now Christian sign of the consummation of all things. Across the chapter Paul displays a mindset that is eschatologically saturated: from the relativizing of what had been his gain in the light of the Messiah's arrival (3:4–7), to his posture of pressing forward towards the goal of experiencing the fullness of being in the Messiah at the time of resurrection (3:8–10, 12–14). Paul's exhortations to his fellow believers press them to take on this kind of forward-focused mindset (3:15–17) rather than an 'earthly mindset' (3:18–19), thereby showing themselves to be 'the true circumcision' (3:3) whose 'commonwealth is in the heavens' (3:20; my translations).

---

66. The NIV varies the translation used for the same Greek word since the two occurrences function somewhat differently in their specific locations. The first is joined closely with *you whom I . . . long for*, and the second functions on its own to conclude the call to *stand firm*.

Paul's entire way of thinking about 'the end' is wrapped up in the reality of resurrection. In a sense, then, we could speak of Paul's frame of reference as a 'resurrection mindset': taken up with the vision and hope of being raised along with the rest of the Messiah's people at the final day. Resurrection – Christ's already accomplished resurrection and believers' resurrection still to come – is not merely an example of God's power at work, although it certainly is that (3:10, 21). Resurrection is itself 'the starting point, the new reality that brings its own ontology [way of being] and epistemology [way of knowing] with it'.[67] Paul, in Philippians 3, embodies this new way of being and knowing. For him, resurrection *is* reality. As Wright puts it, 'The world opened by Jesus' resurrection is the *real* world in its new mode: the new creation which recontextualises and reinterprets the old.'[68]

What Paul values and how he lives has shifted in the light of Christ's resurrection. This is where the deeply personal language of knowing Christ fits into his eschatology. Knowing Christ is Paul's supreme value (3:7–9) and is necessarily joined to resurrection (3:10–11). Of the array of Pauline articulations about Christ across his letters, this is perhaps one of the most personal expressions of his relationship with Christ. Paul desires to know Christ, to be found in Christ, to gain Christ. This language has undoubtedly contributed to the emphasis on 'a personal relationship with Jesus' within evangelicalism and pietism. And these movements offer to the wider Christian tradition just such a personal focus of spirituality, even as they sometimes overlook or underplay Paul's decidedly corporate soteriology, which involves participation in the Messiah's people as integral to participating in the Messiah. Holding together Paul's deeply personal language in this passage with its pervasively corporate context encourages us to affirm both sides of Pauline spirituality – the personal and the communal. As much as Paul uses 'I' language across the chapter, his eschatology makes sense only via the 'we' that begins and concludes the chapter (3:3, 20–21). The 'resurrection of the dead'

---

67. Wright, *Eschatology*, p. 191.
68. Wright, *Eschatology*, p. 190.

(*nekrōn*, a plural) is a corporate vision and hope, as it was in Paul's Jewish context (e.g. Dan. 12:2–3). Knowing Christ more fully involves participating in his resurrection and suffering, which is itself a communal participation – sharing in and with Christ and Christ's people, now and through to that final day.

# 8. SUMMATIVE EXHORTATIONS: TO UNITY, JOY, PEACE, WISDOM AND IMITATION (4:2–9)

## Context

This section of Philippians is contested in terms of the letter's structure. Some understand the early verses (4:2–3) to connect directly with the previous section (e.g. understanding 3:1 – 4:3 as a discrete segment).[1] Most, however, read 4:2–3 – and some 4:1–3 – to go with the series of subsequent exhortations (through to 4:9).[2] Thinking big picture, we can notice a number of connections between the latter part of Philippians (end of chapter 3 and early chapter 4) and the opening of the body of Philippians (e.g. 3:20 with 1:27; 4:1 with 1:27; and 4:2–3 with 2:2–3). Philippians 4:2–9 with its focus on exhortations fits the wider pattern of alternation of exhortations and examples in the letter, and it follows directly after Paul's own autobiographical example in 3:1 – 4:1.

---

1. Fee, pp. 385–386.
2. E.g. Klauck (*Letters*, p. 319) understands 4:2–9 as the closing to the body of the letter and includes 4:10–20 in the letter's conclusion.

While the exhortations in 4:2–9 may at first seem fairly disconnected from one another, it becomes clear from a review of their themes that Paul is revisiting moments of earlier parts of the letter here at its conclusion. The call for Euodia and Syntyche to like-mindedness (*to auto phronein*, 4:2) echoes the same exhortation (*to auto phronein*) to the whole community (2:2). Paul's exhortation to rejoice (4:4) fits that pervasive theme across the letter (1:4, 18, 25; 2:2, 17–18, 28–29; 3:1; 4:10). The call for a stance of 'gentleness' towards all people (4:5) fits the missional posture in 2:14–16, where the Philippians are to live as God's blameless children within society. Paul's exhortation to 'consider' what is good (4:8) connects to earlier calls to a right mindset (2:2, 5) and Paul's example of 'considering' all things from the perspective of the arrival of the Messiah (3:7–8, 13–15). Finally, Paul's example, so prominent in 3:1 – 4:1, recurs in his invitation to act as he does (4:9).

Three of the four believers from the Philippian congregation whom Paul expressly names in the letter appear in 4:2–3: Euodia, Syntyche and Clement (joining Epaphroditus already mentioned in 2:25; cf. 4:18). Although we should be careful about making simple generalizations about the make-up of the Philippian congregation from these four names (especially since people of other ethnicities could adopt Roman names), we can observe that Clement is a Roman name (with *Klēmēs* being the Greek form of *Clemens*), while the other three names are Greek in origin. Oakes notes the potential corroborative value of this information (along with the individuals mentioned in Acts 16: Lydia and her household, a female slave, and a jailor and his household), which fits generally the parameters of the model for the Philippian church he proposes through socio-historical reconstruction. Using evidence such as the history of Philippi and its environs and existing inscriptions, Oakes approximates the make-up of Philippi itself in the mid first century and then the church at Philippi. His proposal for the church is that about a third were of Roman citizenship and two-thirds Greek without Roman citizenship.[3]

---

3. Oakes, *Philippians*, pp. 63–65. His estimate fits within a wider range allowed for in his modelling – Roman citizens (rather than ethnic

*Paul's rhetorical emphases in Philippians 4:2–9:* In this text, Paul focuses primarily on logos as he encourages the Philippians to pursue unity, joy, peace, wisdom and imitation, all from a Christ-centred mindset. He grounds these exhortations, in part, in Jesus' nearness (4:5) and the reality of divine peace (4:7, 9). Paul employs pathos in his appeals to Euodia and Syntyche to 'be of the same mind in the Lord', as he 'pleads' with them and paints a picture of their deep connection with Paul and his mission and their identity as belonging to God (4:2–3). Paul also taps into his own ethos as he speaks of his valued co-workers (4:3) and provides his own lived example (4:9).

## Comment
### A. Shared mindset for two co-workers (4:2–3)

**2.** These opening verses (4:2–3) offer a particular call to unity and a Christ-directed mindset that connects back to the general exhortation to the entire congregation in 1:27 − 2:4, and especially at 2:2–3. Paul addresses quite specifically two of his colleagues in ministry from the Philippian church, Euodia and Syntyche.

Paul clarifies who these two believers are in 4:3: they are Paul's 'co-workers' who have participated with him in the ministry of the gospel. Other than Epaphroditus (already mentioned in 2:25), these two women and Clement (4:3) are the only Philippian believers mentioned by name in the letter. By naming these four from the Philippian congregation, Paul calls specific attention to them and highlights their service – all four are referred to as his co-workers (2:25; 4:3). This attention probably designates them as church leaders, a point suggested by quite a number of commentators, including John Chrysostom (fourth century), and corroborated by the unique feature of the letter's opening where Paul explicitly greets 'overseers and deacons' along with the rest of the church at Philippi (1:1). As Cohick suggests, 'This unusual

Romans only): 25–40%; Greeks: 60–75% (p. 63; with Oakes's definition of 'Greek' including Macedonians and a few slaves of non-Greek origin).

feature, along with mentioning these women by name, likely indicates that the women belong in one of these two [leadership] categories.'[4]

While the matter of Pauline theology and practice related to women in church leadership is debated, often quite heatedly, if Philippians were the only letter we had from Paul, there would be little to contest. In other words, the implied author we encounter in Philippians highlights female leadership within the Philippian church, with half Paul's named 'co-workers' being women. Even if the problem between these women is understood to be a significant conflict (see discussion below for additional possibilities), this only emphasizes the importance of these two women within the Philippian congregation. It is unlikely Paul would take the space to address an issue that had little significance for the well-being of the entire church community.

Further evidence that these two women were leaders within the Philippian congregation (its house churches) is the corroborating testimony of Acts concerning the prominence of women at the founding of the Philippian church. An important person in the Acts 16 narrative is Lydia, who seems to have been the first person in Philippi to respond to the gospel (Acts 16:14). Lydia is described in Acts as 'a woman from the city of Thyatira' (located in the region of Lydia in Asia Minor or modern-day Turkey) and 'a dealer in purple cloth' (16:14). After responding positively to the gospel, she and those belonging to her household were baptized, and she hosted Paul and his ministry companions in her home (16:15). Later, the narrator indicates that the budding church in Philippi gathered in her home (16:40).

In first-century terms, Lydia functioned as a patron to Paul and his colleagues, acting as host during their stay in Philippi and, presumably, receiving benefits in return, such as influence in the believing community.[5] We hear of other women in the early Christian movement who seem to have fulfilled such patronage roles in house churches they hosted (e.g. Acts 12:12; Rom. 16:3–5; 1

---

4. Cohick, p. 210.

5. Cohick, p. 210; cf. Osiek, p. 111.

Cor. 1:11; Col. 4:15). And Paul singles out Phoebe, the letter-carrier of Romans, by referring to her as a 'benefactor' (*prostatis*) of many people, a term used for the specific role of benefaction (Rom. 16:2). In this cultural and ecclesial setting, it is not hard to imagine that the two women Paul corrects and extols in Philippians 4:2–3 could also be patrons and leaders within the Philippian house church(es).[6]

The situation Paul addresses is illuminated by his call to Euodia and Syntyche *to be of the same mind (to auto phronein)*. Importantly, Paul exhorts these colleagues towards a shared mindset *in the Lord (en kyriō)*, with the entire phrase relevant for Paul's meaning. This language closely resembles Paul's earlier admonitions to be 'like-minded' (*to auto phronein*, 2:2) and to share Christ's 'mindset' (*phronete . . . en Christō*, 2:5). These echoes of earlier exhortations help in clarifying the matter that Paul addresses with Euodia and Syntyche. He calls them to a shared mindset, as is usually argued. But that is not all. Given that Paul describes this shared mindset with *en kyriō*, he is calling these co-workers to take on Christ's mindset (2:5) – a mindset characterized by humility and service (2:6–8; cf. 2:2–4). Given that the goal is a sharing together in the Lord's mindset, the problem might be focused on disunity (as traditionally supposed). Or the issue might centre on attitudes or dispositions that would work against humility, attitudes described by Paul in 2:3 as 'selfish ambition' and 'vain conceit'.[7]

Paul does not give details about the exact nature of the issue between Euodia and Syntyche. If, as suggested here, Euodia and Syntyche are leaders in the Philippian church (along with Epaphroditus, Clement and others), then it is likely that their conflict or problematic dispositions centred on something important to the mission of the Philippian church. Euodia and Syntyche may have each had responsibility for and influence over a part of the Philippian congregation, potentially together leading a house church or each being part of the leadership of different

---

6. For the intriguing suggestion that Lydia and Euodia are the same person, see Fellows, 'Name Giving', p. 254.

7. Fellows and Stewart, 'Phil 4:2–3', pp. 226–228; see Cohick, p. 212.

house churches. Their issue may have involved competing ways of envisioning how the community should engage with their common life together – how they should 'work out [their] salvation' (2:12) and live distinctively within the context of Philippi and its adherence to Roman values and priorities.

The tone of Paul's exhortations fits the warmth of the letter more generally. He pleads with or appeals to (*parakaleō*) both women, in equal fashion, using the verbal imperative twice, once for each woman: *I plead with Euodia and I plead with Syntyche*.[8] This may indicate Paul's desire to avoid taking sides and to affirm the agency of both women in moving towards humility and harmony. If so, Paul 'urges each one to equally step close to the other for the sake of gospel unity in mission'.[9] The word order moving from 4:1 to the appeal (4:2) seems significant in discerning Paul's tone. The final word of 4:1 is 'beloved' (*agapētoi*), and the initial words of 4:2 are 'Euodia-I plead and-Syntyche-I plead'. Fee suggests that it is significant that there is no conjunction between these verses and that Euodia's name follows immediately after 'beloved'.[10] These women are integral to the community so dearly loved by Paul.

Paul names the two women, an action best understood in line with Pauline practice more generally. Paul refers to fellow believers by name frequently in his letters. Yet apart from references to his own associates (such as Timothy) or to apostolic leaders (such as Peter and James), most of these named references occur in the initial and final greetings of his letters (e.g. Rom. 16:3–23; 1 Cor. 1:1; 16:19; 2 Tim. 4:19–21; Phlm. 1–2, 23–24) and in remarks about various believers coming and going between Paul and his letter audience, sometimes with Paul's commendation of particular persons (e.g. 1 Cor. 16:10–18; Eph. 6:21–22; Phil. 2:25–30). Seldom does Paul directly admonish specific believers by name, proving true the generalization that 'Paul frequently names his friends and fellow workers but very rarely those with

---

8. For a description of the appeal formula (often with this verb), common in ancient letters, see Weima, *Paul*, pp. 92–93.

9. Gupta, p. 95.

10. Fee, p. 286 n. 12.

whom he disagrees'.[11] So his naming of Euodia and Syntyche signals his positive regard for them, especially given the commendations that follow. As a result, it is unlikely that Paul viewed the situation as dire. Instead, he frames it as an opportunity for these co-workers to come together in Christ for the sake of mission.

**3.** Paul turns from directly exhorting Euodia and Syntyche to addressing someone he refers to as his *true companion* (*gnēsie syzyge*), asking this person (or group) to come alongside these women and assist them: *Yes, and I ask you, my true companion, help these women.* The identity of this *companion* is not made explicit by Paul and so is a matter of some debate. Some interpreters have suggested Paul refers to a specific person named Syzugus (e.g. CJB), although there is no inscriptional or literary evidence for *syzyge* as a proper name. Others have suggested it refers to a specific individual, such as Epaphroditus, although it is not clear why Paul would avoid expressly naming the person if he or she was known to the community. Given these issues, a third line of interpretation understands the addressee to be the church as a whole, with the singular *true companion* standing in for the congregation.[12] If Paul uses *true companion* to refer corporately to the Philippian believers, he would be 'inviting the various members of the church to prove themselves loyal partners in the work of the gospel'.[13]

Determining which of these possibilities is most likely depends to some degree on what Paul is asking this person or group to do.

---

11. Hooker, p. 539. The exception in the Pastorals proves the rule: three named men who are described in wholly negative terms are not directly addressed and are no longer included in the believing community (1 Tim 1:20; 2 Tim. 4:10). The significant admonition to reprove elders who are in error maintains their anonymity (1 Tim. 5:20). As Fee notes, by not naming his enemies, Paul 'denigrate(s) by anonymity' (p. 389 n. 25).

12. A similar use of the singular 'you' (as here) for a letter's audience occurs in Rom. 8:2 ('the law of the Spirit . . . has set you [sing.] free'), with the commonplace use of plural pronouns resuming at 8:4.

13. Silva, p. 193; also Fellows and Stewart, 'Phil 4:2-3'.

The contextually relevant sense of the verb *syllambanō* has to do with helping someone 'by taking part with someone in an activity' (BDAG, pp. 955–956). This suggests that Paul was wanting this *true companion* to come alongside Euodia and Syntyche and join them in pursuing a 'common mindset in the Lord' that overcomes any divisiveness (4:2). While it has been traditional to view Paul asking this *companion* to mediate between Euodia and Syntyche, the *syn* prefix makes it more likely that Paul is appealing for this person or group to join these leaders in the shared mindset already commended (2:2–4, 5). In this light, the identity of *gnēsie syzyge* is more likely to be the whole Philippian congregation.

Paul moves from this appeal to a commendation of Euodia and Syntyche, identifying them as his own (long-standing) co-workers in service to the gospel and as attested members of God's faithful people. He first describes them as having *contended at my side in the cause of the gospel*. Paul uses the same verb here, *synathleō* (*contended at my side*), as he has at the beginning of the letter's body to describe the posture he desires from the Philippian community in relation to the gospel ('striving together', 1:27). He uses the past tense of the verb to indicate that he and these leaders have a history together, possibly going back to Paul's first days in Philippi (e.g. included in the *adelphoi* of Acts 16:40). They have diligently worked alongside Paul 'in the gospel' (*en tō euangeliō*) – a phrase that probably indicates their shared work in the sphere of gospel ministry (NIV: *in the cause of the gospel*).

Paul connects Euodia and Syntyche to a number of other leaders who have worked alongside Paul. He mentions by name Clement, who is the only Roman member (Latin: *Clemens*) of the Philippian church named in the letter (see Context). Paul then refers in another phrase to other co-workers in the Philippian community: *and the rest of my co-workers*. This phrasing (*rest of*) indicates that Paul considers Clement, Euodia and Syntyche his co-workers as well. His reference to co-workers (*synergos*) echoes his earlier reference to Epaphroditus as his 'co-worker' (2:25) and suggests that Paul is using this term to identify leaders in the Philippian church. Later scribes may have found the identification of the two women as 'co-workers' (i.e. leaders) problematic and so adjusted the word order of 4:3. Two early Greek manuscripts include this ordering of the material: 'along with Clement and my co-workers and the rest'.[14] In this sequence, Paul's co-workers are a distinct group that does not include Euodia, Syntyche or Clement. Keown suggests that adjustment arose from 'patriarchal concerns'.[15]

Paul's final affirmation of Euodia and Syntyche, Clement and Paul's other co-workers in Philippi describes them as those *whose names are in the book of life* (*biblos zōēs*). This phrase derives from an image of God inscribing the names of the faithful in a book (see Exod. 32:32–33; Ps. 69:28; Dan. 12:1); and Psalm 69 includes the language of 'life' in its reference to 'the book of the living' (*biblos zōntōn*) (Ps. 68:29, LXX). Paul uses the noun *life*, which explains the metaphor of God's book (so, probably a genitive of apposition): inclusion in the book is inclusion in resurrected life. Given the eschatological context of Philippians 3 along with Paul's allusion to Daniel 12:3 in Philippians 2:15, Daniel 12:1 might be the backdrop for *the book of life*: 'at that time your people – everyone whose name is found written in the book – will be delivered' (Dan. 12:1).[16] In using this language, Paul emphasizes the bedrock of God's faithfulness to God's people.

## B. Joy and peace in the Lord (4:4–7)

**4.** As he begins a section of concluding and more general exhortations (4:4–8), Paul calls the Philippians to rejoicing as a continuing practice: *Rejoice . . . always*. The theme of joy and rejoicing has been pervasive in the letter, with Paul expressing his own joy over the Philippians (1:4; 2:17; 4:1, 10) and in the gospel going forward (1:18). He has encouraged the Philippians to rejoice in their shared ministry (2:18), in the return of Epaphroditus (2:28–29), and as a practice that gives them a secure foundation (3:1). Now, Paul

---

14. The reading found in the NIV (and virtually all English translations) has strong, early manuscript support.

15. Keown II, p. 299. Alternatively, Fee thinks the change derived from an interest in a reading that concluded with all Philippian believers in view, with *and the rest* covering the entire community (Fee, p. 385 n. 4).

16. McAuley, *Scripture*, p. 217.

emphasizes the importance of living out a pattern of joy. And it is a joy found and exercised *in the Lord* (cf. 3:1; 4:10). To highlight the importance of this foundational Christian habit, Paul repeats the command with emphasis: *I will say it again: rejoice!* Noting the contours of this theme of joy across the letter, Wright observes, 'Philippians is itself a celebration, a sustained declaration of joy in God, joy in the gospel, joy in the Lord, joy despite adverse circumstances, joy expressed in faith and hope and love and, above all, unity.'[17]

**5.** To the joy that is consistently to mark their lives as a community, Paul adds another practice that is to characterize the Philippians: *Let your gentleness be evident to all.* The way Paul frames this exhortation – that their gentleness should *be evident* – implies a continuing pattern of behaviour, a disposition, one that is visible 'to all people' (*pasin anthrōpois*). This is not an occasional practice noticed only by a few. Instead, the Philippian believers, as a community, should be marked by this trait.[18] The adjective *epieikēs* means 'not insisting on every right of letter of law or custom', with the following translation possibilities provided for the term: '*yielding, gentle, kind, courteous, tolerant*' (BDAG, p. 371). Paul exhorts the Philippians to a continuing posture of kindness or gentleness in relation to those outside the faith (cf. 1 Pet. 3:15). It is a posture of willingness to let go of rights or customs for the sake of the other, for the sake of mission. In this way, it sounds something like the admonition to 'in humility value others [within the community of faith] above yourselves' (2:3). Paul desires that the Philippians might be known for this kind of gentleness, not just within the family of faith but as a matter of their public reputation (cf. 2:15–16).

Before turning to a third admonition (this one about anxiety, 4:6), Paul provides a brief but compelling Christological affirmation: *The Lord is near* (with the referent for 'Lord' across Philippians being Christ). Given that this line comes at the end of what, in English translations, is verse 5, it is easy to read it as the basis for

---

17. Wright, 'Joy', p. 51.
18. Gupta, p. 96.

the previous exhortation to a missional and communal disposition of gentleness. And this may be quite right. Yet given that there are no connecting conjunctions before or after the affirmation of the Lord's nearness (from 4:4—6a), Paul could be using it to prepare for the subsequent exhortation about anxiety (4:6). And, as we will see, hearing the affirmation to ground either or both exhortations makes good sense contextually.[19]

There is an inherent ambiguity in *The Lord is near*, given that the Greek term (*engys*) as well as its English equivalent (*near*) can refer to spatial or temporal proximity. Does Paul mean to indicate that the Lord (Jesus) is nearby or close to his people? If so, Paul is probably drawing on Psalm 145 (LXX, Ps. 144), a psalm of praise to Israel's God. The psalm extols the Lord's power and the Lord's compassion for every created thing (Ps. 144:9, 16, LXX). The psalmist writes, 'The LORD is near [*engys kyrios*] to all who call on him, to all who call on him in truth' (144:18, LXX). If this is the backdrop for Philippians 4:6, then the affirmation that the Lord is near to believers probably introduces the invitation to turn from anxiety in the subsequent verse.

On the other hand, *The Lord is near* could have a temporal sense, referring to Christ's impending return. This sense fits the strong eschatological cast of Philippians 3 and follows nicely from Paul's affirmation that believers 'eagerly' wait for 'the Lord' to arrive to bring about final resurrection (3:20—21). This reading follows well from Paul's commendation of a posture of gentleness towards outsiders, providing a sense of urgency to this missional stance. Given contextual evidence for both meanings of *near* (spatial and temporal) and the lack of any conjunction to clarify the direction of the affirmation of the Lord's nearness, it may be that Paul intends the Philippians to hear both meanings resonating from this assurance, as it functions as a hinge in support of the surrounding exhortations.[20]

---

19. Fee, p. 407.

20. Fee (p. 407) suggests an 'intentional double entendre', quite unusual in Paul. For the possibility of intentional ambiguity, see also Brown, *Scripture*, pp. 80—81.

**6.** Paul provides a third exhortation in this brief summary list, focused not on a communal pattern to pursue (joy, gentleness) but on something for the community to avoid: *Do not be anxious about anything.* If the previous line is emphasizing that Jesus as Lord is close to believers (see comment on 4:5), then the possibility of being free from anxiety is tied, in part, to the experience of the Lord's nearness. This certainly aligns with Paul's antidote for anxiety: a posture of prayer before God. It is because the Philippians have a God who has drawn near in Christ that they can be freed from the bonds of anxiety. Again, overtones from the Psalms are apparent in Paul's expressions here.[21] Affirming God's attentiveness to the believer's deepest concerns echoes the psalmist's invitation to 'Cast on the Lord your anxiety [*merimna*] and he will sustain you; he will never allow the righteous person to be shaken' (Ps. 54:23, LXX [Eng. 55:22]; cf. 1 Pet. 5:7). Paul may be envisioning particular anxiety-producing triggers for the community, such as the opposition and resulting suffering the Philippians are experiencing (1:28–29).

This is the second time in the letter that Paul has used language of anxiety or concern (*merimnaō*). In his description of Timothy, Paul has honoured him for his 'genuine concern for [the] welfare' of the Philippians (2:20), using *merimnaō* to denote Timothy's care for the other. In his discussion of his co-workers Timothy and Epaphroditus, Paul has used a variety of terms that highlight a kind of 'relational anxiety' existing among Paul, Timothy, Epaphroditus and the Philippian believers (see Theology on 2:19–30). Juxtaposing that relational anxiety with Paul's admonition here to 'be anxious for nothing' (*mēden merimnate*) invites thoughtful reflection on Paul's differentiation among various kinds of anxieties.

Paul's reflections elsewhere lend support for such nuancing. In 1 Corinthians 7:32–34, Paul expresses a desire that the Corinthian believers be 'free from concern' (*amerimnos*) in relation to marriage (7:32). He illustrates this by observing that the unmarried are 'concerned about the Lord's affairs' (*merimnaō ta tou kyriou*, 7:32, 34),

---

21. Fee describes the language of 4:4–7 as characteristic of the Psalter (p. 401 n. 8).

while married persons are 'concerned about the affairs of this world' (*merimnaō ta tou kosmou*, 7:33, 34). Paul, in this passage, aligns the state of being free from concern with a state of having the right kinds of concerns – those revolving around the Lord (*ta tou kyriou*). Later in 1 Corinthians, Paul describes unity in the corporate body of believers in this way: 'its parts should have equal concern [*merimnaō*] for each other' (1 Cor. 12:25). Christians are right to be concerned for one another (for all members of the body, in this metaphor). Paul himself exhibits this kind of properly focused 'relational anxiety' when he writes, 'I face daily the pressure of my concern [*merimna*] for all the churches' (2 Cor. 11:28). It seems that, for Paul, appropriate anxiety or concern is less about its intensity and more about its object. Christ and the welfare of other believers (other people) are the greatest of priorities – the sphere in which stakes are high. As a result, accompanying anxieties are not unexpected and are not, as Paul frames them, to be avoided. As Peters suggests, anxiety is not itself sin but can 'read[y] us for sin'.[22] Returning to the call to turn from anxiety in 4:6, we can see a more nuanced picture of the various kinds of anxieties Paul may have in mind (or may not be addressing) in this prohibition.

Paul's exhortation about anxiety is followed by a strong adversative (*but, alla*) that provides the route to regulating anxieties of all kinds:[23] *but . . . present your requests to God.* When faced with anxieties, Paul invites believers to pray, though not in a way that assumes simplistic overly spiritualized answers to complex problems. What Paul describes is a way of life (*in every situation*, along with the present-tense verb *present*) focused on the freedom to bring before the one true God all matters of concern and of gratitude (*by prayer and petition, with thanksgiving*). Practising dependence on God – recognizing one's own limits and God's limitlessness – can be transformative. As Paul

---

22. Peters, *Sin*, p. 11. Gupta helpfully reminds us that, at Phil. 4:6, 'Paul's counsel is general and theological, not clinical' (p. 103), so we should be cautious about using this verse to presume the spiritual state of those who struggle with chronic anxiety or anxiety disorders.

23. The language of 'regulating anxiety' comes from Sandage, Jensen and Jass, 'Transformation', p. 188.

makes clear in 4:7, this all-encompassing lifestyle of prayer results, not necessarily in the removal of pain or obstacles, but in a transcendent peace that is able to protect believers from overwhelming anxieties.

**7.** The promise arising from habitual dependence on God in prayer is the gift of *the peace of God*. God's peace will guard or protect the whole self of believers (their *hearts* and *minds*). Paul describes this divine peace as a peace *which transcends all understanding*, indicating that it is the *experience* of peace that is being offered, not merely a cognitive recognition of it. The phrasing 'transcending all understanding' suggests something like our English term 'mind-boggling'. Or, to shift the metaphor, God's peace can become a breathtaking reality, even and especially in anxiety-provoking circumstances, when Christians rely on their faithful God.

Paul references *peace* in Philippians only here (4:7, 9) and in his opening greeting formula: 'Grace and peace to you from God our Father and the Lord Jesus Christ' (1:2; see comment). *Peace* (*eirēnē*) represents the Hebrew *šālôm*, which signals holistic, communal salvation. For Paul, 'peace becomes a reality in the death and resurrection of Jesus Christ' (e.g. Rom. 5:1; Eph. 2:14–17),[24] and characterizes believers who live by the Spirit (e.g. Rom. 8:6; 14:17; Gal. 5:22). Paul may be offering an implicit contrast between *the peace of God* – authentic peace – and the 'peace of Rome', known as the Pax Romana. As Tamez suggests, 'this is exactly what the [Philippians] need, a peace that is different from the vaunted peace of the *pax romana* imposed on the conquered'.[25] God's peace, in contrast, is a gift given freely to all who call on the Lord.

## C. Wise evaluation of virtues, imitation of behaviour (4:8–9)

**8.** Using the adverbial *Finally* (*to loipon*; cf. 3:1), along with his characteristic address, *brothers and sisters*, Paul offers his concluding exhortations for the entire letter (4:8–9). As we have already seen, these entreaties recapitulate earlier ones in Philippians (see

---

24. Bockmuehl, p. 248.
25. Tamez, p. 110.

Context). Specifically, the call to 'consider' or assess what is good (4:8) fits the pattern of pursuing a Christlike mindset informed by the gospel (e.g. 2:5; 3:7–8; see Introduction 4d). Such a mindset reorients what these believers consider to be valuable and how they evaluate all aspects of life.

Paul provides a lengthy list of virtues that he commends to the Philippian believers. They are to focus on what is *true, noble, right, pure, lovely, admirable, excellent* and *praiseworthy*. These qualities that Paul catalogues are common values examined in Graeco-Roman moral discourse. As such, these qualities would have evoked for the Philippians the values supported and discussed within their own cultural milieu. As Fee suggests, Paul 'appears to be dipping into the language of Hellenistic moralism, in his case tempered by Jewish wisdom'.[26] Of the first six terms (with each adjective introduced by the pronoun *whatever, hosa*), five occur only here in Philippians (*right [dikaios]* also occurs at 1:7, and is commonplace in Paul). Two terms – translated *lovely* and *admirable* – occur only here in the New Testament and seem to refer to aesthetic rather than strictly moral qualities.[27]

The final two qualities are nouns and are introduced distinctively, each with *ei tis*: 'if anything [is characterized by] excellence, if anything [is characterized by] praise'. As such, and because of their more general senses, they sum up and provide the climax for the entire list. The first term, 'excellence', is the Greek *aretē* that corresponds to Aristotle's well-developed theory of virtue, with his work on this topic, *On Virtues and Vices*, including the term.[28] The second term, 'praise(worthy)' (*epainos*), in this context likely refers to 'what evokes universal approval'.[29] Aristotle ties these

---

26. Fee, p. 416. See his discussion of specific terms and his examples of their use in Jewish wisdom literature (pp. 417–419).

27. With *lovely, prosphilēs*, not used in Graeco-Roman virtue lists; see Bockmuehl, p. 253.

28. This is the only occurrence of *aretē* in the Pauline letters; it does occur in the Petrine writings (1 Pet. 2:9; 2 Pet. 1:3, 5).

29. Willis, 'Virtue', p. 71. Paul uses it at 1:11 of praise to God (his usual usage).

two terms closely together, as Paul does here, by contending that what is worthy of praise (*epaineton*) involves *aretē* or the exercise of *aretē* (*Eudemian Ethics* 2.1.19). Paul's virtue list highlights what is good and best and taps into the cultural conversation of the day about what constitutes these ideals. Paul is evoking this wider cultural conversation, and the question becomes his specific purpose in using this language.

The verb Paul uses directs us towards the answer to this question. Paul exhorts the Philippians to 'consider' or 'reckon with' (*logizomai*) these virtues. While the NIV and many other English versions render *logizomai* as 'think' (*think about such things*), in this context Paul is more probably calling his audience to deliberation and discernment about these virtues, and to consider them in the light of the gospel (see 4:9). Paul's other use of *logizomai* in the letter fits this sense. In 3:13, he has described his own eschatological mindset related to final resurrection and full salvation: 'I do not consider [*logizomai*] myself yet to have taken hold of it.' Paul's use of *logizomai* in the sense of 'consider' or 'evaluate' fits a wider pattern of language in the letter around pursuing a Christlike (gospel-focused) mindset, including usage of *phroneō* and *hēgeomai* (see Theology below). Paul borrows the *categories* but not necessarily the *content* from Greek culture, with the 'if' clauses opening up space for theological reflection on what is *truly* excellent and praiseworthy. 'Learning how to discern what is truly excellent in God's eyes as opposed to what merely appears excellent according to common convention is a crucial task in creating a Christian discourse.'[30]

**9.** Paul concludes by providing a parallel exhortation to the previous one: *tauta logizesthe . . . tauta prassete* ('these things consider . . . these things practise', 4:8–9). The referent of *tauta* ('these things') in each case is distinct. In 4:8, Paul has called the Philippians to an evaluative mindset for the *range of virtues* extolled within wider society. They are to consider and assess 'these things' (well-known virtues) from the mindset of Christ (cf. 2:5). In 4:9, Paul refers to his own teaching of the gospel and his example of living it out, and calls the Philippians to *put . . . into practice* 'these things'.

---

30. Fowl, p. 188.

The specific language Paul uses centres on the gospel preached and enacted: *Whatever you have learned or received or heard from me, or seen in me* ... The first two (or three) verbs focus on what the Philippians have gained from Paul, when he was with them (e.g. Acts 16:14, 17, 31–32), along with his message in the letter he now sends to them. They have learned (*manthanō*) from him, certainly with a focus on the gospel and the way to embody it in the life of the community (with one sense of *manthanō* involving learning through experience or practice, BDAG, p. 615). The verb *received* (*paralambanō*) can be used to refer to the passing down of tradition (i.e. a set of teachings), and, in this case, focuses on the message of the gospel as the central tradition passed down from Paul to the Philippians (1:5–7; cf. 1 Cor. 15:1–3). The third verb (*heard*) is more general and either provides a general conclusion to the first two verbs focused on Paul's message of the gospel, or should be understood as paired with 'see' and the prepositional phrase that concludes the verbal list (*en emoi*). The NIV reflects the latter understanding by including a version of the prepositional phrase with both final verbs: *heard from me, or seen in me*. In this reading, Paul's words and deeds point in unified fashion to the truth of the gospel. Paul's reference to his own example fits the recurring theme in Philippians of imitation (e.g. 3:17; see Introduction 4f).

Paul concludes the dual exhortation to a gospel-informed mindset (4:8) and a gospel-infused praxis (4:9) with a theological promise: *And the God of peace will be with you.* This last line not only corresponds to Paul's exhortations in 4:8–9, it also forms an *inclusio* with 4:7, where Paul promises 'the peace of God' as the Philippians bring their prayers to God. Paul refers to *the God of peace* at other points in his letters (Rom. 15:33; 16:20; 1 Cor. 14:33; 1 Thess. 5:23; 2 Thess. 3:16; cf. Heb. 13:20). Here, Paul moves from affirming peace as a divine gift to peace as a defining characteristic of God. Those who practise dependence on God in prayer (4:6) are promised God's peace (4:7). And as believers live wisely with a gospel mindset in society and live out the gospel in practice (4:8), the presence of the God who is peace will be in their midst. Such a vision corresponds to the wider canonical portrait of the God of *šālôm*. As the psalmist affirms, 'surely the LORD will declare peace / to his people, his faithful ones', looking ahead to a time when 'righteousness and peace will embrace' (Ps. 85:8, 10, CSB).

*Theology*

Paul's concluding exhortation to the Philippians takes an interesting turn as he delineates a catalogue of cultural values and presses his audience to consider a true understanding of these values in the light of the gospel (4:8–9). Migliore suggests that we might call Paul's interest here at the letter's conclusion his 'theology of culture'.[31] Paul has already prepared the way for this line of reasoning in his exhortations to communal discernment or a 'shared mindset'. This communal mindset is a disposition oriented around the gospel. Paul has used three key terms to express this distinctive disposition: *phroneō* ('mindset'; 1:7; 2:2, 5; 3:15, 19; 4:2, 10), *hēgeomai* ('consider'; 2:3, 6, 25; 3:7–8) and *logizomai* ('consider'; 3:13; 4:8). If we trace the theme of communal discernment across the letter, we see Paul calling his audience to the new pattern of thinking and living that emanates from the gospel of Christ and that reframes their past understandings and their previously held values and priorities.

Already in his opening prayer, he has prioritized love with knowledge leading to 'discern[ing] what is best' (1:10). This kind of communal discernment can happen only when the Philippians pursue a shared mindset (*phroneō*), free of self-aggrandizement and individual ambition (2:2; 4:2). By emulating Christ's mindset of humility and service to the other (2:5) and by reframing all of life through this lens (3:7–8, 13), they will grow towards maturity as a community (3:15). To demonstrate what living with a gospel mindset looks like, Paul provides his own example of reframing all things in the light of his relationship with Christ ('considering' from *hēgeoma* or *logizomai*; 3:7–8, 12–14). Now, in 4:8–9, he raises key categories for affirming what is valuable in life. Paul encourages the Philippians to bring an evaluative eye to these already known categories, asking them to 'consider' them afresh in the light of the gospel.

---

31. Migliore, p. 166.

This kind of discernment involves listening for the ways cultural values might align with or differ from the ways of the gospel. As Migliore suggests, 'determining what is true, just, and praiseworthy is not for Paul a matter that can simply be read off the customs and practices of a particular society or culture'.[32] We can see examples of Paul's own discernment practices in Philippians. For example, the calls to rejoice and to address anxiety (4:4–7) find resonance in, for example, Seneca (a Roman philosopher), who commends tranquillity of mind characterized by joy and peace (*De tranquillitate animi* 9.2.4–5). Yet Seneca's means of reaching this goal is quite distinct from Paul's. Seneca commends that people pursue balance, learning to be reconciled with their lot in life, to avoid complaining and to emphasize the good they do have (9.10.4). In contrast, Paul presses believers to find their joy *in the Lord* and turn *to their God* in prayer and thanksgiving. Paul's rationale is decidedly theological and Christological. On the other hand, the Christian virtue of humility (2:3) sits quite at odds with the philosophy of the day (see comment on 2:3–4). It would certainly not be considered 'excellent or praiseworthy' within Graeco-Roman moral deliberation. Yet in the light of Christ's profound act of humility (2:8), Christians are to evaluate humility as central to what is right, what is lovely, what is excellent.

And this discernment is best done in community, which Paul highlights in his language of a 'shared mindset' (*to auto phronein*, 2:2; 4:2; cf. 3:15). Believers pattern their life together by taking on the mindset of Jesus the Messiah. And this patterning involves continuing communal, theological deliberation as the realities of the gospel are discerned and lived out in any particular cultural context.

---

32. Migliore, p. 167.

# 9. PAUL'S SITUATION AND PERSPECTIVE CONCERNING THE PHILIPPIANS' GIFT (4:10–20)

## Context

In this final passage of Philippians leading into its concluding greetings (4:21–23), Paul expresses (implicitly) his gratitude for the monetary support the Philippian church has provided for him.[1] The location at the end of the letter of what has been called Paul's 'thankless thanks' is not accidental.[2] For example, in the light of the letter's characteristics related to orality and rhetoric, Fee argues that Paul intentionally places these sentiments at the end of the letter to leave the Philippians with an emphasis on his gratitude to them for their partnership ('the last words left ringing in their

---

1. Although the final greetings (4:21–23) are treated separately (see Comment section there), no discrete Context or Theology segment is included for the letter's concise ending. The Theology section on 4:10–20 has been placed after the brief discussion of 4:21–23, as a conclusion to the entire commentary.

2. Hawthorne, p. 259.

ears').[3] Fowl suggests that Paul has already communicated his gratitude in the letter (e.g. 1:3–5; 2:16–18) and any extended discussion of Paul's response to their gift (with some length required due to cultural expectations) would have needed to wait until a later point.[4]

Key themes that connect 4:10–20 with earlier parts of the letter include an emphasis on Paul's rejoicing (4:10; cf. 1:18; 2:17–18; cf. 4:1); a right 'mindset' informed by the gospel (4:10, 'concern'; 2:2, 5; 3:15; 4:2); the partnership of Paul and the Philippians (4:14–15, 'share[d]'; 1:5, 7; 2:1); and the framing of ministry – specifically the sharing of resources – using the metaphor of a temple sacrifice (4:18; cf. 2:17; see also comment on 2:25).

Given the complexity of expectations regarding reciprocity and gift-giving in the Graeco-Roman world (see comments on 4:10, 11, 17), the rhetorical flow of this passage includes a number of concessive turns in the argument where Paul qualifies a previous statement to bring greater nuance to his meaning. First, Paul tempers his reference to the Philippians' renewed concern for him by noting it was their lack of opportunity, not their lack of concern, that slowed the sending of their gift (4:10). Paul immediately turns to explain his joy in their gift by using a strong negative, *ouch* ('not', which begins the sentence), to indicate that he did not 'need' the gift itself, since he has learned the secret of contentment (4:11–12). He then tempers any potentially perceived lack of gratitude, using the concessive conjunction *plēn* ('Yet', 4:14), by commending the way they shared in his troubles. Finally, after delineating how the Philippians had shared with him through sending aid, Paul once again uses *ouch* ('not') to provide the qualification that he is not desirous of the gift for himself but for the credit accrued to them, since it functions as their gift to God (4:17). At the end of this carefully navigated argument, Paul lands on the theological nature of their gift and of their partnership with Paul in the gospel.

*Paul's rhetorical emphases in Philippians 4:10–20:* Paul relies on ethos in significant ways in this passage, evident in his first-person

---

3. Fee, p. 17.

4. Fowl, p. 190.

expressions throughout. Even as he navigates the complicated waters of gift-giving and reciprocity, he personally affirms the Philippians' actions on his behalf (4:10), their longstanding commitment to him and to the gospel (4:14–16), and how, in the end, he has been 'amply supplied' by their gifts to him brought by Epaphroditus. As already noted, Paul's logos or argument is finely tuned towards a carefully expressed gratitude that avoids obligating the Philippians further (see comment on 4:11). His argument concludes with the affirmation that their gift is 'pleasing to God' (4:18), and that God, drawing out of the divine riches, is the ultimate gift-giver (4:19–20).

*Comment*
## A. Joy in their gift and contentment in all circumstances (4:10–13)

**10.** Paul turns to the final topic of his letter (4:10–20): the gift the Philippians had provided for Paul and sent through Epaphroditus (4:15, 18). As he has done at earlier points, Paul frames the discourse in terms of his practice of rejoicing (cf. 1:18; 2:17–18). Paul has just exhorted his audience to rejoice in the Lord (4:4) and now demonstrates his own practice of joy: *I rejoiced greatly in the Lord*. The basis of Paul's joy is Christ (*the Lord*) and the focus is the Philippians' renewed concern for Paul. That *concern* translates *phronein*, a term used across Philippians to express an appropriate mindset formed by the gospel. Paul uses it here to affirm the Philippians' disposition towards Paul in their support for his work in the gospel. The phrase *to hyper emou phronein* is reminiscent of Paul's justification of his own disposition towards the Philippians: 'It is right for me to *feel this way about . . . you*' (*touto phronein hyper . . . hymōn*, 1:7 [emphasis added]). Paul's way of thinking and feeling about the Philippians is now being matched by the Philippians' way of thinking and feeling about Paul.

Paul speaks of the Philippians 'renewing' their concern for Paul, using the verb *anathallō*, which sometimes describes the (re)-blooming of plant life (e.g. Ezek. 17:24). In other occurrences it is used metaphorically, as it is here for the revived concern the Philippians have shown to Paul through the gift they sent him. Yet Paul immediately qualifies this idea by noting that their concern (*phroneō*) did not need revitalization but opportunity: *you were concerned, but you had no opportunity to show it.* It is not clear how long it had been since Paul had last received financial support from the church. In this passage, he will reference gifts he received on more than one occasion from the Philippians when he was in Thessalonica (4:16), presumably shortly after his initial work in Philippi (cf. Acts 17), and possibly thereafter. In 2 Corinthians 8:1–5, Paul mentions the generosity of the Macedonian churches, which would have included the church at Philippi as well as the churches of Thessalonica and Berea (Acts 17). Paul commends their giving in the face of a 'very severe trial' and in spite of 'their extreme poverty' (2 Cor. 8:2). He refers to their giving as a *koinōnia* ('sharing'), as he does in Philippians 1:5 (with cognates used in 4:14, 15; see comments). If Philippians is written from Rome in the early 60s, there could have been quite a span of time (close to a decade) between earlier gifts and the one sent through Epaphroditus to Paul in his imprisonment.

It may seem strange that Paul does not explicitly thank the Philippians for their gift, although his expression of joy functions as something of an implicit 'thank you'. Nowhere in this passage (4:10–20) does Paul express his gratitude directly. The indirect way Paul thanks them (4:10, 14, 18) fits the social conventions of giving and receiving, of patronage and friendship. As Fowl notes, 'A straightforward expression of thanks would invoke the very social conventions about status and reciprocity that Paul seeks here to circumscribe, if not undermine.'[5] Instead, Paul acknowledges indirectly that he is grateful for their financial support and tempers these expressions so as not to put the Philippians or himself in the awkward position of further obligation (see comment on 4:11).

**11.** Paul explains why he rejoices over their gift by providing his own perspective (his own mindset) on his circumstances. The Greek word order of this explanation emphasizes what he is *not* saying (*ouch hoti*, 'not that'). It is not an experience of need (*hysterēsis*) that leads Paul to rejoice over their giving. Quite the opposite: Paul

---

5. Fowl, p. 192.

has *learned to be content whatever the circumstances*. It can sound odd to
modern ears to hear Paul tempering his expression of joy, which
itself functions implicitly as a word of gratitude. It would have been
an important qualification, however, for Paul and the Philippians.
In the Graeco-Roman context (and between those of equal
standing), offering an explicit expression of gratitude by mentioning
one's need could be perceived as an appeal to fill that need, in this
case obligating the Philippians to additional giving.[6] Paul would
also have wanted to avoid the implication that he himself had an
obligation to 'respond in kind to their gift', as could be expected
within social convention.[7] Paul wants to demonstrate implicitly
his appreciation for their gift without centring his own need for it.
In 4:17–19, he will foreground the divine benefit the Philippians
have received.

Paul's contentment is something he has learned (*manthanō*), a
term he has just used (4:9). It can connote learning through experience or practice (BDAG, p. 615), which fits well in this context, in
which Paul refers to learning contentment *whatever the circumstances*.
Paul's self-described track record elsewhere demonstrates he had
become practised in situations where he was hungry and thirsty,
and without adequate shelter, clothing or sleep (1 Cor. 4:11; 2 Cor.
11:27; cf. 11:23–29). Learning to be *content* (*autarkēs*) in such circumstances (or in situations of plenty, 4:12) would not have been the
only possible outcome. In fact, Stoic philosophers, such as Seneca
and Epictetus, describe two ways of life: one characterized by
frustration with the way things are, and the other defined by
contentment and so 'with a gentle spirit awaiting anything that may
yet befall, and enduring that which has already befallen' (Epictetus,
*Discourses* 4.7.12–13). In Stoic thought, the difference between the
two ways comes down to a person's perspective towards what
cannot be controlled (e.g. external circumstances). As long as a

---

6. Peterman, *Paul's Gift*, pp. 134–135; also pp. 88–89 (see Seneca, *De
   beneficiis* 2.2.1–2; 7.24.1–2).

7. Cohick, p. 242. For an extended discussion of Graeco-Roman
   conventions about patronage, friendship and giving, see Cohick,
   pp. 237–244.

person does not tie his or her sense of the good to these external situations, that person can be 'content' (or 'self-sufficient'). As Epictetus vividly expresses it,

> 'Would you have me bear poverty?' Bring it on and you shall see what poverty is when it finds a good actor to play the part ... 'Well, and would you have me bear troubles?' Bring them on too. 'Well, and exile?' Wherever I go it will be well with me, for here where I am it was well with me, not because of my location, but because of my judgements, and these I shall carry away with me ... and with the possession of them I am content, wherever I be and whatever I do.
>
> (*Discourses* 4.7.13–15)[8]

Paul differs from the Stoic philosopher, not in his contentment in whatever the situation, but in the *source* of his contentment, which sits outside himself and comes from Christ (see 4:13 and comment).

**12.** Paul expands on his assertion that he has learned to be content whatever his situation by delineating a series of contrasting circumstances in which he has found contentment. He speaks of

> being *in need* (*tapeinoō*)  and  having *plenty* (*perisseuō*; as in 4:18)
> being *well fed* (*chortazō*)  and  being *hungry* (*peinaō*)
> *living in plenty* (*perisseuō*)  and  living *in want* (*hystereō*; cf. *hysterēsis*, 4:11)

The middle terms focus on Paul's specific (and distinct) experiences of lacking food and having an abundance to eat. The first and last verbal pairings are more general. The first verb, *in need* (*tapeinoō*), is a status term and has been used already by Paul to describe Christ's action of self-humbling (2:8). Here, it refers to the humble and abased circumstances that Paul has endured (e.g. his imprisonments

---

8. See also Seneca, *De vita beata* ('On the Happy Life') 6.2: 'The happy man, therefore, is one who has right judgement; the happy man is content with his present lot, no matter what it is, and is reconciled to his circumstances; the happy man is he who allows reason to fix the value of every condition of existence.'

and beatings; 2 Cor. 11:23–25; cf. 4:7–12), with likely echoes of Christ's decision to humble himself and the call for believers to be humble-minded (2:3). Paul has been prepared to live in the humblest of circumstances because he follows a Messiah who 'humbled himself by becoming obedient to death' (2:8).

Paul expresses these polarities of circumstance and indicates that he 'knows' the experience of both extremes. He then emphasizes that *in any and every situation* he has *learned the secret of being content* (with *of being content* implied from 4:11). Paul makes an unusual word choice here, *myeō*, a *hapax* in the New Testament (and only occurring once in the Septuagint, 3 Macc. 2:30). It was a technical term for being initiated into a mystery religion, of which there were many in the Graeco-Roman world (e.g. the Eleusinian mysteries, the Isis cult). It could be used in a more general sense (BDAG, p. 660), functioning as a metaphor for gaining knowledge 'through religious insight';[9] and it seems Paul uses it with this kind of 'revelatory nuance' to highlight the wisdom he has gained from God for a contented life.[10]

If we follow the verbs in Philippians 4:11–12, we hear Paul affirm that he has 'learned' (*manthanō*) through experience how to be content in all situations. He 'knows' how to live in both humble circumstances and situations of abundance. And he has 'gained such wisdom' (*myeō: learned the secret*) from God. If this is Paul's meaning, then he does not bifurcate the practical wisdom of lived experience from the wisdom given by God. The two aspects are integrated to guide his mindset and grant him the gift of contentment. And both are available to all believers, not just to a select few.[11]

**13.** Paul culminates his expression of contentment in any situation by pointing to the source of his capacity to live equally well

---

9. Holloway, p. 187.

10. Cohick, p. 247; Bird and Gupta, p. 189 (citing Philo, *On the Cherubim* 48–49).

11. In this way, Paul might be using *myeō* with some amount of irony, 'reframing' its technical usage concerning mysteries limited to those initiated into a religion to signal instead a revealed knowledge that 'is open to all believers in Christ' (Keown II, p. 412–413).

with little and with abundance: *I can do all this through him who gives me strength*. Paul 'is able' (*ischyō*) to be content only through Christ. The NIV's *all this* (*panta*, 'all' [plural]) rightly points the reader back to Paul's catalogue of his diverse experiences, through which he has practised and been granted contentment. This affirmation makes it clear how Paul's perspective on contentment diverges from that of Stoic philosophers. For Paul, being content (*autarkēs*) is not at its core a matter of self-sufficiency, since it is enabled only through the one who 'gives strength' (*endynamoō*) to believers. While Paul has quite deliberately played on Stoic terminology in this passage, 'no reader of Philippians could fail to be struck by the powerfully Christ-centered redefinition of [Paul's view of] contentment'.[12]

Some Greek manuscripts add 'Christ' in 4:13. While this reading has early attestation, internal evidence, along with solid external support, favours the view that a scribe added *Christō* to make explicit the identity of the one who empowers Paul's contentment. This is not ultimately unclear, however, since Christ has been central to Paul's teachings in Philippians 4 (e.g. 4:7); Paul has regularly been referencing Christ as 'the Lord' across the chapter (4:1, 2, 4, 5, 10). As such, the Philippians would almost certainly hear *him who gives me strength* to refer to Christ himself.

## B. The Philippians' participation with Paul and God's abundance (4:14–20)

**14.** This section continues closely from the previous one (4:10–13), with the whole of 4:10–20 providing a single and cohesive argument. As Paul has already qualified his expression of joy over the Philippians' gift to indicate that his need is not the driver of his response of joy (4:11–13), he now qualifies that qualification! His capacity to be content in Christ should not imply to the Philippians that he is ungrateful. So Paul again offers an implicit expression of thanks: *Yet it was good of you to share in my troubles*. Paul refers to their 'co-participation' in his troubles with the term *synkoinōneō*. Paul has used various cognates of this word across Philippians to emphasize

---

12. Bockmuehl, p. 187.

the partnership of Paul and the Philippians in the gospel and in Christ: *koinōnia* (noun: 'partnership' or 'sharing'; 1:5; 2:1; 3:10), *synkoinōnos* (personal noun: 'sharers' or 'co-participants'; 1:7) and *koinōneō* (verb: 'share'; 4:15). Paul considers the gift sent through Epaphroditus a tangible demonstration of the Philippians' partnership with Paul – a 'partnership in the gospel' (1:5) as they together 'share in God's grace' (1:7).

Paul's reference to *my troubles* (*thlipsis*) is probably a general nod to his imprisonment with its accompanying difficulties (cf. 1:17), including, we should presume, a regular deficit of resources. It bears noting, especially for readers whose lives are marked by fairly comfortable circumstances, that the experience of the imprisoned Paul and of many Philippian believers would rightly be described as being 'in need' and 'in want' (4:12). In his socio-logical modelling, Oakes approximates that one-quarter of this church were in poverty ('in habitual want') and many more would have lived at or near subsistence level,[13] cohering with Paul's char-acterization of the Macedonian churches elsewhere: 'their overflowing joy and their extreme poverty welled up in rich gener-osity' (2 Cor. 8:2). As Tamez describes the relationship of Paul and the Philippians, 'Paul knows that the majority of the members of the community of Philippi are poor, that their support of him is solidarity among the poor.'[14]

**15.** Paul recalls for the Philippians their longstanding relation-ship and partnership (*as you . . . know*) and narrates something of that history. He calls them *Philippians* here (uniquely) since he wants to distinguish them from other churches in their generosity towards Paul: *not one church . . . except you only*. This direct address is a Latinized form – *Philippēsioi* – of the Greek *Philippēnoi* or *Philippeis* (BDAG, p. 1057). It could refer to residents as well as citizens of Philippi and provides additional evidence of the significant influ-ence of the Latin language in Philippi (also the Latin loanword *praitōrion*, 1:13; see Introduction 2b[i]).[15]

---

13. Oakes, *Philippians*, pp. 48, 60–61.

14. Tamez, p. 115.

15. Oakes, *Philippians*, pp. 66–67.

Paul's rehearsal of their shared history in 4:15–16 starts at the very beginning: 'in the beginning of the gospel' – a shorthand for their introduction to the good news by Paul and his associates (cf. Acts 16). Paul references leaving Macedonia, a Roman province in northern Greece that included Philippi, Thessalonica and Berea (Acts 16:1 – 17:15), to continue his mission. According to Acts 17:16 – 18:17, he travelled to southern Greece and preached the gospel in Athens and Corinth. Paul highlights the Philippians as the only church who participated with Paul *in the matter of giving and receiving*. Although he affirms the generosity of the Macedonian churches more generally in 2 Corinthians 8:1–5, here he focuses on the pattern of generous exchange provided by the Philippian congregation, which seems to have been unusual.[16] And he returns to the language of 'sharing' or 'participating' (*koinōneō*) to describe that pattern (see comment on 4:14), drawing on terms that would have been at home in financial accounting: *giving, receiving,* 'credited to your account' (4:17), 'received full payment' (4:18). While a few commentators have suggested that this language indicates Paul and the Philippians have a kind of business partnership, it is more likely that Paul uses 'these financial terms metaphorically as a medium for social exchange'.[17]

**16.** As support for his characterization of the Philippian church as co-participants in the gospel, Paul references the resources sent early on by the Philippians when he was in Thessalonica, immediately after his time in Philippi (Acts 17). The pattern of their giving is signalled by Paul's phrase *more than once* (*kai hapax kai dis*). This phrase (woodenly: 'once and twice') is idiomatic for something occurring more than once but without further specification.[18] Paul either means that the Philippians *sent . . . aid* to him on more than one occasion when he was in Thessalonica (NIV and other English versions), or he indicates that they sent gifts both when he was in

---

16. Paul himself references more than once his practice of not drawing support from the churches he established (e.g. 1 Cor. 9:1–18; 2 Cor. 11:7–9; 1 Thess. 2:9; cf. Acts 18:1–3).

17. Osiek, p. 122.

18. Morris, '*Hapax*', pp. 205–208.

Thessalonica and more than once after that time (with *kai . . . kai hapax . . .* indicating 'both in Thessalonica and more than once [after that]').[19] The latter makes more sense of Paul's emphasis on their pattern of giving across their earlier history (not just in Thessalonica shortly after the Philippians received the gospel).

While Paul has been careful to avoid the impression that he rejoices in their gift because he needs it (*hysterēsis*, 4:10–11), he has no difficulty here affirming that the Philippians gave in order to address his need: *when I was in need* (*chreia*). He has already highlighted the role of Epaphroditus as the congregation's 'messenger . . . sent to take care of my needs' (*chreia*, 2:25). And he will point to God as the ultimate provider who 'will meet all your needs' (*chreia*; 4:19).

**17.** Paul again qualifies his affirmation of the Philippians' gift by frontloading the negative particle *Not* (*ouch*; cf. 4:11). Paul clarifies that what he desires (*epizēteō*) is not the gift itself but how they benefit from giving it. As we have noted, a delicate balance was required in that social context to convey Paul's appreciation for their gift, while avoiding the impression either that Paul was required to return the favour or that the Philippians ought to give more in the light of Paul's continuing need (see comments on 4:10–11). This is the first time in the letter he uses the language of 'gift' (*doma*), although their provision of resources (through Epaphroditus) has been reflected more than once (2:25, 30; 4:10–11, 15–16; cf. 1:5).

Continuing to use financial language, Paul portrays the gift of the Philippians as accruing to their *account* or ledger. Specifically, he ties their gift for him to an increased profit for them. By what logic does Paul arrive at this connection? It is important to recognize that Paul's sentiment goes beyond a conventional understanding of reciprocal giving and receiving in the Graeco-Roman world. In that context, the focus is on a back-and-forth reciprocity of giving that would involve exchanges of physical gifts as well as gifts of honour. In the process, the tendency was towards 'out-giving' the other party to accrue greater honour for oneself. While Paul does focus attention on the gain the Philippians themselves will receive

---

19. Morris, '*Hapax*', pp. 205–208; Reumann, p. 665.

because of their gift, he turns it in a quite different direction. Crucial to this metaphor of financial gain is the one in charge of their account: Paul implicitly brings God into the equation with this reference. As Fee suggests, Paul is referring to the Philippians' 'accrual of "interest" against [their] divine "account"'.[20] This will become very clear in 4:18–19, where God becomes the central figure providing the balance of reciprocity between the Philippians and Paul. Paul 'implicitly recognizes the Greco-Roman social conventions inherent in giving and receiving while at the same time subverting these conventions in light of the three-way relationship that obtains between Paul, the Philippians, and God'.[21]

**18.** Paul's final word about his own situation affirms that the gift given by the church has been more than sufficient. The Philippians can feel satisfied that they have no further obligation to give now that Paul has received *from Epaphroditus the gifts* sent by them. Paul's choice of language emphasizes the complete fulfilment of obligation: *I have received full payment and have more than enough. I am amply supplied.*

As he turns to the conclusion of his argument, Paul makes explicit that God is deeply engaged in the reciprocal relationship and profound partnership between the Philippians and Paul – a partnership embodied in their gift sent to Paul through Epaphroditus. Paul describes their gift with three theologically rich phrases: it is *a fragrant offering, an acceptable sacrifice, pleasing to God.* Together, they function to paint a picture of a sacrifice offered on an altar that God accepts as suitable and pleasing. The first Greek phrase, *osmē euōdias* (*a fragrant offering*), is used routinely in the Septuagint for a sacrifice whose aroma pleases God; that is, it is an acceptable offering (e.g. Gen. 8:21; Exod. 29:18, 25, 41; Lev. 1:9, 13, 17; LXX). In Ephesians 5:2, Christ himself is called an *osmē euōdias* ('a fragrant offering' to God); and Paul draws on *euōdia* elsewhere to affirm, 'we are to God the pleasing aroma [*euōdia*] of Christ' (2 Cor. 2:15). The second phrase, *an acceptable sacrifice*, highlights the importance of offering only sacrifices that are acceptable to God;

20. Fee, p. 447.
21. Fowl, p. 200.

that is, those which fit particular parameters (e.g. unblemished). Paul has already used the image of a sacrifice (with *thysia* at both 2:17 and 4:18) as a metaphor for the Philippians' faith and faithfulness (*pistis*, 2:17). Here, their gift to Paul is one expression of their faithfulness, and an important one. The image of an acceptable, sweet-smelling sacrifice culminates in its goal of being *pleasing to God* (cf. Rom. 12:1). These images, with their Septuagintal flavour, would have resonated among Jewish audiences. They would also have been fully understandable among the primarily Gentile Philippian congregation, whose past loyalties and practices of worship would have involved offerings and sacrifices to their former gods.

By interpreting the Philippians' gift theologically, Paul brings God into the centre of the relationship he has with the Philippians. The recipient of the gifts sent by the Philippians is not only or even primarily Paul. Although given *for Paul*, they are given *to God* as an expression of their faith. Peterman refers to this configuration as a 'social triangle' (versus a dyad) and emphasizes that this framework is congruent with the Old Testament.[22] For example, we read in Proverbs 19:17,

> Whoever is kind to the poor lends to the LORD,
> > and he will reward them for what they have done.

This kind of theological triangulation complicates and re-orients conventions of giving and receiving by highlighting God's central and necessary role in the relationships within the Christ community.

**19.** Paul continues this theological emphasis with the promise that *my God will meet all your needs*. Paul now refers to their need for the first time in the passage. While he has not framed his need for their support in terms that would require them to give more (4:10–11), he has referenced his need that has been fully met by their gift (4:16; cf. 2:25). By turning to highlight their needs, Paul could be obliged, according to convention, to address those needs. He does,

---

22. Peterman, *Paul's Gift*, p. 36.

though in an unconventional way. He places the responsibility for this provision not on himself but on God. As God has been the happy recipient of their gift for Paul (4:18b), God will be the giver as well.[23] Paul connects closely and reciprocally God's provision for the Philippians to their own giving by using the same verb, *plēroō*, for both: 'meet' (4:19) and 'amply supplied' (4:18).

Paul accentuates that God gives in line with the expanse of *the riches of his glory in Christ Jesus*. The phrase *of . . . glory* (*en doxē*) could be adjectival (i.e. 'glorious riches'); and, while some argue this is not the natural reading, it is the way the phrase *en doxē* is used in 2 Corinthians 3:7–8, 11. If adjectival, then Paul is highlighting the divine wealth as 'magnificent, eye-catching, splendid, renowned'.[24] The phrase could also be read locatively, identifying the sphere of God's riches and indicating that God's riches derive from the divine glory – the vastness of God's presence, power and benevolence.[25] The final phrase – *in Christ Jesus* (*en Christō Iēsou*) – is Paul's routine shorthand (e.g. 1:1; 2:1, 5; 3:14; 4:7) to express the relational union believers enjoy with Christ and which involves communally sharing in the defining experiences and benefits of Christ (see comment on 1:5). God's riches arise from God's own magnificent benevolence and are imparted to believers 'in the Messiah'.

**20.** Paul's description of God as the ultimate and gracious giver propels Paul to praise: *To our God and Father be glory for ever and ever. Amen.* Paul provides doxologies at various locations in his letters (for examples of mid-letter doxologies, see Rom. 11:36; Gal. 1:5; Eph. 3:21; and 1 Tim. 1:17). Since Paul does not routinely conclude his letters with doxologies, this line is anything but perfunctory (for instances of doxologies at the conclusion of Pauline letters, see Rom. 16:25–27; 1 Tim. 6:16b; 2 Tim. 4:18b). Paul has just referenced

---

23. Cohick helpfully frames this in terms of Graeco-Roman patron–client relations. Given Paul's argument, 'the Philippians are less likely to think of themselves as Paul's clients who must continually pay back a great debt', and 'Paul prevents them from imagining themselves to be his patron' (p. 252).

24. Hawthorne, p. 274.

25. Bockmuehl, p. 267.

God's glory as the basis of God's benevolence; now he ascribes glory to *our God and Father*, drawing on the same language that began the letter (cf. 1:2). Paul has indicated that God's glory – God's inexpressible presence, power and benevolence – is the foundation of all divine gifts (4:19). So it is truly right and fitting, as Paul does here, to return glory to God, to whom it belongs.

## 10. CONCLUDING GREETINGS (4:21–23)

*Comment*

**21.** Paul follows standard convention in providing concluding greetings to and from each side of the communication. Paul encourages the Philippian congregation to greet each member of *God's people* (singular: 'each saint', *panta hagion*) on his behalf. This language follows closely the way Paul began the letter: 'To all God's holy people' (*pasin . . . hagiois*; see 1:1 and comment). Paul describes the people of God as *in Christ Jesus*, namely, those who belong to and are found in the Messiah (see comment on 4:19). Paul's greeting is joined by the greetings of *the brothers and sisters who are with* Paul. We have heard relatively little about this (probably small) group who are able to help Paul in his imprisonment. Timothy is the only member of this group expressly named in the letter (1:1; 2:19–24), but we can imagine others who have come to help Paul in prison, as Epaphroditus had done on behalf of the Philippians and like the co-workers Paul mentions in Philemon 24.

**22.** Here, Paul broadens his reference to offer greetings from *all God's people* (*pantes . . . hagioi*) who reside on his side of the expanse between Rome and Philippi. Paul has the Roman church in view. Paul's greeting from the entire faith community in Rome (i.e. its multiple house churches; cf. Rom. 16:5, 10b, 11b, 14, 15) would include the 'brothers and sisters' (*adelphoi*) he has earlier mentioned who have increased their preaching efforts since Paul's imprisonment (1:14–17). While we do not know precisely how Paul connected with this wider group, it would be plausible to imagine some of those Paul knows in the Roman churches (e.g. who are listed in the greetings in his letter to the Romans, 16:3–16) to have been able to see or communicate with Paul, at least occasionally, and to pass along those communications to the wider Roman faith community. As Tamez suggests, 'Early Christian prisoners had the advantage of having brothers and sisters from the nearby ecclesia who usually took on the responsibility of attending to their needs.'[1]

In the greetings he passes along, Paul highlights *especially those who belong to Caesar's household*. The household of Caesar (*tēs Kaisaros oikias*; Latin, *domus Caesaris*) was not limited to family members; it included 'all persons in the emperor's service, whether slaves or freed[people], in Italy and even in the provinces'.[2] Nevertheless, the location that makes most sense for this referent is Rome itself, especially for a large enough contingent of Christ-followers among the imperial household to warrant mention here and to inspire believers who are living in such an influential Roman colony as Philippi (see Introduction 2c). For Paul and the Philippians, both experiencing pressure or persecution related to Roman power and influence, 'it will have been a source of hope and reassurance to know that the gospel was penetrating into the very heart of the Roman imperial apparatus'.[3]

**23.** Paul concludes the letter with an echo of where he began:

*The grace of the Lord Jesus Christ be with your spirit.*
'Grace . . . to you from . . . the Lord Jesus Christ' (1:1).

---

1. Tamez, p. 13.
2. Lightfoot, p. 171; see pp. 171–178.
3. Bockmuehl, p. 270.

In addition to 1:1 and 4:23, Paul has also used 'grace' in his opening prayer, there as a cipher for the gospel, the good news about Jesus the Messiah (1:7; cf. 1:5). This Messiah had willingly humbled himself to the point of death on a cross and was now resurrected and exalted by God. Paul and the Philippians were worshipping and waiting for their Lord who, unlike Caesar, would resurrect and exalt them as he himself had already been resurrected and exalted (3:20–21). This is the good news; and it is truly the grace granted to all Christians. Paul prays that this grace would be with the Philippians' *spirit* (*pneuma*). The use of the singular noun here could echo the singular *pneuma* in 1:27, used to express Paul's desire for the Philippians to 'stand firm in one spirit' (NIV footnote), potentially signalling at this final turn the unity Paul has desired for the Philippians across his letter.

Paul's concluding *Amen* – from the Hebrew affirmation *'āmēn* (e.g. 'surely'; cf. Neh. 5:13; 8:6) – has already been used to conclude the doxology in 4:20. Its presence here at the very end of the letter has early external support (as does its omission), although its inclusion would fit scribal tendencies to add such liturgical markers and so it is probably not original to the letter (see NIV footnote).

### Theology
Paul draws on the theme of partnership (*koinōnia*) across the letter to express the relationship he shares with the Philippians, and this theme culminates in the discussion about the Philippian gift in 4:10–20. Already in the first line of his opening prayer, Paul has identified their longstanding 'partnership in the gospel' as the reason for his joyful gratitude (1:3–5). And he justifies his disposition towards them by virtue of their partnership (their role as 'sharers', *synkoinōnoi*) 'in God's grace' (1:7). For Paul, the reality of the gospel – the story and work of Jesus – binds them together in the deepest of ways; together they share 'in the Messiah' (*en Christō*; e.g. 1:1; 4:21). This reality is the reason Paul can bank on their experience of unity 'with Christ' (2:1, *en Christō*) to propel them towards unity with one another (2:2). Union with Christ is a communal existence that envelops together all who trust in Christ.

In 4:10–20, Paul applies the reality of the Philippians as his fellow sharers in Christ and in the gospel to the gift he has received from the church. He commends their willingness 'to share' in his troubles (*synkoinōneō*, 4:14) and emphasizes their history of this kind of participation (*koinōneō*, 4:15). For Paul, the characteristic practices of 'giving and receiving' between them are integral to their gospel partnership (4:15). This framing of financial and material support as a gospel practice is augmented by Paul's theological grounding in 4:18–20. Giving and receiving is not a two-way transaction, because God is the first and primary gift-giver. Paul relies on God to meet the needs of the Philippians (materially and otherwise). Paul, it seems, holds a theology of abundance: the conviction that God is a God of abundance and 'that our lives will end in God, and that this well-being cannot be taken from us'.[4]

This talk of abundance could easily be (and has been) leveraged in the direction of a prosperity gospel, in which God is presumed upon to meet all financial and material needs that the Christian has (usually predicated on an unwavering faith in divine provision). This theological perspective is often accompanied by an expectation that generously giving to a particular ministry will yield rewards far beyond what one has sacrificed to give. Paul's letter to the Philippians does not allow such a reading, when understood in its historical context.

The social reality of the Philippians and of Paul is one in which neither party has an abundance out of which they give. Both Paul and the Philippian church are closer to a state of impoverishment than prosperity (2 Cor. 8:2; see comment on 4:14). The Philippians' gift to Paul is truly an expression of 'solidarity among the poor'.[5] And Paul's portrait of God as an abundant God is deeply intertwined with his assumption that God has worked precisely through the Philippians to make sure that Paul has been 'amply supplied' (4:18). Such interconnectivity is essential to any theology of abundance we might offer for contemporary reflection.

Brueggemann highlights the biblical motif of abundance (e.g. Ps. 104) and claims that it is antithetical to 'the story of scarcity' promoted by the present powers. He suggests that the issue facing

---

4. Brueggemann, 'Abundance', p. 343.

5. Tamez, p. 115.

Christians especially in the wealthy West (and in the USA particularly) is whether we will actually choose the good news, the gospel.

> We [the USA] who are now the richest nation are today's main coveters . . . we must confess that the central problem of our lives is that we are torn apart by the conflict between our attraction to the good news of God's abundance and the power of our belief in scarcity – a belief that makes us greedy, mean and unneighborly.[6]

Especially for Western Christians, most of whom benefit from an abundance of resources on a daily basis, working against greed and un-neighbourliness and working for an equitable distribution of wealth – locally, nationally, globally – should be a matter of habitual gospel practice. As Works suggests from the Christological vision of Philippians, 'By standing with the powerless and testifying to the hope of the gospel, the church exhibits the mindset of Christ and bears witness to God's kingdom.'[7] A prayerful posture appropriate to the letter of Philippians might consider: How can we participate with God in the divine design to provide for a world in need 'according to the riches of [God's] glory in Christ Jesus'?

A prayerful posture grounded in Philippians will place Christ Jesus at the centre, as Paul has made clear throughout Philippians (e.g. 2:5–11) and as he does in the conclusion of the letter. It is God's riches 'in Messiah Jesus' that are offered to humanity and that are able to meet every need (4:19). And the people of God are marked by and participate 'in Messiah Jesus' (4:21). Paul's concluding line (4:23) offers a greeting of grace that resonates with the grace believers have already received from God (cf. 1:7) because of the Messiah: 'The grace of the Lord Jesus Christ be with your spirit.'

---

6. Brueggemann, 'Abundance', p. 343.

7. Works, p. 584.